The Managerial Imperative
and the Practice of Leadership
in Schools

Hight - Art of teaching
Jackson - Life in
Classrooms
John Dewey
Horace Mann

SUNY Series in Educational Leadership
Daniel Duke, Editor

The Managerial Imperative and the Practice of Leadership in Schools

LARRY CUBAN

State University of New York Press

We acknowledge excerpts from *The Real Teachers* by Philip Sterling. Copyright© 1972 by Philip Sterling. Reprinted by permission of Random House, Inc.

Published by
State University of New York Press, Albany

For information, address State University of New York
Press, State University Plaza, Albany, N.Y., 12246

Library of Congress Cataloging-in-Publication Data

Cuban, Larry.
    The managerial imperative and the practice of
leadership in school.

        (SUNY series in educational leadership)
        Includes index.
        1. Teacher-administrator relationships.   2. School
management and organization.   I. Title.   II. Series.
LB2831.5.C83   1987   371.2   87-6512
ISBN 0-88706-593-7
ISBN 0-88706-594-5 (pbk.)

10 9 8 7 6 5 4 3

To my brothers, Norty and Marty, who mean so much to me. Separated by years and distance, the bonds remain strong.

And to my oldest friends, Yus Merenstein and Dave Mazer; each has given and received the love of a friend.

Contents

Figures and Tables   ix

Preface   xi

Introduction   xiii

Part I. The Crucible

1.   Teaching: Images and Roles   1

2.   Drifting into Teaching and Staying Awhile   41

3.   Principaling: Images and Roles   53

4.   Perverse Incentives: Moving Back and Forth   85
        Between Classroom and Administration

5.   Superintending: Images and Roles   111

6.   From High School Teacher to Superintendent   149
        to Professor

Part II. Meanings

7.   From Images and Roles to Leadership   179

8.   Summary and Implications   219

        Notes   251

        Index   287

Figures and Tables

Fig.   1   Conceptions of Teaching in Public Schools,   3
1800s to Present

Fig.   2   A Model of Teacher Thought and Action   6

Fig.   3   Core Roles of Thelma Katz, Kindergarten   39
Teacher

Fig.   4   Conceptions of Principaling in Public Schools,   55
1850s to Present

Fig.   5   Relationship Among District, Principal, and   68
Teacher Functions; Student Entering Behavior,
Classroom Behavior, and Year-End Achievement

Fig.   6   Core Role Patterns Among Principals   83

Fig.   7   Conceptions of Superintending, 1870s–1950s   117

Fig.   8   Core Role Patterns Among Superintendents   146

Fig.   9   Organizational Commonalities Bonding   181
Teachers and Administrators

Fig. 10   Organizational Leadership: Elements,   195
Relationships, Settings, and Outcomes

Table 1   How Principals Spend Their Time in Schools,   62
1911–1981

Table 2 Percentages of Superintendents Holding Three 121
Major Conceptions, as Drawn from Department
of Superintendence and American Association
of School Administrators, 1871–1950

Table 3 Percentages of Superintendents Holding Three 122
Major Conceptions, as Drawn from the Writings
of 251 Big-City Superintendents, 1881–1950

Table 4 Distribution of Superintendents' Time Devoted 127
to Various Functions as Reported by City and
Rural Chiefs, 1950

Table 5 A Comparison of School Superintendents' 130
Activities and Contacts

Preface

Over the last decade and a half, I have been fortunate enough to pursue what Rebecca West said of her work: "I write books to find out about things." Of the books that I have written, I found this one the most exhilarating and tiring. I do not know why. In talking with Dan Duke, the editor of this series, he suggested that I might be bringing to a close a period of my life. Perhaps.

Between 1955 and 1981, I either taught high school history or administered school district programs. Since 1981 I have taught and administered in a university and have had the good fortune to think, study, and write. In writing I have had the time to rework the meaning of the last thirty years as a teacher and administrator. Both are compelling activities that I have combined in one career. I have come to see that teaching in a conventional and larger sense is central to thoughtful administration. They are wedded together, although few policymakers or practitioners might see them as I do. In writing this book, I have wrestled with the issues that bind and separate these two essential tasks in schooling. I discovered new insights about my life and my career by writing. This book is the product of that reflection.

Every author piles up debts. Mine are many and I wish to recognize the colleagues and friends that helped me work through the ideas in this book. Mike Atkin gave me the idea of alternating scholarly and practitioner chapters by lending me a book that contained the germ of that idea. I prevailed on a number of practitioners, scholars, and my

xi

students to read either the whole or parts of the first draft, and they were kind enough to share many comments: Beverly Carter, Todd Endo, Elisabeth Hansot, Milbrey McLaughlin, Scott Pfeifer, Paul Sakamoto, Steve Swerdlick, and David Tyack. A number of the ideas in this book emerged from two classes I taught in the Stanford University School of Education. The intense discussions in Education X290 renewed my excitement for teaching and the ideas in this book. It is not modesty that impels me to declare that I learned a great deal from my students; for me, it is simply saying what is true.

Introduction

No longer are teaching and administering viewed as one career. They are divorced from one another. Few see these occupations anchored in a common history sharing core roles. I do.

I begin with this assertion because exploring it is vital to any understanding of why, over the last century, periodic designs for school improvement and calls for more leadership have persistently disappointed well-meaning reformers.

So many reforms in the twentieth century have tried to alter what teachers and administrators do. Planned changes have been thrust upon schools. Most teachers and administrators complied at some level. Many did so because they believed in the mandates. Others complied because it made little difference in their work lives. Some fearless teachers and occasional principals voiced complaints for being the objects of changes that were misdirected, ill-advised, or simply inappropriate; fearful teachers and principals swallowed their objections and ignored or adapted the designs aimed at them. In short, most teachers and administrators had little room to shape the content or packaging of reforms. In a word, they had little chance to lead. To explore the splitting apart of teaching from administering, then, is also to probe at the basic premises of reforms aimed at improving what happens in schools and why management rather than leadership has dominated schools.

The separation of teaching from principaling and superintending is evident at every turn in the world of practice. Few common bonds tie them together now. Finger-pointing dominates much of the discussion about public schools. Divisions between teachers and administrators, reformers' efforts to improve schooling, and social scientists' research have somehow frayed further what few friendly ties may have existed among educators.

Administrators berate teachers for losing their dedication to serving children while seeking more dollars, fewer hours in classrooms, and more privileges. Teachers flail administrators for their high salaries and dim understanding of the classroom as a workplace. Rhetorical darts dipped in the vocabulary of late nineteenth century labor-management struggles are thrown at one another. The tensions, the adversarial spirit, and the social distance between teachers and administrators surface tangibly when a superintendent on a tour of a school enters a teachers' lounge for a chat and finds a chilly silence. Or the principal, in plowing through an agenda filled with announcements during a late afternoon monthly faculty meeting, exceeds the contracturally stipulated hour for the meeting. The mumbles, the shifting in seats, the rustling of papers that teachers were grading while half-listening tell the principal that the faculty meeting is over.

Petty irritations and smouldering slights seal the differences among teachers and administrators. Teacher strikes, "sick outs," and "working to the rule" register what many see as the incompatible interests of the two occupations. Uncertainty over just whose interests principals and district office staff serve arises in those places where unions of administrators form to protect their concerns. Yet teachers, principals, and superintendents entered education to, among many reasons, help children learn; they share a common purpose. They are educators.

Sporadic surges of reform aimed at improving social and economic ills often spilled over into the schools. Curing today's national problems by dealing with tomorrow's adults is a favored reform tactic. Sincere advocates calling for more leadership and school improvement often deepened the fractures among educators. Professional and amateur reformers eager to improve schooling frequently spotlighted flaws in classrooms and districts in order to boost a favored solution. Over the decades, we have heard how intransigent teachers were reluctant to use radio, film, instructional television, and other technological innovations, or that administrators who relaxed standards caused test scores to slip. For reformers, blame is the coin of the realm. Teachers and administrators, defensively protecting themselves from the blamers point to others as the *real* cause. The foundation for school reform is often constructed out of the narrowly perceived inadequacies of those who work in schools.

Academics help not a bit. The growth of specialized university research also has contributed to the divisions among teachers and administrators. Academic careers are built upon finding a disciplinary niche from which to experiment, interview, collect data, and publish articles. Social scientists in education have subdivided like cells undergoing mitosis. Psychologists, sociologists, economists, anthropologists, and political scientists have so splintered the concept of teaching (while separating it thoroughly from learning) that distinct journals, conferences, and research agendas divide academics up into intellectual fiefdoms. Researchers who label themselves as educators, claiming no disciplinary niche, copy their brethren by creating applied subspecialties. Page after page in school of education catalogs document the unchecked spread of specialization, further distancing teachers from administrators and researchers.

These splits among academics and educators that have grown over the years, of course, have failed to isolate all teachers, administrators, reformers, and professors from one another. Many have built bridges; some work together, emphasizing the commonalities, not the differences. Furthermore, at times of fiscal crisis, coalitions of educators frequently form. Setting aside differences, teachers and administrators will resurrect the rhetoric of common purpose and collaborate. Nonetheless, even in the face of many instances of cooperation between groups of educators, any informed observer of public schooling in the waning decades of the twentieth century would be hard-pressed to deny the existing fractures and the animosities that color relationships among educators.

Whether sporadic impulses to reform education, grafting of corporate labor-management practices upon public schooling, or social science researchers studying fragments of the schooling process fully account for the divorce of teaching from administering, I do not know. This unintended outcome nonetheless shattered a professed sense of unity in purpose and function into warring specialties. For adults who have worked in schools over the last century, the core experience of schooling has splintered.

Over a century ago, this unity, honored far more in words than practice, still gave people who worked with school children a common mission. True, rhetorical flourishes by administrators and academics

who glowingly spoke of teaching as a noble crusade to eliminate ignorance while building a democratic citizenry often masked intentionally
designed inequities in teacher status, salary, and working conditions.
Although such words often rang hollow in teachers' ears, they still
spoke to a deeply felt need for a shared vision about the role of schooling among those who worked with children. Even the earliest unions
to organize educators included teachers and administrators united
against school boards. The unintentional transformation of school
communities into contentious factions over the last century has diminished a shared sense of purpose, replacing it with suspicion, antago-
nism, and a heightened sense of self-interest rather than a nurturing of
the public good. The fissures that I see in the educational terrain that
divide educators into factions have over the last three decades in which
I have taught and administered widened and deepened.[1]

PURPOSE AND PLAN OF THE BOOK

This book reexamines the organizational experiences that bond
teachers and administrators; reaffirms the enduring legacy teachers,
principals, and superintendents jointly inherited once they entered
classrooms; and, finally, argues that reconstructing that sense of common purpose about the role of schooling that both teachers and administrators seek, even in the face of an unpredictable environment
that few can influence, is an essential task in improving what happens
in classrooms and schools.

These purposes may appear to some readers as mildly romantic,
out of touch with the hard-core realities that have permeated public
schooling in the last half of the twentieth century. Perhaps. But I do
want to build more sturdy bridges between teachers and administrators. My thirty year career as an educator documents a shuttling between classrooms and administrative offices. That shuttling taught me
far more about mutual rather than separate interests.

This Introduction presents the argument that frames the book.
The argument is a series of propositions anchored in various research
findings, historical studies of school occupations, and personal experiences. These arguments are, however, assertions, not factual statements. While I will synthesize much empirical data and conceptual
knowledge, I do make leaps from the data, which may trouble researchers. Such leaps, I identify. Also, I combine empirical generaliza-
tions from many sources to invent different ways of seeing familiar

phenomena. In this book, then, I draw from practice, conceptual knowledge, and empirical data and blend these ingredients into a broader view of teaching and administering. My aim is to persuade, perhaps convince, readers that what teachers, principals, and superintendents do in schools, shaped inexorably as it is by the environment in which they work, is cut from the same fabric and needs to be rewoven anew into a coherent tapestry rather than remain in tattered fragments.[2]

THE ARGUMENT IN BRIEF

TWO DOMINANT IMAGES—THE TECHNICAL AND THE MORAL—HAVE DOMINATED BOTH TEACHING AND ADMINISTERING OVER THE LAST CENTURY AND A HALF. Images portray what should be. What people picture in their minds influences what they become. By picturing what can be and trying to move towards it, images inspire practice. Two images of what teachers, principals, and superintendents should be like have colored the history of these occupations. From each occupation's origins, a bureaucrat/technocrat image called for compliance with orders from above, the establishment of routines, and the use of technical expertise to achieve both efficiency and effectiveness in transmitting knowledge to children. Frequently, as a consequence of larger social forces in the culture (e.g., industrialization, enthusiasm for scientific management) influencing public schooling, reformers, teachers, and administrators for decades pursued productivity, order, routine tasks, and low-cost pedagogies.

Another image attracting both teachers and administrators at the same time was that of craftsman/artist. Present from the earliest decades of each occupation, the craftsman/artist, or moral* image, aimed

---

*As used here, *moral* does not imply that the technical conception is either value-free or amoral. The technical image contains values that prize accumulated knowledge, efficiency, orderliness, productivity, and social usefulness; the moral image, while not disregarding such values, prizes values directed at molding character, shaping attitudes, and producing a virtuous, thoughtful person. This ideal also encouraged teachers and administrators to expand their discretion in bureaucracies, to pursue less uniformity in how things should get done. Both the technical and moral conceptions of teaching and administering intersect in the image of the professional. The notion of a professional working in a bureaucracy calls for both compliance and independence, technical expertise and intuition, universal treatment of others and deliberate partiality.

at transforming the child by instilling virtue and character. While the moral conception also called for technical expertise, it demanded far more: a repertoire of knowledge and skills that required independent judgment, autonomy, invention, imagination, and performance. Teachers and administrators seeking to fulfill this image concentrated on the instructional side of each occupation. The teacher sought freedom to teach children in a manner consistent with their beliefs. Administrators concentrated on the instructional side of their jobs: creating and sustaining the conditions that would improve curriculum and pedagogy for children.

These pictures of what teaching and administration should be resurfaced throughout the history of public schooling, often reflecting larger cultural forces while inspiring and shaping what actually happened in schools and classrooms. These images persist today in the minds of policymakers, administrators, teachers, and the lay public, still influencing the direction that schooling should take. These conceptions are buried within policies, programs, and novel proposals from competency-based curricula, effective schools, and mastery teaching to the superintendent as instructional leader, the principal as school-site manager, and competency testing for new and veteran teachers.

TEACHERS AND ADMINISTRATORS SHARE THREE ROLES IN COMMON. If images give direction to what teachers and administrators should become and shape to a degree what they practice, they fall short of determining the core activities of each occupation. Socioeconomic and cultural forces that shape the larger goals for schooling also affect local communities, which, in turn, have a direct influence on schools and classrooms. For example, the graded school, self-contained classrooms, fifty-minute periods, tests, certification requirements for teachers, all were organizational innovations introduced over a century ago in response to reformers' efforts to improve schooling and, thereby, the larger society. They have become part of the familiar terrain called public schools and influence the daily practice of teaching and administering.

The substance of what teachers and administrators do daily, then, is derived from a number of sources (including the images). What they do, however, can be reduced to three roles that both occupations share in common: instructional, managerial, and political. For the instructional and managerial roles, there is little explanation needed now. A word, however, is necessary for using *political* in reference to teachers and administrators. To the degree that teachers, for example, use their legitimate authority to allocate scarce resources to children, govern minors through a series of techniques, negotiate order, and bargain with members of the class, teachers act politically. Determining who gets what, when, and under what circumstances in order to achieve desirable ends—a classic formulation of political behavior—occurs in classrooms, schools, and districts. Although the settings differ for a kindergarten teacher and a high school principal, the core roles are the same.

Overlapping and complex, these common roles contain within them values, expectations, and obligations that teachers and administrators, over time, use to build patterns that others come to call a "teaching style" or an "administrative style." These core roles are discharged daily by each in varied patterns regardless of the organizational structure, available technology, and relative power of the incumbent. What teachers in classrooms and superintendents at district headquarters do appears so different because common roles are displayed in dissimilar settings. Each stage may differ, but the roles that are performed are the same.

By understanding these three basic roles for teachers and administrators, carried out in varied settings, we can begin to make sense of the complexity of their tasks, and how some educators become leaders and many do not, and, most important, we can also begin to see in a slightly different way how teachers and administrators may adapt to periodic surges of reform as they sweep across schools and classrooms.

THE WORKPLACE NOT ONLY FORGES BONDS AMONG TEACHERS, PRINCIPALS, AND SUPERINTENDENTS BUT ALSO CREATES THE POTENTIAL FOR LEADERSHIP. If teachers and administrators share these images and three core roles, it is due, in part, to the nature of the organizations within which they work. In the shared purposes about the role of schooling, in the common roles they discharge, in the pace and rhythm of the work they perform, they are alike. Moreover, teachers and administrators are both bosses and subordinates. They direct others while obeying orders. They are solo practitioners. They prize autonomy. They manage conflict. They also are expected to lead.

Opportunities for leadership among teachers and administrators arise from the nature of the school district organization and the tasks they are called upon to perform. The complex tasks that teachers and administrators are called upon to discharge extends far beyond what any one individual could ever do. Organizational expectations and obligations that demand compliance from the teacher, principal, and superintendent must be tempered by the expectations and obligations that ensue from the clients (parents and students) that each occupation serves. Moreover, expectations and obligations derived from professional norms and personal beliefs compete with other demands.

Totaling up these crosscutting, often incompatible, obligations yields a situation in which no person could find the time and energy to satisfy all of these demands. Hence, if there is insufficient time and energy to do everything, choices must be made. From choice comes autonomy. Autonomy is the necessary condition for leadership to arise. Without choice, there is no autonomy. Without autonomy, there is no leadership.

From choice, then, comes the potential for leadership. In whatever manner leadership emerged from the complex roles teachers and administrators performed, those inside and outside school organizations have *expected* teachers, principals, and superintendents to lead, at the minimum, their primary organizational audience (i.e., teachers > students; principals > teachers; superintendents > principals). Simply exerting authority as teachers and administrators do, however, is not the same as leading. Subordinates are not necessarily followers. For leadership to exist, followers must agree to be led.

WITHIN THE SCHOOL AND DISTRICT WORKPLACES, THE MANAGERIAL IMPERATIVE, NOT THE IMPULSE TOWARD LEADERSHIP, DOMINATES BEHAVIOR. By leadership, I mean influencing others' actions in achieving desirable ends. Leaders are people who shape the goals, motivations, and actions of others. Frequently they initiate change to reach existing and new goals. Occasionally they lead in order to preserve what is valuable, such as, protecting core school functions during the Depression from budget cutters anxious to reduce the general tax burden. Such leadership, when it occurs, takes as much ingenuity, energy, and skill as starting an innovative program.[3]

I do distinguish, then, between leading and managing. Managing is maintaining efficiently and effectively current organizational arrangements. While managing well often exhibits leadership skills (see above example), the overall direction is toward maintenance rather than change. I prize both managing and leading and attach no special value to either one since different settings and times call for varied responses.

While there are problems with these definitions, they have the advantage of being familiar and close to what most people would define as leadership and management in daily affairs. I chose a broad definition of leadership because I assume that leaders exist in every organization and that each person is capable of leadership depending upon time and setting. What produces variety in how individual teachers and administrators handle their multiple organizational roles is, in part, due to the conception of leadership each has, whether constraints or discretion dominate each perspective and the ineffable mix of these beliefs with personal traits and the specific setting.

I argue that schools as they are presently organized press teachers, principals, and superintendents toward managing rather than leading, toward maintaining what is rather than moving to what can be. The structures of schooling and the incentives buried within them produce a managerial imperative. The images, roles, and practices dominant in teaching, principaling, and superintending, shaped largely by the ways that public schools have been designed over the last century and a half, shrink the margin for the practice of leadership further.

Thus, for teachers and administrators to join together in leading efforts to alter the present role of schooling, that is, to have schools cultivate the talents of individuals so that they can contribute to society and live fruitful lives—regardless of background—rather than have schools continue to reinforce advantages children bring with them, existing organizational arrangements, and incentives would need to be substantially altered as a necessary prior condition. For those largely satisfied with the present role of schooling and its outcomes, including the salience of the managerial imperative in classrooms, schools, and districts, no fundamental changes need occur.

I view this entire argument as one half of a dialogue with the reader. As a practitioner/academic, I have learned that valuable knowledge gained from experience and research intersect over issues of practice. I will present research findings and will share my experiences as a teacher and administrator to illustrate points. Both, however, are offered in the spirit of probing to get the reader to question, counter, or expand the argument. Thus, the other half of the dialogue comes from the reader. The danger in writing a book that is an argument that draws from the practitioner and scholarly sides of my career is to slip into polemics, particularly when facts are uncertain and values are deeply felt. Both ambiguous information and noisy values often erode a reader's will to turn the page. It is a danger I acknowledge and will try to avoid.

The book is organized in the following manner. Part 1, "The Crucible," describes the dominant images of teaching and administering from the earliest days of both occupations to the present and their influence upon what occurred in classrooms and schools. In these chapters (1, 3, and 5), I explore how images of teaching and administering arose, how they flourished, and how they created a set of constant tensions that have continued to inspire and plague both occupations. I examine the gap between the ideal and the real, between what teachers, for example, do daily and what nonteachers expect them to do. While the images offer direction to the people who hold these positions, it is the core roles that are basic to each occupation. The political, managerial, and instructional roles, conflicting as they often are, emerge as central to the work done by teachers, principals, and superintendents. Yet, as I also argue in these chapters, there is a DNA to teaching and administering and a set of perverse incentives that shape these roles and steer daily activities toward the managerial.

Separating these scholarly chapters will be three chapters (2, 4, and 6) that draw from my teaching and administrative career. Believing as I do that knowledge I have gained, examined, and used over thirty years as a teacher, administrator, and academic is just as valuable as the coin of empirical research, I have included experiences drawn from my years in classrooms and administrative offices to illustrate how I combined managing and teaching in one career and how I tried to finesse the managerial imperative that inevitably shaped what I did over the last three decades. Also, I include these chapters to suggest how one person became socialized as a teacher and administrator. I do not suggest that my career was typical; I do suggest that the impulses I responded to, pressures I felt and ignored, the uncertainties I experienced were common.

The images, roles, and patterns of leadership and management that emerged in my career as a teacher and administrator was one way of responding to what I faced. With so few career histories combining both teaching and administration that what appears as an atypical pattern may still offer clues to the many puzzles embedded in organizational socialization and the adult development of educators.

Part 2, "Meanings," (chapters 7–8) distils the argument and explores the significance of seeing teachers and administrators as sharing common experiences and performing similar functions within different settings. Using a number of examples drawn from teachers and administrators, I show how each acts as a leader. I explore possible answers to the following questions: How did teaching get separated from management? Why does interest in instructional leadership for principals and superintendents rise and fall like hemlines. Why have administrators since 1900 expressed remorse when reporting how little time they spend in classrooms? Why do most teachers and administrators adopt a predominately managerial pattern in enacting their three roles? In Chapter 9, I consider the implications of institutions designed to school masses of children containing structures and incentives that push teaching and administrative behavior toward the managerial while reformers dedicated to improving what occurs in classrooms create policies that ignore these fundamental organizational arrangements. Finally, I assess the implications of the arguments in the book against the periodic reform impulses aimed at school improvement that have seized national attention and have evaporated like dew in the early morning sun.

I
The Crucible

1

Teaching: Images

- On the fifteenth anniversary of the U.S. Supreme Court decision legalizing abortion, a San Jose area junior high teacher showed three of his classes a graphic anti-abortion film. More than half of his fellow teachers, angered by the showing of unborn fetuses being swept up in suction tubes and vivid shots of bloody parts to seventh and eighth graders, complained to the central administration. The twenty-three teachers said that their colleague had exceeded his authority since the film did not fit into the district curriculum for either language arts or social studies.

Richard Schmidt openly opposed abortion. He claimed that the state law required him to instill in students respect for all living creatures and he had the academic freedom to choose what to teach. He also said that he wanted to show "what is going on and what a young girl goes through, the dangers she faces." One teacher who supported Schmidt said, "I'm very pro-life and, frankly, I feel abortion on demand is infanticide." She felt the film to be "very realistic and very appropriate."[1]

- Beginning in the late 1970s, Washington, D.C., teachers received from their superintendent a new curriculum. Designed by experts and tested extensively in hundreds of classrooms across the District, lessons stressing specific objectives (e.g., identifying beginning sounds of words, adding two-digit numbers, recognizing synonyms and antonyms) were written with scripts for teachers to follow detailing what methods they were to use for which content. Teachers tested students either daily or weekly to assess how much students had learned. They recorded each student's progress indicating when

1

each student had mastered the prescribed skill before moving on to the next one. Elementary school students who had not achieved levels of performance set for the third and sixth grades were retained.

Sitting on Dorothy Porter's desk is a large red binder that she calls her "bible." In it are daily lessons with precise aims for what the students will cover. What the teacher is expected to do, what the students are expected to achieve, even the quizzes that the teacher must give to determine whether students have mastered the skills rest within the binder. The second-grade teacher at Bruce-Monroe Elementary School in Washington, D.C., consults the "bible" over the course of the day to check if the students are progressing as expected. With thirty-one students in class, Porter, a twenty-five-year veteran in the District schools, organizes the activities of the day around small groups, large group instruction, and seatwork. She has a checklist of which students need help on the skill of recognizing synonyms, which have mastered it and can do other work. Porter believes that the Pupil Progress Plan which tells the teacher what they should teach and allows students to progress at their own rate is "the best thing that I have seen in the system."[2]

• Mrs. Eleanore J. of Rhode Island describes her teaching in elementary and secondary schools since 1937:

I extend myself intensively in teaching; I do it because I enjoy it and I like the response. . . . There was Jimmy, a 17-year-old who hadn't been working at all, but when I told him in the spring that I would pass him if he could just work hard till the end of the year, he was elated, just beaming. I tried to keep him motivated. Then I had another boy, a 10th grader, who wanted to drop out of school at 16. I had a terrible time trying to motivate him, to get him to appreciate that as long as he was in school he should make something of his time. I got nowhere. He was getting bored and became a class disturbance; he wanted my attention. I told him to stay out of school the last two weeks and after marks were in, he came in and said, "You know, I've been thinking of all the things that you told me. I'm going to come back in September," and he went on and talked about how much he appreciated me. And he said, "You know, Mrs. J_____, I love you," and he kissed me. The first day of school that next fall I looked over and there was Michael standing in the doorway. . . . I think that as educators we have to know when and how to approach the students.[3]

Different images of teaching emerge from these descriptions. There is a planned, highly rational view of instructional materials and techniques constructed by experts and delivered to teachers to use in classrooms. There is a picture of a teacher as a professional drawing from a blend of artistry, science, and personal beliefs to make independent judgments about what should be taught and toward what ends children should be guided. Images of teaching come as much from notions of what teachers *should* do as much as from what they actually do.[4]

There is a history to these images of teaching. Because conceptions of teaching express purpose, guiding and inspiring action rather than determining it, I begin with the dominant images.

Drawn from an array of historical data on how teachers were expected to teach, how they taught, and reform movements to alter existing practices, I have extracted two dominant conceptions of teaching: teaching as giving knowledge and applying rules (the technical image) and teaching as transforming students (the image of teacher as a moral actor).[5]

The technical conception anchored initially in an early nineteenth century metaphor of a factory and a machine captured those teachers and nonteachers who concentrated upon producing masses of children armed with knowledge and attitudes appropriate to being citizens and workers. Aiming to control what teachers did, policymakers directed practitioners to employ routine procedures in a systematic manner. By the turn of the twentieth century, this bureaucratic conception, spurred by a fascination with corporate efficiency as applied to teaching and administering, gave way to a technocratic conception which emphasized the application of scientifically produced knowledge ("laws of learning") to the classroom.

The image of a teacher as classroom bureaucrat/technocrat, for example, matches the needs of large organizations impelled to provide standardized services to many students. Instruction concentrates on rationally, systematically and uniformly achieving specific aims. Curriculum is like a staircase, students climbing content step-by-step with no hallways or landings to ease the climb to the top floor. I use the hyphenated term because it captures the essence of the organizational role that teachers are expected to play; that is, the teacher is a subordinate, expected to carry out faithfully instructions from superiors—bureaucrats. But the teacher is also the boss of the students, the executive who is expected to know more than subordinates, possess skills that they lack, and get a product out of the door—technocrat.[6]

The technical conception of teaching continues strongly in the waning years of the twentieth century. Advocates of "direct" or "active"

Figure 1: Conceptions of Teaching in Public Schools, 1800s to Present*

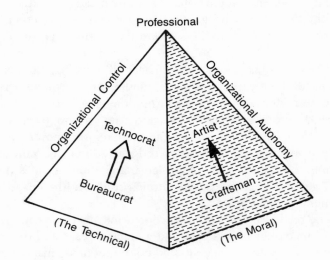

*I make no claim that this figure is empirically or historically valid; it is a device that tries to make sense of the available evidence. I use it to begin organizing existing information about conceptions of teaching.

instruction and teacher effectiveness research seek those methods that work for most students. Administrators restlessly pursue those teaching approaches that can be installed in district classrooms. Collective bargaining agreements with grievance procedures and specific clauses on what can and cannot be done in classrooms further fasten a technical perspective upon teaching practice.[7]

The moral view of teaching traces its origins to the establishment of formal schooling in Western culture. This view holds that the aim of teaching is to transform the individual. Teaching is a moral activity that requires skills, knowledge, critical judgment, and an eye cocked on imagining what each person can become. Those who hold this view sweep up the technical, artistic, and scientific findings—anything that can be used to help. Those holding a moral view of teaching use technical skills in classrooms and accommodate the imperatives of organizational life while persistently seeking to turn children into individuals of high moral character.

An example might help to further distinguish the two conceptions of teaching. A teacher searching for a way of bringing more orderliness to a class marked by frequent outbursts from a few students considers a new system based upon rewards allocated by the teacher for acceptable behavior (e.g., candies, paper money redeemed later for privileges). Careful records of behavior supplemented by increased surveillance and social distance from the students are part of the novel package.

A teacher with a dominant technical view who is determined to reduce the disorderliness of a few students will grasp and implement the behavioral modification materials. A teacher holding a dominant moral image will consider what impact such an instructional approach will have on student relationships with the teacher, a bond sought for both its rewards and links to learning. The teacher will weigh the trade-offs inherent in using this approach or some variation of it and the potential damage to the individual students and the existing relationships. Whether the costs are tolerable if used for a short time would be considered also. In short, the teacher calculates gains and losses as measured against a desired goal. Obviously both images can be held simultaneously by the same teacher in an uneasy equilibrium. I simply offer this example to suggest how images can get translated into practice. Graphically, it would look like this.[8]

Figure 2: A Model of Teacher Thought and Action*

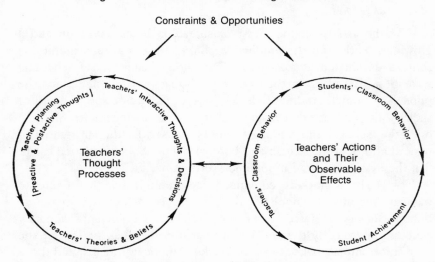

*Christopher Clark and Penelope Peterson, "Teachers' Thought Processes," in E. Wittrock, *Third Handbook of Research in Teaching* (Washington, D.C.: American Educational Research Association, 1986), p. 257.

Both conceptions merge in the image of teacher as a professional, where the technical intersects with the moral. The image of the professional dates from the late nineteenth century with the attempts of teachers and administrators to improve the training and status of both occupations. Further education and stiffer certification requirements nudged salaries upward (as did market forces). Harnessing these efforts to the early twentieth century passion for scientific knowledge applied to schooling fueled the drive for professional status. By the midtwentieth century, the marriage of both conceptions of teaching into the image of teacher as a professional was complete in the minds of many practitioners who viewed teachers as either semiprofessionals or civil servants.[9]

Because both images of the teacher as classroom bureaucrat/technocrat and craftsman/artist date back to the origins of public schooling in this country, I argue that these visions of what teaching should be not only surfaced and submerged throughout the history of formal schooling, often mirroring larger socioeconomic forces, but also gave purpose to what actually occurred in the nation's classrooms. Present today, these images persist in the minds of policymakers, administrators, teachers, and the lay public, still inspiring practice.[10]

TEACHER AS CLASSROOM BUREAUCRAT/TECHNOCRAT

Monitorial Schools

By the 1820s, in the midst of spreading industrialization and a growing affection for the productive power of the machine, monitorial schools dominated educational debate over what forms of schooling were best. Based upon their work in British private schools for the poor, Englishmen Andrew Bell and Joseph Lancaster spread word of their work. Lancaster's evangelical fervor and organizational skills in operating schools and training teachers, backed by the substantial financial efforts of the British and Foreign School Society, helped establish the system across Europe and North America.[11]

By 1818 promoters convinced the Pennsylvania legislature to mandate monitorial schools for the poor. In 1825 the New York Free School Society operated eleven monitorial schools for approximately 20,000 children. By the end of that decade, the peak period for the innovation, monitorial schools for blacks, American Indians, and those wishing to continue their education dotted the countryside.[12]

What happened in such a school? While practice differed among monitorial schools, still common patterns were evident. A master headed the school. Responsible to him were a series of monitors, older boys who carried out his instructions according to a manual. For example, there was a general monitor of order who was responsible for insuring orderly behavior; other deputies of the master were monitors for reading and arithmetic. There were also subordinate monitors, boys in charge of teaching small groups, who inspected pupils' writing, and examined each class of boys (i.e., first through eighth). The master often chose monitors for the younger boys from the fifth and higher classes.[13]

In a large room, along each wall within semicircles carved out on the floor (called "draft stations"), subordinate monitors taught groups of ten to twelve children, spelling, reading, arithmetic, and grammar. Instead of books, large individual lesson cards on each subject hung from the walls around which the monitor and students gathered. Monitored followed a prescribed set of questions and answers drawn from manuals. When a student answered correctly he received a reward (a ticket to be redeemed for a prize) and moved to a higher position within the group; if he moved to the top position ("first boy"), he would then move on to another draft station with a different monitor. Thus, students were not assigned to groups for a year or six months and expected to remain there; they were graded separately for performance and behavior in reading, spelling, writing, and other subjects. Each was promoted, retained, or put back to a more suitable group. Competitiveness (or emulation) and rewards drove the system.

Punishments also were given within the monitorial group. Idleness, talking, unwashed face or hands, tardiness, inattentiveness, and other "misdemeanors" prompted monitors to give cards to students stating their infractions; the boys then had to present the cards to the schoolmaster. Levels of punishment ranged from carrying a five pound log around their necks, wearing leg shackles, to the worst punishment, sitting in a cage suspended from the ceiling in full view of the other students, who, as Lancaster writes," "frequently smile at the birds in the cage." To late twentieth century sensibilities, such punishments may seem inhumane; however, the alternative, in early nineteenth century America was a birch rod, or the teacher's open palms or fists.[14]

At the front of the room the schoolmaster used an elaborate system of written initials to communicate with monitors. When the master, Joseph Lancaster wrote, "wishes to know if every boy is provided with a pencil, 'show pencils' is the command given, and instantly the whole school hold[s] up their right hand[s] and exhibit[s] pencils. . . ." The more common messages requested of monitors by the teacher were such commands as T.S. (Turn Slates), C.S. (Clean Slates), L.D.S. (Lay Down Slates).[15]

The central aim of this hierarchial organization immersed in explicit rules and bent upon regimenting behavior while transmitting both knowledge and skills was to invest the poor with the values of compliance, punctuality, cleanliness, and knowing one's place in society. In doing so the monitor, the person actually engaged in formal instruction, is both a bureaucrat following a manual and a boss. The schoolmaster is also head of the school but is a bureaucrat/technocrat nonetheless since he is the expert exercising managerial authority by following instructions in operating the school. What excited nineteenth century reformers was the systematic organization of a school, the school's capacity to handle many students cheaply, a pedagogy that seemingly instilled basic values and knowledge with admirable machinelike precision, and a clear set of rules for teachers and those planning to enter the occupation.

Within monitorial school can be seen the dreams that drove reformers then and since toward constructing planned, bureaucratic systems of schooling that promised uniformity in both how students were taught and what they were taught, while delivering results efficiently. Organizational success depended upon obedience to the system, not the personality or judgment of an individual teacher. Teacher as classroom bureaucrat/technocrat was an image born in the early decades of the Industrial Revolution when the love affair with the machine and the factory still entranced Americans.

By the 1840s, however, monitorial schools waned. Other pedagogies and systems of organization, swept across the educational terrain burying Joseph Lancaster's innovations. But the Lancasterian legacy of an hierarchial organization processing large numbers of children and the image of the teacher as an efficient agent of that organization persisted in subsequent decades.

Big city schools at the turn of the century

A half century after monitorial schools disappeared, a system of tax-supported compulsory schooling for boys and girls of all social classes had grown and expanded to become the marvel of the world. Within big cities, in the midst of massive migration, districts with boards of education and superintendents, had principals who administered buildings housing scores of classrooms, each with a teacher and many students.

By 1910 the twin migrations from Europe to America and from farm to city swelled towns into large, inadequately financed and over-extended urban school districts coping with the consequences of poverty, unfamiliar cultures, and overcrowded neighborhoods. These large urban districts had come under heavy fire from journalists, academics, civic reformers, and others who saw these large schools as factories inefficiently and mechanically producing regimented and unimaginative instruction.

These critics no longer saw the machine or factory as a proper metaphor for schooling. Francis Parker, John Dewey, and others, building on the work of earlier European reformers such as Pestalozzi and Froebel, saw schools as communities where teachers drew upon children's interests to transform minds, emotions, and bodies, where teachers built a school around children rather than stuffing subject matter into little people. They wanted fundamental changes in the purposes of schooling and the role of teachers. Prior to World War I, they remained a vocal minority. Not until the two decades between the World Wars did they become the mainstream of established educational thought.

Such critics visiting urban schools at the turn of the century saw instruction as mechanical, determined by the rules generated out of administrative convenience and a passion for saving dollars with little relevance to teachers or children. Holding a very different image of what teachers should do, these critics passionately rejected the view of teachers as classroom bureaucrats/technocrats.[16]

The published reports of pediatrician turned school reformer Joseph Rice, who visited 1200 classrooms in thirty-six cities between January and June 1892, illustrates this critical voice.

> In St. Louis we have an example of how sad the lot of the child may become when the superintendents not only do practically nothing toward raising the standards of the teachers by instructing them in the science of education, but where they do much to depress them by examining their classes and judging them by results alone. . . .

The consequence is that the teachers at all times labor under a high degree of pressure for results. To secure desired results is now their aim, and to secure them the children are ever relentlessly pushed. The fact that a child is a child is entirely forgotten, and the characteristic feature of the St. Louis schools—absolute lack of sympathy for the child—ensues.

During several daily recitation periods, each of which is from twenty to twenty-five minutes in duration, the children are obliged to stand on the line, perfectly motionless, their bodies erect, their knees and feet together, the tips of their shoes touching the edge of a board in the floor. The slightest movement on the part of a child attracts the attention of the teacher. The recitation is repeatedly interrupted with cries of "Stand straight," "Don't bend the knees," "Don't lean against the wall," and so on. I heard one teacher ask a little boy: "How can you learn anything with your knees and toes out of order."[17]

Other critics, however, still believing in productivity, saw massive school bureaucracies as inefficient machines in need of scientific retooling. They looked to the managerial revolution that streamlined corporations into efficient profit making machines. They sought standardization through the use of science applied to schooling.[18]

As with the other critics, they, too, saw instruction as mechanical, regimented, and unimaginative. What they sought, however, were improved bureaucracies, the use of information rigorously applied to problems, and scientifically derived policies that would produce better instruction for less money. They wanted college educated, state certified professionals to bring to schools and classrooms technical expertise, yet still remain responsive to superiors in terms of what and how to teach. These critics aimed at modernizing organizations. In effect these critics wanted sharper, better-educated classroom technocrats, not simply unthinking clerks implementing procedures. They proved to be far more influential in touching schools and classrooms than their fellow critics who saw the teacher as an artist changing individual children.[19]

Stanford professor Ellwood P. Cubberley, an admirer of corporate efficiency and one of the leaders in the movement to apply scientific principles to schooling, visited many districts across the country in the decades before and after World War I to evaluate their performance. His textbooks became standard fare in college courses for teachers and administrators. What Cubberley saw in Portland, Oregon, in 1913 when he and his associates surveyed the district for a committee of taxpayers illustrates this line of criticism.

> The influence of the system, rigidly centralized, mechanized and mechanically administered . . . is quite manifest in all the classroom work of the grammar grades—in the attitude of principals, teachers and pupils. In these grades everywhere there is a noticeable absence of any feeling of educational responsibility. Teachers are convinced that many of their efforts are futile, that much that they are attempting is of little or no value to their pupils. But what can they do about it? They have no responsibility, no right to depart from the rigidly uniform prescriptions of the course of study, reinforced by inspection from the central office, and by the important term examinations. . . . Any system that compels, encourages, or permits passivity to become the prevailing attitude in the schools, at once deprives itself of the best powers of teachers and limits the education of pupils. . . . That the Portland system is chiefly responsible for this condition in the grammar schools, there can be no serious doubt.[20]

Both sets of reformers saw the same mechanical instruction, but they prescribed very different cures. Cubberley and other like-minded reformers wanted science applied to schooling. They wanted to count and categorize. They wanted students placed in appropriate classes taking suitable subjects. They wanted intelligence and achievement testing, curricula matched to student differences, and guidance counseling. They wanted teachers, principals, and superintendents to become trained and certified to become educational experts. The shift from bureaucrat to technocrat to a professional begins with this movement to apply science to schooling.

Rationalizing Instruction in the 1960s and 1970s

While historians are uncertain as to what caused another surge of popular interest in making public schools again more efficient and productive, the civil rights movement, beginning in the South in the 1950s and spreading north and westward in the 1960s, provided the context for rising concern over school results. Publishing of school-by-school test scores in the late 1960s shocked professionals and fueled growing criticism of teachers and administrators' inability to teach effectively minorities and the poor.

Merging with the clamor for desegregation, legal remedies to improve schools' performance, and federally subsidized compensatory programs (e.g., Title I of the Elementary and Secondary Education Act of 1965) were other federal efforts to introduce budgetary accountability and program productivity. Planning, Programming, and Budgeting Systems (PPBS), mandated by President Lyndon Johnson in 1965, spilled forth from Washington to state capitals and, ultimately, to school districts. The notion of rational approaches to increase efficiency and productivity, again, entranced educational policymakers who either anticipating the future or transfixed by public criticism sought means of both controlling what teachers did and converting them into technical experts.

As applied to schooling, PPBS and similar designs produced schemes that included competency-based curricula, teacher-proof instructional packages containing behavioral objectives and scripts for teachers to follow, minimum competency tests, and the like. One representative experience with accountability in the early 1970s occurred in Oregon. I use it to illustrate the persistent image of teaching as a technical activity.

In 1969 a group of University Oregon researchers persuaded a nearby superintendent to adopt a version of PPBS. Concerned about fiscal and instructional accountability, the superintendent wanted to manage the curriculum more closely. He embraced the researchers' design and the School Planning, Evaluation, and Communication System (SPECS) was born.[21]

The heart of SPECS was material designed for teachers. Teachers received numerous sheets consisting of directions and spaces to write lists of objectives for each class and subject, student names, the outcomes they expected, and the tools they would use to judge student performance.[22]

The central role of testing was apparent in the materials. Teachers were expected to test students (and record results) before instruction began; they were expected to indicate when students had mastered the objectives, and they were expected to rate each student's effort as well. An example follows:

D. When interpreting *mastery* on the basis of pre-and/or post-test scores, refer to the specific criteria defined in each objective.
1. If the program or unit is so designed that all students move through it, under the same time constraints, their levels of mastery

will inevitably vary. Therefore, use one of the following to designate the degree to which each student mastered the objective:

MB—The student performed the desired behavior with *mastery before* instruction.

MA—The student performed the desired behavior with *mastery after* instruction.

CP—The student failed to achieve mastery, but made *considerable progress* toward it.

SP—The student failed to achieve mastery, but made *some progress* toward it.

LP—The student failed to achieve mastery, and made *little or no progress* toward it. (emphasis in original)[23]

How did teachers react to SPECS? Anthropologist Harry Wolcott listened to teachers in classrooms, lounges, before and after school and recorded the following mix of responses. I have selected an illustrative sample:

I'm now more aware of seeing if I achieved the objectives I set in the beginning of the term. But it's terribly time consuming. I spin a lot of wheels. And in my field, changes occur so fast that I can't write something to last.

I think SPECS helps teachers to plan. Right now the state superintendent of schools is trying to push through some kind of accountability program. In our district it's going to be SPECS; somewhere else it will be a different program.

Regardless of what I turn in, from the department head on up they want to change it. Just the other day they wanted me to combine two objectives that couldn't be further apart. They shouldn't be making those judgments. It's like having vocational education people tell you how to teach art or music.

SPECS doesn't work for my subject. I think it was started from the wrong end. It served administrators' needs, but not teacher needs. And it still doesn't meet student needs. It required a new language and a new sequence. I wish instead they had asked teachers, "what have you already done that's working?" It seems strange that in two years they haven't asked us anything. We are just told to do it or get out. But a teacher's program can't be all set up in advance. It's got to be flexible. I never know for sure what I'm going to do with a class until I get them.[24]

Ideas about teachers as artists and teachers as professionals emerge in these comments. By 1973, when the professional association presented the option to phase out SPECS, 31 percent of the teachers strongly favored (15 percent simply favored) and 19 percent strongly opposed (12 percent simply opposed) ending the program. One-quarter of the teachers were neutral on the proposal.[25]

A program designed by university researchers for teacher use and mandated by the superintendent contained within it the image of teacher as bureaucrat/technocrat. The split in teacher opinion over SPECS mirrors both acceptance and rejection of that image. Those teachers rejecting or even partially holding this view, believed that teaching requires autonomy, independent judgment, and the necessity of making decisions tailored to a specific setting.

In the waning years of the twentieth century, the bureaucrat/technocrat image persists. Concern over the nation's eroding economic primacy and foreign success in what had been American markets turned attention anew to public school performance. National reports became a growth industry. Recommendations for holding schools accountable for academic achievement as measured by standardized test scores, wedded to efforts at improving teacher performance, triggered state reforms. State after state mandated tests for both teachers and students; stiffer graduation requirements; curriculum that specified what content was to be taught; and new procedures for educating, recruiting, evaluating, and rewarding teachers. Buried within these national reports and state laws to improve schooling was an image of the teacher. The National Commission on Excellence in Education's report, "A Nation at Risk," offered a glimpse of that image when it called teachers "the tools at hand."[26]

The effective schools movement, another effort to improve schooling for low-income, minority students, also contains within it an image of the teacher as bureaucrat/technocrat. Mastery learning, direct instruction, competency-based curricula (staples of the movement) lean heavily upon instructional materials that have behavioral objectives, pre- and post-tests, frequent monitoring of student performance, and, in some cases, scripts for teachers to follow. Recall District of Columbia teacher Dorothy Porter's "bible."[27] Yet, within the effective schools movement and elsewhere in the nation's schools are individual classrooms where teachers use small group instruction, encourage student choice, and nourish creativity. These classrooms offer much play for both teacher and student decision making. Similarly, there are alternative schools where special curricula aimed at cultivating students' talents draw teachers who seek opportunities to express their artistry, their professionalism. The images endure.

TEACHER AS CRAFTSMAN/ARTIST

If bureaucratic/technocratic images permeated what both non-teachers and teachers saw as appropriate for classrooms since the late eighteenth century, then similarly, images of the teacher as craftsman/artist, drawing out from pupils the finest they have to offer, has a long history.

Socrates, Buddha, Jesus of Nazareth, Rabbi Hillel are often cited as exemplars of great teaching in the artistic tradition.[28] While each had what today would be called schools with pupils as disciples and while each had qualities that went far beyond communicating knowledge and skills—indeed, they transformed those that came to learn—I will concentrate on teaching in formal settings (i.e., classrooms, where public authorities determined that the young must be schooled prior to entering adult society). My point is to show that if the innovative monitorial schools of the early nineteenth century contained the bureaucratic/technocratic view of teaching, other views also competed for attention at the same time and since.

In combining the terms *craftsman/artist*, I go beyond notions of teaching as a trial-and-error search for specific solutions to practical problems or what some writers have labeled the routine application of particular procedures to classroom problems. Instead, the conception of teacher as craftsman/artist (I use *gender* generically) means a repertoire of skills organized around a body of knowledge that aims to transform children into better human beings. Reflection, systematic thinking, and imagination occur among teachers seeking desired ends. A craft image, then, includes technical skills drawn from experience and reflection independently applied in both prosaic and creative ways to develop content and character in children.[29]

The image of the artist has a long, esteemed history although few writers distinguish between the practical arts with a scientific basis (e.g., medicine, engineering, weather forecasting) or those that draw from folk experience (e.g., cooking, coaching, fishing, law) and fine arts (e.g., music, art, and drama) where aesthetics and performance dominate. I combine the fine and practical arts because both involve ideas of craft within artistic practice and the need for teacher invention, analysis, and improvisation.[30]

The merging of craftsman and artist acknowledges the importance of experience, technique, reflection in action, and autonomy in pursuing goals. This conception of teaching is embedded deeply in the image of the teacher as professional. Professionals render independent judgments based on a repertoire of skills, accumulated formal knowledge, and direct experience. Yet in judging, professionals know full well that invention and imagination and timing and tempo are critical in coping with the unknown and the unpredictable.[31]

The interplay in teaching between science and artistry, between technique and feeling, opens the window for independent judgment, personal autonomy, and professional expertise. The notion of teacher as decision maker, determining what to teach and how to communicate content and skills to students, becomes central to instruction. Transforming the young into mature youth of substantial character inspired the artistic vision. These images of craftsman/artist within public schools date back to the early decades of the nineteenth century.

NINETEENTH CENTURY EDUCATORS. Evangelist for public schools, Horace Mann, appointed secretary in 1837 to the newly created State Board of Education in Massachusetts, frequently included his ideas of what teaching is and what teachers should do in his annual reports on schooling in the state. Writing in the waning years of the Lancasterian enthusiasm, Mann offered his views of teaching:

> He imparts vigor; he supplies knowledge; he ripens judgment; he establishes principle; and he then bends them on their way to fulfill the great duties of earth, and to be more and more prepared for another life.

> He cannot impart, unless the child consents to receive. What, then, is the state of mind most receptive of knowledge and most cooperative in acquiring it? Surely, it is a state of confidence, of trustfulness, of respect, of affection. Hence it follows that the first great duty of a teacher is to awaken these sentiments in the breasts of his pupils. . . . Does not the farmer break up the soil, and open it to the sun, before he commits the seed to its bosom in expectation of a harvest? Have not celebrated artists owed their fame as much to the

careful preparation of their materials as to the skill with which they afterwards combined them?[32]

Cyrus Pierce, also from Massachusetts, who ministered to a congregation (a career common to many school reformers), left to become a private school teacher, then accepted a post as high school principal in Nantucket, and finally, in 1839, accepted, upon Horace Mann's urgings, the headship of the first normal school in America.

When asked in 1851 about what his aims were as head of a normal school, Pierce replied:

> Yes, to make better teachers; teachers who would understand, and do their business better; teachers who should know more of the nature of children, of youthful developments, more of the subjects to be taught, and more of the true methods of teaching; who would teach more philosophically, more in harmony with the natural development of the young mind.
>
> The old method of teaching Arithmetic, for example, by taking up some printed treatise and solving abstract questions consisting of large numbers working blindly by what must appear to the pupil as arbitrary rules, would now be regarded as less philosophical, less in conformity to mental development than the modern way of beginning with mental Arithmetic, using practical questions which involve small numbers, and explaining the reason of every step as you go along.
>
> And the teacher who should attempt to teach reading by requiring a child to repeat from day to day, and from month to month, the whole alphabet, until he is familiar with all the letters, as was the fashion in former days, would deserve to lose his place and be sent himself to school. Teaching is based on immutable principles and may be regarded as an art.[33]

Pierce, Mann, and other reformers saw that while teaching may be a practical art, those who wished to teach should be schooled both in subjects and pedagogy. Nineteenth century normal schools nourished the notion that there is a body of knowledge about the art and science of teaching that can be used reliably in classrooms. The transforming of craftsman/artist into professional begins in these years.

By the closing decades of the century, the issue of how scientific the art of teaching was still puzzled educators. In 1881 the National

Council of Education discussed a committee report prepared by distinguished academics and superintendents that answered the question, Is there a science of teaching?

"Yes," they answered. "A science," the committee stated, "is a systematized aggregate of knowledge relating to some special important subject." Just having an "aggregate of knowledge" is insufficient; scientific knowledge is orderly, connected, and systematic. Given these definitions, the committee concluded that teaching or "pedagogics" is a science.

> It embodies in the first place, an aggregate of knowledge gathered through thousands of years, and so well known in many of its features, that it has become the commonplace experience of the race. Child-nature has been the object of study of every mother and every teacher. The pedagogical knowledge derived from experience and thought has been systematized by many thinkers and teachers. . . . There is also one central point to which all of these centralized data relate, namely, the Child. . . . The science of pedagogics consists of maxims or ethical axioms and of data arranged systematically and causally or logically connected.[34]

The committee's wrestling with the relationship between science and art were, of course, part of the larger struggle to professionalize the craft. Certifying those who completed their schooling and urging teachers to continue their education were central to nineteenth century reformers' efforts to elevate both the status and practice of teaching. Converting the craft of teaching into a science, or if that was too ambitious, at least to give instruction a scientific veneer, was tied closely to the growth of the National Education Association (1870), expansion of universities, and a growing self-consciousness among educators. Whichever impulses drove reformers, the notion that the teacher needed more freedom to make classroom decisions was essential.[35]

The freedom that teachers needed to guide students was implicit in the conception of teaching that John Dewey put forward in the 1890s and later. Dewey's influence on how teaching should be done continues to shape thinking about classrooms and teachers in the remaining decades of this century. It was Dewey who offered a fuller, broader, and compelling image of teacher as a combination of artist, scientist, tacit reformer, and moral actor. His writings not only changed the terms of the debate about what teachers ought to be but also offered critics the vocabulary of criticism for any shortcomings that subsequently emerged from classrooms.[36]

To Dewey the teacher was the instrument for turning a sterile schooling into a potent education. The drawing out of a student's full mental and emotional powers and connecting learning with social change could now happen within the four walls of a classroom. Learning could be socially useful, by developing the mind and character of a child while removing the worst excesses of an industrialized and urbanized society. What Dewey expected of teachers was far more than what they did in the nation's classrooms at the turn of the century. He saw teachers and children engaged in a process of mutual learning in a highly moral enterprise. No longer the single authority, the teacher helped students link formal knowledge with the larger culture.

To do this, teachers had to know about the psychology of child development, the principles of learning, how groups worked, subject matter, theory, and the philosophical foundations of education. The teacher had to become a professional with knowledge anchored in the sciences, philosophy, and history. In 1897 Dewey published *My Pedagogic Creed*. In it the transforming image of a teacher emerges clearly.

> The school is primarily a social institution. Education being a social process, the school is simply that form of community life in which all of those agencies are concentrated that will be most effective in bringing the child to share in the inherited resources of the race and to use his own powers for social ends.
>
> Education, therefore, is a process of living and not a preparation for future living.
>
> The teacher is not in the school to impose certain ideas or to form certain habits in the child, but is there as a member of the community to select the influences which shall affect the child and to assist him in properly responding to these influences.
>
> The discipline of the school should proceed from the life of the school as a whole and not directly from the teacher.
>
> The teacher's business is simply to determine, on the basis of larger experience and riper wisdom, how the discipline of life shall come to the child.[37]

The conception of the teacher that Dewey set forth expects much of the men and women that enter classrooms. They need to construct daily experiences that, while permitting children to figure out for themselves what is necessary to learn, still connect to the ethical ends that education seeks. The conventional view of the teacher as a formal authority presenting the student with content, in Dewey's perspective, shifts toward joint student and teacher planning, more physical movement in the classroom, and active involvement in tasks that make sense to the students—all of which are linked to the larger culture. Such fundamental shifts in expectations for what teachers should do imposes different obligations upon the teacher, obligations that require much teacher knowledge, skill, creativity, imagination and freedom to act. Could such an image of teaching survive in the existing world of urban and rural schools?

Hardly. Only in private schools, where the teacher is most free to teach, and occasional rural one-room schoolhouses, an institution reformers sought to eliminate, could such a vision of teaching survive intact. In the early twentieth century one-room school, the teacher faced twenty or more students of varying ages, scattered across at least eight grades, for five or more hours a day and six or more months a year. She was expected to teach all of the subjects. An occasional visit from the county superintendent constituted supervision. For many teachers, isolated from colleagues and ill-trained for the low-paying position, teaching became a mechanical series of recitations devoid of meaning to most students. Such instances of unimaginative instruction became grist for reformers intent upon consolidating one-room schools into larger units, in effect, modernizing rural schools to make them replicas of urban ones.[38]

But for some teachers in these settings, isolation became precious freedom. Lack of supervision led to instructional risk taking, trial and error. Few materials sparked ingenuity in many teachers, including Marian Brooks.

After graduating high school in 1924 at the age of fifteen, Brooks began her first job in a New Hampshire one-room school located in a small Irish farming community. To prepare herself she spent the summer at a nearby normal school. That September she faced eleven children in grades 1 through 8, of whom one boy, a repeater of earlier grades a number of times, was waiting until he turned sixteen to leave school.[39]

I was required to follow the teaching guide issued by the State Department of Education and the textbooks in reading, math, spelling, grammar, history, and geography. There were very few resource materials such as maps, games, supplementary reading books; these the teacher had to supply if she wished to have them in the classroom. I was also required to have posted a detailed timetable of each day's program, and I still recall the struggle I had in making a timetable that would include all the content areas: ten minutes of first grade reading, ten minutes of fourth grade reading, ten minutes of fourth grade math, and so on. But it was a greater and more frustrating struggle to follow it each day. I finally gave up, ignored it and went about establishing an organization that seemed to make more sense to me and the needs of the children.

We read together at the same time or did math together. I would work with one child, such as the little boy in first grade who needed my help in beginning to read, or with the group; the rest of the children would help each other. The fourth graders would read from their history text together as a group or individually if they wished, helping each other with the study problems at the end of the chapter. . . . My very competent little girl in the eighth grade often read with the children in the second grade, then later I would work with them on the reading skills.

As I look back on those years I realize what a great learning experience it was for me as a beginning teacher. Sure if I had had an experienced teacher to confer with and give me some sympathetic guidance and support I, no doubt, would have done a better job in reassessing my practices and making changes. But it was equally important for my own development that I was free from many outside pressures and had the time to find my own style of responding to the children and to discover ways of making learning and school an experience that they could become excited about and enjoy.[40]

By the 1920s reformers interested in modernizing rural schools had introduced to country schools bureaucratic organization, supervision, a planned curriculum with accompanying texts, and large buildings housing hundreds of students listening to college educated and state certified teachers. But beliefs in teachers making independent judgments about content and methods of instruction persisted in the growing professionalization of the craft.

Invariably the belief that teachers, as professionals, should have the autonomy to create motivated learners was wedded to the child-centered wing of the progressive education movement. The broader view of the pupil as more than a mind that needed molding to the contours of an adult-generated curriculum gained increasing currency among teachers and administrators in the years between the two World Wars. For the most part, these reformers wanted instruction and curriculum tailored to children's interests; they wanted instruction to occur in small groups or individually; they wanted programs that permitted children more freedom and creativity than existed in urban schools; they wanted school experiences connected to activities outside the classroom; and they wanted children to help shape the direction of their learning. Accompanying these progressive ideas about schooling was the idea of the teacher as a careful decision maker qualified to decide what students needed, when, and under what conditions.[41]

In the 1920s, for example, Denver Superintendent Jesse Newlon, a leader among pedagogical progressives, initiated an experiment in teacher decision making that combined the image of the teacher as craftsman/artist with the image of a professional. Newlon believed that involving teachers directly in determining what they would teach would lead to a staff "that would teach better and with more understanding and sympathy than they could ever otherwise teach."[42] Why did Newlon believe this?

> It is only by actively engaging in the process of curriculum construction that a teacher can attain his greatest effectiveness. There is no substitute possible for a maximum of teacher participation if teacher growth and effectiveness . . . are to be expected from classroom procedures. Since teaching is a professional job, the practitioner can be master of his profession only if he is conversant with the theories that underlie practice.[43]

Participation meant that teachers chaired subject matter committees on which principals and central office administrators served. Substitutes replaced teachers on those days when committees met. Each committee prepared objectives, selected content, designed instructional methods, including which questions to ask, and suggested varied projects and materials that their colleagues might use. After syllabi were written, they were used in classroom trials, and with further comments from teachers, revisions were made.[44]

Such teacher involvement was rare in the 1920s. Bureaucratic curriculum-making reigned. Most districts designed curricula in the central office, shipped it to principals, and ordered that it be implemented. Supervisers inspected classrooms to determine if the curricula were being taught. Denver's experiment placed teachers at the center of curriculum design. Essential to this process was the belief that teachers had to understand how a curriculum was put together if they were to teach it well. What went on in teachers' minds, their intentions, became crucial to teacher improvement.

Teacher participation in curriculum development spread as a result of the Denver experience but seldom with the intensity that Newlon and his successors brought to it. Of course, teacher associations and, later, unions made this assumption central to their professional activities. But they were private groups openly serving teachers' material interests. For administrators to nourish that conception was unusual in the post-World War I decades.

The notion of teacher as craftsman/artist persisted in ensuing decades. Gilbert Highet's *The Art of Teaching* (1950) continued the familiar dialogue between art and science. "I believe," he wrote, "that teaching is an art, not a science." Acknowledging the orderly and systematic work that is part of teaching, Highet believes, is not science. "Teaching involves emotions which cannot be systematically appraised and employed, and human values, which are quite outside the grasp of science."[45]

If Highet's book draws from the great teachers of the past, Philip Jackson's classic, *Life in Classrooms,* captures the complex society of thirty children and one adult that exists for six hours daily within a small room. In contributing to the discussion of art and science, Jackson concludes:

> People who are interested in the application of learning theory or the engineering point of view to teaching practice often have as their goal the transformation of teaching from something crudely resembling an art to something crudely resembling a science. But there is no good evidence to suggest that such a transformation is either possible or desirable. An equally reasonable goal . . . is to seek an understanding of the teaching process as it is commonly performed before making an effort to change it. As we learn more about what

goes on in these densely populated hives of educational activity it may turn out that we will seek to preserve, rather than to transform, whatever amount of artistry is contained in the teacher's work.[46]

Other recent books continue the tradition of viewing the act of teaching as some ineffable mix of science and practical art. Louis Rubin devotes an entire book to teachers as artists. Ken Macrorie found twenty teachers and professors who were "enablers," people who did more than transmit the knowledge of the world and get it back from students on tests; these were people who "help others to do good works and extend their already considerable powers."[47]

The image of teacher as craftsman/artist continues to inspire researchers, practitioners, and policymakers. It also continues to compete with the image of teacher as bureaucrat/technocrat. No single public image captures a consensus among teachers and nonteachers over what teaching should be. Among educators, however, the conception of teacher as professional merges the technical and moral images, sacrificing clarity for a blend, but one that has come to be the preferred metaphor, blurred and unaccepted by many researchers and other professions as it may be.[48]

Over the last century and a half, academics, policymakers, and citizen reformers have viewed the classroom as a place where teachers *ought* to do one thing or another in the quest to raise the next generation correctly. Often holding the same views, teachers also have entered classrooms with private images of how they should go about their work with children. These contending images rose and fell in popularity depending, it seemed, on the larger social forces at work in the culture and the particular experiences and values that teachers had. The uneasy coexistence of these pictures in people's minds continues to this day. What these pictures of teaching suggest is that images have a potent influence on policies and practices. In effect, the pictures help shape teaching behavior.

After all, teachers do so many things in classrooms. The image of bureaucrat/technocrat inevitably conveys a fraction of the essential classroom tasks. There *is* a rule-governed and technical set of tasks in managing a crowd of children for six hours a day. Attendance has to be taken; tests have to be given; homework policies have to be complied with at some level. Moreover, there are techniques that need to be mastered by teachers to construct tests, to question, to praise and reprimand, and scores of other mundane but essential classroom tasks that constitute what a skilled classroom teacher should do.

Similarly, the craftsman/artist image fits another portion of classroom activities. Improvising when emergencies arise with students or when planned activities go awry; sensing that special moment of when *not* to proceed with the next planned task and, continuing with what is going on instead; deciding when there is too much planned, too much crowded into too little time, and figuring out how to better pace the lesson.

Within a six hour day a teacher may proceed in a technocratic manner in drilling students, assigning and monitoring seatwork, and similar tasks; yet at other portions of the day, that same teacher will work with groups, handle an outburst by a tense child, confer with an individual student while the rest of the class is working, and lead a soaring discussion. Both images of teaching then, like two-dimensional Egyptian paintings, depict portions of the teacher's duties. But a third dimension is needed to give depth to the classroom portrait. If the history of these images of teaching helps us understand something of classroom instruction, we have yet to find out how teachers teach and the varied roles that they play in the classroom.

TEACHING: WHAT HAPPENS IN CLASSROOMS

How Teachers Taught

Few historians have written about what teachers have done in classrooms. The enormous task of recapturing classroom descriptions from student recollections, teacher autobiographies, school reports, photographs and paintings, accounts from visitors, and other sources intimidates most researchers, save for those determined to reconstruct what happened.

Barbara Finkelstein, using many of the above sources, described teaching in rural and urban elementary schools between 1820 and 1880. In those classrooms teachers talked a great deal. Students either recited passages from textbooks, worked at their desks on assignments, or listened to the teacher and classmates. Teachers expected uniformity in both behavior and classwork. According to Finkelstein, teachers told students "when they should sit, when they should stand, when they should hang their coats, when they should turn their heads." Frequently students entered, stood, sat, wrote, and spoke as one.

Documenting these patterns, Finkelstein richly detailed monitorial schools established in cities in the 1820s, where group recitations and standardized behavior were routine in rural one-room schools, where individual students sat before the teacher on the recitation bench and raced through their memorized text.

Finkelstein found three patterns of teaching in these classrooms. The "Intellectual Overseer" assigned work, punished errors, and had students memorize. The "Drillmaster" led students in unison through lessons requiring them to repeat content aloud. The "Interpreter of Culture" located only occasionally, clarified ideas and explained content to the children.[49]

My research on both elementary and secondary classrooms between 1890 and 1980, using similar sources, extended Finkelstein's work into the closing decades of the twentieth century.

In studying over 7000 classrooms, urban and rural, black and white, poor and nonpoor, at times of peak efforts to alter classroom instruction (e.g., progressivism in the 1920s and 1930s and open education in the 1960s), I found the persistent domination of teacher-centered practices before, during, and after each of the intense surges of reform aimed at installing student-centered approaches.[50]

Changes did occur. Reforms left their marks on chalkboards, desks, and teachers' repertoires. Some teachers, mostly in elementary schools, created their versions of student-centered instruction where pupils could move about freely to work at learning or activity "centers," where clustered desks encouraged cooperation, and where student-teacher planning occurred.

Other teachers—a much larger number—used certain student-centered practices for part of a day or once a week. They felt such innovations would benefit children and not unsettle existing classroom routines. Some, for example, began grouping students for certain periods a day; others established a science or reading center in a corner of the room. Some pulled desks into a circle so that children could talk to one another as they worked; others choose a unit on American Indians and tried to integrate many subjects into the three weeks spent on the project. These new practices were often used slowly on a consciously selective, piecemeal basis. Over time, practice altered.

But most teachers, especially at the secondary level, retained the general teacher-centered pattern of instruction. Studies of teaching behavior in the 1980s confirm these dominant teacher-centered practices.[51]

Such studies fail to capture the rhythms and busyness of classroom life; the complex repertoires that teachers use in varying what they do in different settings; the daily ebb and flow of emotions that tie teacher and students to one another; the unique culture that develops for thirty-six weeks and disappears when the school year ends. The nature of that classroom culture adds an important dimension to understanding the realities that teachers face daily. I now turn to what some classroom observers have found.

Teaching and Learning in Classrooms

When the state compels a group of students to spend six hours a day absorbing certain information and learning particular skills from an adult certified to teach, the DNA of classroom life emerges. Implacable imperatives drive much of what occurs between students and teachers, regardless of what pedagogy is used, or the personal traits or philosophy of the teacher.[52]

Walter Doyle detailed concisely these classroom facts of life.

MULTIDIMENSIONALITY. The classroom is a crowded place where many tasks have to be done. As Doyle states, "Records must be kept, schedules met, supplies organized and stored, and students' work collected and evaluated." With limited resources available to achieve many goals, complex choices must continually be made against this backdrop of shifting school circumstances.[53]

SIMULTANEITY. Many events occur at the same time. A third grade teacher, for example, listening to Barbara read aloud in the top reading group, scans the class. With a snap of her finger, she signals Jose, who had left his desk and worksheet, to return to his chair. Barbara makes two mistakes and the teacher questions Barbara. A messenger from the office delivers lunch tickets. Two students come up to the teacher and whisper in her ear. She nods and they pick up the wooden pass hanging by the door and leave for the lavatory. Elapsed time: thirty seconds.

IMMEDIACY. Classroom events swiftly begin and end. Seldom do teachers have time to deliberate before acting. Researchers estimate that an elementary teacher daily has over 500 exchanges with individual students. Reprimands or praise for the conduct of students occurs almost ninety times a day.[54]

UNPREDICTABILITY. Interruptions occur frequently. Lesson plans get diverted by student inattention, minor crises, or simple distractions. Announcements from the principal's office over the classroom's public address system compete with a child's sudden illness or a flare-up between two students over crayons. What becomes predictable is the unexpected.

PUBLICNESS. All classroom behavior is on display. Favoritism or vindictiveness on either a child's or teacher's part is noticed as is a spelling error on the chalkboard or a soup stain on the teacher's necktie. A class is an audience for whom a teacher or child can perform, where isolated misbehavior or singular achievement get amplified like an echo in a cavern. Few secrets exist in classrooms.

HISTORY. Over thirty-six weeks, a teacher and students develop a relationship that has a beginning, middle, and end. Norms, rituals, ceremonies, and myths arise and mature in a class. From class applause for a student giving a sterling oral report, to placing a special inked stamp in the shape of a star on the back of a child's hand for good behavior, to the shared (and perhaps mistaken) belief of a junior high history class that the teacher was once a major league baseball player—a culture grows within a class. A history is jointly created and lived by a teacher and class.[55]

All of these characteristics form the DNA of classroom life, the man-made genetic material that creates the scaffolding for one adult and two dozen or so pupils to live together in a confined space for six hours daily, thirty-six weeks a year. Between the earlier reconstruction of how teachers taught and the characteristics described above—what Willard Waller called the "human nature of the classroom"—the varied and complicated roles that teachers must play in order to teach students emerge more clearly.[56]

ROLES TEACHERS PERFORM IN THE CLASSROOM. Because most teachers picture themselves as professionals and because they work in a bureaucratic organization, crosscutting demands inevitably arise. Expected to work alone in a classroom applying expertise and expert judgment to instruction, teachers must also respond to organizational mandates that send rules, materials, students, and supervisors into their rooms.

Moreover, teachers must struggle with what they believe professionally is best for students, the values they prize, and the special needs, diverse abilities and behaviors that students bring to the classroom. That internal battle over how to reconcile professional norms and personal beliefs with the realities of students' differences gets sharpened when parents or other constituencies lobby the teacher or principal to respond to these differences. These considerable obligations to students, organizational demands, professional norms, and personal values produce a mind-bending melange of tasks from which a teacher must choose. From this complexity of conflicting obligations, the nature of the classroom as a workplace, the variation that exists among students, and the incomplete history of what teachers have done in classrooms, I have extracted what I believe are three primary and interdependent roles that define the teaching core: instructional, managerial, and political.[57]

THE CORE ROLES OF CLASSROOM TEACHING

Instructional

This role is the familiar one of the teacher planning the subject matter of the lesson, determining the materials and methods to use, motivating students to learn, harnessing their energies, and determining if students have learned what was intended. What some researchers label as logical (explaining, comparing, concluding) and strategic (planning, counseling, questioning) acts of teaching are instructional. This is the role for which the teacher has been trained: to convey to students the formal knowledge, skills, and values designated as important by the community.

The description of how teachers taught in the last century frames the role's crude outline. Pedagogical routines wedded to subject matter give content to the role. Yet how teachers use recitation, seatwork, lectures, computers, and a dozen other approaches vary. Public and private images of what teaching should be like compete with researchers' findings and practitioners' folklore. While there are numerous models of how teachers have taught and should teach, no clear agreement exists on the "shoulds." Lacking a consensus over how teachers should teach, within the instructional role exist numerous approaches. Many teachers concentrate upon the subject matter of lessons; some focus on getting students to learn how to learn; other teachers adopt a highly personal approach that is nurturing or caring. Grade levels and subject matter also affect the enacting of the instructional role: a kindergarten teacher and a calculus teacher with a class of college-bound seniors differ dramatically in instructional style.[58]

Managerial

The primary focus of this role aims to achieve both crowd control and instructional order. Because students are required to attend school, the imperatives of classroom management generate rules and routines. Teachers set standards for acceptable behavior and academic performance; establish procedures for doing homework and going to the bathroom; organize the flow of paperwork, from keeping attendance and grading quizzes to completing reports for the principal; pace such varied classroom activities as individual seatwork, small group work at learning centers, and total group lessons; they also punish children for violating school rules. Nicknames for the managerial tasks that teachers assume in this role capture its range: traffic cop, referee, supply sergeant, and gatekeeper. The managerial role is central to the image of teacher as bureaucrat/technocrat.

Managerial styles vary among teachers. Some classrooms are exemplars of Prussian efficiency, while others display cluttered desks, file drawers, and book shelves and chunks of unplanned time. Despite differences in style, crowd management serves professional purposes of reaching classroom instructional goals and the larger society's goals of compliance with authority, impersonal application of rules, and learning to live in a community. While in some instances the initial aim may be to establish order (e.g., a new teacher entering a classroom in December after a succession of substitutes), once maintenance of order and the establishment of routines occurs, the basic purpose of formal schooling—classroom instruction—can take place. Both the managerial and instructional roles demand that choices be made by the teacher. How those decisions are made, the content of the decisions, and the actions to put those decisions into practice constitute the political role.

Political

The sense of the word *political*, as used here, is generic: how to get done what is desirable in an highly contested, unpredictable world. Yet how can one link political action to dealing with children in classrooms? After all, a primary assumption is that political behavior occurs between adults who vote and choose to freely join or exit a group. I argue that minors compelled to attend schools where teachers and principals are invested with formal authority over them are special instances of a political system.

Inequality in status, knowledge, and skills prevent children in classrooms from choosing freely among options. They are expected to comply with adults' requests. But compliance is seldom automatic. Teachers must negotiate a classroom order with students who influence what teachers decide to teach and the pedagogy used. Teachers must determine when to act, who in the class to cultivate, how to arrange tasks to maintain calm and encourage learning. In these and other classroom decisions, teachers act politically—although they would call their behavior "classroom management" or "maintaining discipline." In the sense that teachers use a political process with minors to achieve desired ends, the teacher acts politically.

Many educators still wince over the use of the word *political* in reference to schools, much less a teacher. A century ago, in many parts of the nation, elected public officials appointed school board members, principals, and teachers. In some cities school board elections produced scores of trustees who would look upon administrative and teaching positions as jobs to distribute among the faithful like food baskets given to loyal voters just before election day. The schools in many cities were part of a patronage system. Contracts with book publishers or desk manufacturers went to those companies that had the most influence with school trustees. School affairs were indistinguishable from the machine politics that governed the police, public health departments, and street repair.[59]

With turn-of-the-century progressives eager to apply science to city government, a major shift in school governance placed the operation of schools in the hands of small boards of education dominated by business and professional men (and later college educated housewives) predisposed to delegate responsibility to educational experts (i.e., superintendents and principals). The language and the open practice of partisan politics among school officials was banished. Shielded from public view by a wall constructed by school boards to separate educational affairs from the rest of city government, political behavior continued, of course, but was referred to by another name. Moreover, professional norms emerged that made partisan activity in the community and the very use of political vocabulary virtually taboo. While those taboos have eroded over the last few decades, strong feelings about schools being special and removed from the familiar tussles within the larger political arena continue among many educators.[60]

Apart from these historically understandable responses by educators, there is no escaping a central fact: The teacher works within a publicly financed institution governed by noneducators. Teachers, then, are agents of the community (through the school board and administration), authorized to carry out its expectations for schooling the young. This means the teacher uses formal authority, rules, control, and influence to move students toward a desired end. Hence, teachers, not only work within a political institution but they act politically in their classrooms as they try to achieve the goals they have set for their students.

Schools, for example, are expected to teach children about the Declaration of Independence and fortify their sense of right and wrong. Respect for adults is to be learned from teachers along with the periodical table of chemicals. Parents expect their children will learn how to read and how to find a job. Aiming to improve the character, knowledge, and skills of children makes schools intensely political places.

For teachers to make political choices, they, in effect, will make moral ones also. While not all political choices have moral values embedded within them, choosing one value over another in seeking a desirable end for students is a moral decision. At times, when a controversy surges through a community's schools, such as whether to teach the biblical or scientific accounts of life's origins, political decisions anchored in moral values emerge clearly. For a teacher to decide that Darwin's discoveries are not only inaccurate but antireligious, means the teacher is acting both politically and morally in sharing those views with students. How different that is from the teacher who must decide what factors caused the Great Depression; except to a Marxist, such a decision carries little or no moral freight.

But in a larger sense, teaching children in of itself is a moral act. By having an adult authorized to exercise power on behalf of the state to instruct the young, who are compelled to attend, an unequal relationship between a child and teacher is legitimized. A teacher who accepts the dominant position assumes a moral responsibility for moving children toward desirable goals. For decades courts have recognized the special moral relationship that teachers have in regard to personal behavior, speech, and what they choose to teach.[61]

Hence, politics (and therefore morality) enters the classroom in the daily and weekly choices teachers must make about tactics in assuring student compliance, responding to bureaucratic demands, and determining what content and methods to use. The actions they take to implement those choices, the process of converting what ought to be into what is taught, I call political.

When teachers, for example, punish an entire class for the misbehavior of two students, that is politics in action. When teachers give gold stars to second graders who scored highest on an arithmetic test, that is politics in action. When teachers disregard a principal's request to enter into their roll books what lessons they taught each day, that is politics in action. Or when Richard Schmidt showed the anti-abortion film to his junior high classes, that is politics in action.

Teachers stand between what policymakers intend, what administrators direct, what students and parents expect, and what occurs in classrooms. By their decisions and actions, teachers determine the degree to which a policy is implemented faithfully, transformed to fit the classroom, or ignored. Within classrooms, then, teachers engage in political acts. A few examples should help make clear this important point about the political nature of a teacher's decision making and actions.[62]

Consider what many researchers have discovered (but practitioners knew through experience) in secondary school classrooms where teachers and students negotiated tacit deals over how much work will be assigned and completed in exchange for student orderliness. Such deals, where they exist, reveal anew how the teacher's managerial and political roles intertwine. Some bargains constructed by intensely engaged teachers (e.g., band director, football coach, advanced placement biology teacher, or auto mechanics instructor) extract large quantities of work and superior performance from students. Many bargains, however, are what Theodore Sizer calls the "conspiracy of the least." These informal contracts, struck quietly between consenting parties representing contested interests, are political deals that teachers and students negotiate to create a stable environment where resistance and conflict are reduced.[63]

Another example is testing. Arising from a public clamor for evidence that school district performance is satisfactory, many districts directed their schools to prepare students for periodic tests. Individual teachers must decide the degree of adherence they give to such organizational mandates. Teachers ask themselves how much student preparation for tests is enough. Teachers calculate the instructional trade-offs in estimating how much time needs to be set aside for test preparation, how similar the practice items are to the ones in the actual test, and how comfortable they feel professionally with that degree of match. A first grade teacher must decide whether the standardized achievement test mandated by the district or state is an accurate measure of what a six-year-old child has learned.[64]

Using the limited powers at their disposal and working within a unique setting where children and adults are unequal, teachers parse public policies to fit the grammar of the classroom in order to reach goals that they have set for their students. Thus, teachers not only work within an unusual political arena but they act politically as they negotiate how to achieve their goals in an unpredictable and complex setting.

These three overlapping, but nonetheless distinct, roles form the teaching core. From conflicting obligations generated by professional norms and personal values, the nature of the workplace, the historic images of what teaching should be and what has occurred in classrooms, and student variation, a cluster of three interdependent roles frame the broad outlines of what teachers do daily in classrooms. Let me make these interdependent roles clear by illustrating how one teacher's ideas and performance combine the three.

A Kindergarten Teacher

In her all-day kindergarten (a "magnet" class that draws from a public housing project) Thelma Katz has twenty-four children evenly split between black and white, boys and girls. Completing her eighteenth year as a teacher and her sixth at Westwood Elementary in Pittsburgh, she usually arrives at school at 7:15 A.M. to get ready for her class which arrives at 8:30. Since she has an aide for only twenty minutes a day, she spends the hour getting materials in place for the score of activities that will unfold during the day: salt and sugar containers for a science lesson, art materials and a new puppet for centers that the five year olds will use later in the day. Records need to be in place for the many songs that she and the children sing.[65]

Except for a quick lunch and forty minutes in the afternoon (a period when the class goes to music, art, or physical education—an arrangement that Katz negotiated with the principal), Katz has no breaks until 2:35 P.M. when school ends. She usually leaves around 3:10 P.M.. The only other daily help she will have are two parent volunteers whom she recruited.

Mornings are structured and fast paced. After the pledge to the flag, Katz will lead the class in the first of many songs. She then moves to a large calendar, sounds out the letter *m* for March, and through coaching and vigorous choral responses the children tell her the day of the week, the date, and that St. Patrick's day is coming soon. She then gathers the five year olds in a circle around her and asks each child to share news. Jennifer tells the class how she smacked her little sister. In a rush of words, John spills out quickly that he received a toy car for a birthday present, and on it goes for five minutes as different children volunteer information.

Without missing a beat, Katz shifts to a familiar song and students join in singing. As she sings, she picks up a stack of number and color cards and moves to the large calendar. Here she announces at the end of the song, "We will review what we learned this week." The entire class, still seated in a circle, repeats in unison the colors and numbers at Katz shows each card. She asks the class to count by tens to one hundred and name the days of the week and the months of the year. They respond eagerly. Katz scans the class continuously and, on occasion, will correct a child on his behavior. The kindergarteners are tuned into Katz's tone of voice, hand signals, and facial expressions. And her reprimands focus on the child's behavior, not his or her character.

The transition to telling time on a clock comes easily after reviewing days and months on the calendar. She picks up a stack of paper plates she has converted into clock faces with movable hands. Katz chooses two children to pass out the "clocks" to the rest of the class as they continue to sit on the rug. As she watches the children, she moves again to the record player, turning on a song about the hours of the day. As Katz sings along with the record, each child moves the hour hand in time with the singer's directions. When the song ends, the two children jump up to collect the clocks. Not losing the tempo, she directs the class's attention to a bulletin board that contains the daily schedule. Each activity for the remainder of the morning is covered slowly. As children raise their hands to ask questions about an activity (if they call out, Katz gently reminds them of class rules about hand-raising), she answers questions with a smile and, frequently, with a compliment.

The class will color a paper filled with suns and balloons—they are working on various number and color words and this is a reading worksheet; they will then do "first grade" work on a sheet (lots of "ooohs" and "aaahs" from the class), and they will be assigned to work in the three centers for the rest of the morning: art, math, and reading.

She explains that for the art center there is a special activity. They will make a shamrock for St. Patrick's Day. She shows the class how to paste a cutout shamrock on a paper plate and how to put yarn through holes, which will give the plate a look of a woven green border. Finally, Katz brings out two new language games that will be added to the puzzle center for the afternoon. In preparing for the many daily lessons and weekly changes in the centers, Katz has spent over $300 a year out of her own pocket above the district's allocation of materials.

After almost ten minutes of explaining and answering questions, the preview of coming attractions ends. Katz asks the class to stand. She goes to the record player and the words and music of "Disco Mickey Mouse," a class favorite, begin. As they stand in a circle, Katz and the children sway, touch parts of their body in time with the singer, snap fingers to the music, and sing the lyrics with the verve that would bring a smile to the songwriter's face. To a casual observer, what appears to be a routine (but enjoyable) activity is for Katz a way to teach the names of various body parts. After the record ends, Katz reviews the day's activities and the children return to their tables to begin on the worksheets. Katz moves around the room helping children and then moves to the reading center to work with individuals on the alphabet.

When the worksheets are completed, the "managers" of the three centers move to their assigned centers. Managers change daily. They know their duties: giving out pencils, collecting them, and straightening out the center. Katz wants the managers to independently carry out their duties. The class is divided into three groups that will rotate through the centers at a given signal from the teacher. For the rest of the morning, the children work contentedly. By this time in the school year, each child knows the routines, what materials to use, and what tasks to do. Five-year-old managers help when needed. While Katz usually stays in the reading center, she also moves quietly from center to center helping students, comforting a little boy on the verge of tears, or complimenting a girl for completing a center task so well. If a recalcitrant student doesn't respond to these teacher signals, Katz sends the child to the "Time Out" corner to think about what has happened.

After lunch, students choose from a broader array of centers: the doll house, puzzles, music, math, perceptual motor skills, blocks, the puppet center, the store, art, or science. Students go over to each center, where strands of color necklaces identifying the activity hang.

The child picks a necklace and goes to the appropriate center. Thus, at a glance Katz knows where each of the students should be and what he or she should be doing. Usually, all-day kindergartners have a rest period in the afternoon. But Katz believes a rest period is unnecessary after the first month of school and uses the time for centers. If a child is sleepy or cranky, Katz lets the child rest. Near the end of the day, the class goes to music, art, or physical education, depending upon the day of the week. When they return, Katz will alternate each day with a snack, a story, or a game; then they prepare to go home. Another school day ends for Thelma Katz.

Both children and teacher face a busy, crowded day between 8:30 A.M. and 2:35 P.M. Art, music, reading, and math come together in a set of imaginative activities that five year olds enjoy. She makes tasks into games so that work and play merge. "Most of the time," she says, "the kids don't even know they're learning." But it takes a lot of her time. "Last night, I was thinking of how I could teach rhyming words to make it fun for the kids."

Katz groups and regroups children throughout the day. All twenty-four students work as a group for an hour in the morning and then move into small groups at each center for the rest of the morning. After lunch, twenty minutes may be spent together as a large group for listening to a story, but most of the afternoon is spent in the centers or in small groups. Why the mixed pattern of grouping?

"I began using centers in the early 1970s and I found small groups got kids to learn, be independent, and make decisions. Also, I found them personally satisfying," she said. "I can get them enthused about learning," she added. With more intensity, Katz said, "I need the closeness of a small group; there is warmth and excitement which I lose in the total class." With a group of eight or less, "I can spend time on getting kids to feel good about themselves; also if I am losing someone, I can see who it is."

With the emphasis of the Pittsburgh Board of Education and superintendent on accountability for content and skills taught in the elementary schools, I asked Katz how this shift had affected her use of centers and her approach to teaching.

> I feel the pressure. You are accountable. We have to give the Monitoring Achievement Test three times a year. It has 20 skills in it for kindergartners and I go over each child's work on the test. If items are missed, I find out which skills are involved. It is like a bible. Also

my principal calls us in to go over the results. Yes, I feel the pressure, but I don't really worry because I believe the kids will do well and be ready for the first grade. They always have in my class. There's far more stress on academics. They tell you what to cover but they don't tell you how to do it. You work around what they want. Homework, for example, is optional. I give it to them because I use it to build in routines for the first grade. It gives kids a sense of responsibility. We discuss that it is not their mom's responsibility to bring to school the homework but theirs. I work on them to be independent.

Kids should learn how to get along with one another. They should feel good about themselves. I work on these goals through the academics. Before they leave at the end of the day, I'll ask them what they have done that day and how do they feel about what they did. Now, that is important.

Katz works also on the link between home and classroom. She writes notes and phones parents weekly. "PR [public relations] is extremely important," she says. When she speaks with parents, she says that she begins with "I need your help." The two parent volunteers that work in the classroom daily create the basis for a parent network. When a volunteer will be absent, she will call another parent to substitute. But it is not only PR that motivates Katz to work with parents. She sees the results with the five year olds. When parents get involved with the child's work, "I can see how the kids do so much better the next day."

Thelma Katz enacts the three interdependent roles as a kindergarten teacher. The pattern she displays illustrates how the instructional and managerial roles intersect in grouping decisions, arranging the centers, organizing the traffic flow in the classroom, and the dozens of other seemingly routine acts of teaching. The political role emerges in her work with parents, in negotiations with the principal, and in the adaptations she makes to the mandates of the school district concerning tests and academics. In each of these areas, Katz uses her formal and informal power to accommodate competing interests in order to achieve her goals. Figure 3 suggests the particular configuration of roles for Thelma Katz.

Those teachers who work in schools for five, ten, or more years and move into administration carry with them these three interdependent roles. Over time, teachers-turned-administrators adapt these core roles to the broader arena of administration. That is what happened to me over the last thirty years as a practitioner.

Figure 3: Core Roles of Thelma Katz, Kindergarten Teacher*

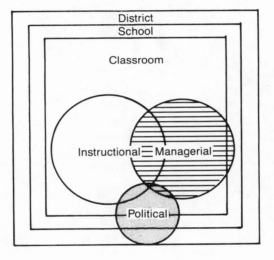

*The pattern of core roles is how I, as an observer, would align these roles into a pattern. This is a device to illustrate how roles converge and diverge. It is *not* meant to represent precisely how Katz carries out her three roles. Other teachers would have different patterns. In some instances, for example, the political role might be absent, overlap hardly at all. For other teachers, the managerial role might be dominant, overshadowing the instructional.

2

Drifting into Teaching and Staying Awhile

So often we discover the meaning of what we do and have done by looking backwards. And so it was with how I became a teacher.

After wandering through three years of undergraduate schooling in the early 1950s, sampling pre-medical and journalism courses at the University of Pittsburgh, I decided on history. In retrospect, the decision to major in history was understandable. As a high school student at Taylor-Allderdice High School, a twenty-minute trolley car ride from Pitt, my highest grade was a "C." Yet the one class that captivated me was world history.

The class was taught by Bertha Mitchell, a no-nonsense, by-the-book teacher. She introduced me and thirty classmates to the ancient world, medieval Europe, and the Renaissance. It was 1948; I was 13, in the tenth grade, and far more interested in finding out the secrets of popularity than attending classes, most of which I feared (I had failed Algebra) or didn't care a whit about.

Except for world history. It was the only class that I can recall in which I did homework, read beyond what the teacher assigned, constructed models of pyramids and castles, and drew elaborately detailed maps with mountains drawn to scale and arcane legends. That passion for studying history and that memory of Bertha Mitchell resurfaced in my junior and senior years of college. I majored in American and European history as I prepared to become a teacher.

Drift rather than intention is how I recall applying for the School of Education. I barely made the required "C" average. The courses

41

that I took, except for history, philosophy, and one methods course in social studies teaching, were forgettable. These particular courses led me to connect ideas with experience, testifying to the quality of the professors and my readiness to make connections. My peak experience as an undergraduate was the four months in the spring of 1955 when I student-taught American and world history at Peabody High School.

Because I worked fulltime at the post office from 11 P.M. to 7 A.M., I would teach the two classes at Peabody in the late morning and early afternoon; I spent all of my available time preparing detailed lesson plans that were virtually scripts for me to follow. My supervising teachers at Peabody High School, like Bertha Mitchell, pursued the conventional teacher-centered practice. I was expected to assign students pages to read in the textbook and questions to be answered; in class I was expected to lecture, have students recite answers to the assigned questions, and lead discussions.

I did all of this with passion. Frightened by the responsibility, yet eager to do well, I looked forward to every lesson I had to teach. Andrew Jackson's fight with the national bank became a test of how I could get students to understand the points in the text and to keep them interested in it. No easy task I discovered.

Within three weeks, my supervising teachers, either confident that I could do a minimally decent job or simply eager to have an additional period for themselves, left me alone with the two classes. I cannot remember much of the details of what occurred, although a warm glow still remains. What I remember is the theatrical flavor of teaching. Every day was a dramatic performance and I had to be ready. My lines, just as when I appeared in Pitt Player productions, had to be memorized; I had to entertain; audience participation was essential. Before each class, I could feel my stomach muscles tense. I was wired for action.

I could write that I entered teaching to improve the lot of under-educated children, to serve the community, or a similar noble sentiment. While such motives may have been buried within my psyche, what really appealed to me initially was performing and the challenge of conveying to others what I believed to be crucial information.

Response from students, only several years younger than me (I had just turned twenty years old), must have been either neutral or mildly positive because I recall much laughter and genuine helpfulness whenever my university professor and my supervising teachers entered the room. I cannot recall any problems in managing the class. While I attributed that to my natural talents in dealing with people, the more convincing explanation might be that the two veteran teachers whose classes I had taken in January had set down rules which I religiously followed.

I enjoyed student teaching and, according to all reports, did an adequate job, but I entered a job market in 1955 that had a surplus of social studies teachers. Because I wanted to stay in the area, I applied for numerous jobs in western Pennsylvania, eastern Ohio, and Pittsburgh. In those years teaching in the city was prized. High salaries and better workplace conditions attracted many to Pittsburgh. The hiring process was rigorous. I took the National Teachers Exam, which I barely passed. I taught a class for two central office social studies supervisors and, according to them, did a superior job; finally, I interviewed with a panel of district office staff and failed.

Told to get more experience and to reapply in three years, I substituted in Pittsburgh schools for two months while desperately seeking a job in or out of teaching. The youngest of three sons, the only one in my family to have gone beyond high school—my parents had emigrated from Russia—I was embarrassed to have a college degree and be only marginally employed. Finally I was hired to teach biology (my college minor) at McKeesport Technical High School to replace a teacher who suddenly quit six weeks into the school year. My salary was $3000 a year and those biweekly checks of $98 swelled me with pride.

MCKEESPORT TECH HIGH SCHOOL

Located in a small city about twenty miles from my home, McKeesport Tech drew 2000 students from all segments of the community. The recession of the mid–1950s had hit the steel industry in western Pennsylvania hard and was reflected in the high rate of unemployment.

Handed a room key, the two texts that I was to use, and given a handshake from the principal, I was sent to the classroom to begin teaching five classes of biology and general science, from which my predecessor had made a hasty escape. I saw my department chairman a few times during the year to beg for supplies; my next-door neighbor, a science major, had been at the school two years and helped me over some rough spots in the months that followed. That year was a blur.

What I do recall are fragments. I remember staying up late every night at my desk with different biology textbooks spread before me preparing minutely detailed lessons to use the next day. Those lessons listed the questions I would ask, how I would motivate students, what tasks I would assign. Before class I held them as tenaciously as Linus hugged his blanket in "Peanuts." They were blueprints that pumped me up with confidence giving me an illusion of control until I discarded them in the middle of the lesson.

I recall that without any laboratory space, I found textbook learning about animals and plants severely limited, especially for my students who had little interest in biology. So every weekend I would gather live specimens of whatever lessons of botany and zoology that we were studying. I collected salamanders, and using paper towels and knives on tablet-arm chairs (we had no laboratory tables), we dissected amphibians. It wasn't in the text, but we learned the lessons the book was trying to teach; moveover, it fueled my enthusiasm and that of my students more than any of my lesson plans could anticipate.

I also clearly remember both the fear and fun of teaching. Keeping order troubled me in two of my five classes. In general science, where the content still handcuffed me, I trembled in anticipation of a sharper student revealing to the class how incredibly little I knew. Every mistake I made fed my resolve to succeed.

Even though the two unruly classes and I struggled over the next eight months, I still recall with affection that initial year of teaching. Teaching was an intellectual challenge. I had to figure out how to make clear what I decided the students needed to know. Getting the class to understand and reading the elusive signals that learning occurred was so strong an impulse in me that I could almost touch it, yet could find few words to capture its intensity. I was elated when the impulse was satisfied and stung when it went unfulfilled. Also, I grew attached to certain students and they to me. A few of my students shared my passion for bringing animals and plants into class and we formed a close group.

But I was anxious to teach history. In the spring of 1956 I applied for jobs in Cleveland and Los Angeles. The Los Angeles interviewer who came to town told me that I could never teach there because I bit my nails. I never found out if such a requirement existed, but the humiliation of that interview still rankles. The day before the next school year began, I received word from the Cleveland public schools that a social studies job awaited me at Glenville High School. For the next seven years, I taught in a predominately black school. It transformed my career and the direction of my life.

GLENVILLE HIGH SCHOOL

When I reported to Glenville, however, I had no idea that the school was 95 percent black. In the early 1950s, when whites fled the area to the suburbs, middle-income blacks had moved in. The transition was so swift that by the late 1950s another shift toward low-income black families was already well underway.

Oliver Deex, promoted to principal at Glenville from the same position at an adjacent junior high, took me to a nearby delicatessen the day I reported and began my informal education about segregated Cleveland schools. Although I had grown up in Pittsburgh's black ghetto, my memories of being one of a handful of white children in the neighborhood elementary school was less than pleasant and not calculated to instill sensitivity. Moreover, the popular film *Blackboard Jungle,* featuring Glenn Ford as a high school teacher and Sidney Poitier as a lethal delinquent, was fresh in my mind. I can only guess what went through this principal's mind as he heard an inexperienced newcomer spill out fears and innocence about the world. Being twenty-one and on my own for the first time in my life, I had little choice than to take a deep breath and learn to teach.

For the next seven years, I taught economics, government, and world and American history. Two intersecting developments, neither intended but simply emerging from daily experiences, accounted for a shift in my values and career direction. I continued to study history at Case Western Reserve University part-time, getting my master's degree in 1958 and completing all doctoral requirements except for the last few chapters of a dissertation on twentieth century black leadership in Cleveland. Coincident with or arising from graduate work (I don't know which) was my growing interest in ideas and their consequences.

My principal proved to be my first intellectual mentor. None come to mind from either my undergraduate or part-time graduate work in Cleveland. A voracious reader and charming conversationalist, Deex introduced me to books and magazines I had never seen: *Saturday Review of Literature, Harpers, Atlantic, Nation,* and dozens of others. When we were at his home, he would often lend me books from a wood-paneled library that looked as if it were a movie set. At our rushed lunches or in his office as I would return what I had borrowed, we would talk about what I had read. I have no idea why he took an interest in the intellectual development of a naive novice, but his insistent questioning of my ideas and gentle guidance left me with a great hunger for further intellectual growth.

The other development was the uneasy awareness that what I had been taught about teaching, what I had been taught about schooling, little of it seemed to match my daily experience at Glenville. I was like a child trying to blow out a light bulb as though it were a candle. I had to learn anew.

These were the years *before* the civil rights movement had moved northward. Martin Luther King, Jr., was in the midst of his Montgomery ministry; Rosa Parks had just triggered the boycott of Jim Crow buses in that city. These were the years before the mislabeled "culturally deprived" students were discovered. Neglect of the most malign form blanketed Cleveland's racially segregated schools. As the years passed, I became more aware of the double standards, the two-tiered schooling in the city. But it was slow going for a white teacher who gradually learned from his students and black colleagues what was happening. Also being teacher-centered in my instruction concentrated my attention upon content in the classroom.

At the same time, in either 1957 or 1958, I began to add materials to the assigned American history text (David Saville Muzzey's *History of Our Country* [Boston: Ginn and Co., 1955] had no entry for *Negro* in the index). Drawing from my graduate courses, I began to type up excerpts, duplicate them on ditto machines, and assign them to a few classes at a time. For example, in a textbook chapter on colonial America, where the origins of slavery were dismissed as unimportant, I would duplicate copies of readings from historians that spelled out the complicated historical and moral issues surrounding the introduction of Africans into the colonies. In addition, the librarian gathered the few books on Negro history that we had in our school and nearby public libraries and put them aside in a special section.

By the second year at Glenville, I had found that gaining students' interest in U.S. history, a required course for graduation, was only half the struggle. Student response to nontextbook ethnic materials was mixed. The novelty of studying Negro figures triggered deep interest in a few students, but many students felt that such content was substandard because textbooks omitted references to what we studied.

Many students expressed puzzled concern over being different from other classes where only the text was used. Periodically a few students would ask me to work only in the text. But overall I felt that response was mildly positive. Discussions were spirited, interest was a notch or two higher for most (but by no means all) students. While I leaned less and less on a text and more on study guides and materials that I had created, daily classes still followed the familiar teacher-centered pattern. I did spend more time in framing open-ended questions, learned to listen better to what students said, and to manage a discussion in classes of thirty-five to forty students. Occasionally I would experiment by dividing the class into groups to work on tasks.

Also, as I learned the methodology of the historian in my graduate courses, I introduced more and more lessons on analyzing evidence, determining which sources of information were more or less reliable and assessing what makes one opinion more informed than another. Even with purple-smudged hands and mountains of ditto paper to hand out each week, the excitement of creating materials, using them, and checking students' responses was exhilarating. Increasing student interest in history drove me to prepare even more materials. When lessons died in front of my eyes, I blamed myself and tried to figure out what had happened. What limited me most was the sparsity of tools—ditto masters, a duplicating machine, and reams of paper.

Fortunately my principal used a petty cash fund to help fill my insatiable appetite for reams of paper. One district office supervisor heard of my work and, in 1959 or 1960, quietly allocated a small sum of money for me to purchase books, paper, and a ditto machine.

By 1963 I had completed a U.S. history course that included readings about blacks in every chronological period. Drawing from my graduate work and my work at Glenville, I wrote my first article, "Jim Crow History," in 1961 and saw it published in a small professional journal. Also, I enlisted in the infant movement to make social studies inquiry-oriented, or what was later labeled as "discovery learning." One of the founders of that movement asked me to do a paperback book on the history of the Negro using readings that I had developed.

I enjoyed working with the students as advisor to the student council, as senior class faculty advisor, and the dozens of activities that throw students and teachers together outside of class. Also, I joined a small number (about eight to ten out of a faculty of around forty) of like-minded teachers, black and white, who expected minority students to work hard and achieve, and who shared deep concerns over the consequences of segregation. Encouraged by the principal who often joined us and set aside his home as a place to get together, we also created a stock investment club, a social venture that provided far more laughs, food, and camaraderie than dividends. Working with these colleagues strengthened the values I had about teaching and the capacities of minority youth to learn.

MAKING CHOICES ABOUT TEACHING AS A CAREER

I was now teaching, writing, and working daily with students and like-minded faculty. Yet in 1963 I left Glenville. Even with the teaching, writing, collaborating with kindred teachers, sponsorship of a mentor, and my bonds with students, I became frustrated by what I later defined as the limits of classroom teaching. Although I enjoyed working with Glenville students and teachers, the intellectual growth I had experienced both at the school and in graduate work (I passed my doctoral orals in history in the spring), wedded to a growing determination to improve the quality of schooling that my students received, produced a gnawing sense that teaching five classes a day was not enough. The bureaucratic reluctance of the Cleveland schools to renovate the curriculum or recognize the needs of minority students annoyed me and I can only guess that I must have irritated my superiors at the board of education who heard from me. My marriage to Barbara Smith in 1958 and Sondra's birth in 1962 probably fueled my discontent with teaching. Earning $5000 a year combined with a panicky scramble each summer for work left me uneasy. Ambition, ego, and small successes served to increase my dissatisfaction with the system. I gained self-confidence in my teaching skills, which I came to see as more extensive than what I did in Room 235.

I saw that teaching was influencing others, and I did it well. But I wanted a larger stage. Already I had worked for five years as a summer camp counselor and then later as a head counselor. Those summers as head counselor gave me my first taste of organizational leadership beyond the classroom. I liked the experience and convinced myself that I did a first-rate job. To be sure, the discontent that I felt with "just" teaching and the growing confidence that I experienced after seven years in classrooms happens to many teachers: we begin to ask ourselves what we will do for the rest of our working lives. What kind of legacy do we want to leave others?

I found that high school teaching was less and less of an intellectual challenge for me. I had experienced the excitement of creating lessons that worked with students; I also had trained five student teachers. Through my graduate courses in history and with the gentle but firm touch of Oliver Deex, I became deeply tied to ideas and their consequences in people's lives, although at the time I doubt whether I could have expressed it as I do now. Also, the emerging civil rights movement had engaged me. Sit-ins, demonstrations, and especially the Birmingham church bombing triggered strong feelings in Glenville students and me.

In 1963 I was torn between staying in public school teaching and finding another outlet for the agitated energy, the insistent impulse to learn, grow, and work in a setting consistent with the values that I had come to embrace as a result of teaching at Glenville. Only as I think now about those entangled impulses can I see that I was approaching a fork in the road.

After passing my doctoral orals in history in 1963, I applied for a number of college teaching positions. A small liberal arts college in Connecticut offered me a three-year appointment as an assistant professor of history. After much discussion with Barbara and friends I considered what it would mean to leave public school teaching, the years of work in developing history lessons, and my growing convictions about the inadequate schooling that low-income minorities received, I turned down the offer. It was a road I did not take for another eighteen years until I came to Stanford in 1981.

Two months later, I was invited to apply for a position of master teacher of history in a federally funded project that would take returning Peace Corps volunteers and train them to teach at Cardozo High School in Washington, D.C., I applied for the position and was hired. My request for an unpaid leave of absence to work in the one-year project was denied by the Cleveland superintendent. I resigned from the system, and the day before the March on Washington, driving a faded purple Rambler pulling a U-Haul trailer, I arrived in the city to set up a home for Barbara and two-year old Sondra.

CARDOZO HIGH SCHOOL

The Cardozo Project, as it came to be called, was conceived in the heady days of the Kennedy administration to reduce high numbers

of dropouts from inner-city high schools and meet the dire need for
new teachers in ghetto schools. The informal criteria then in use—a
pulse rate and a college degree—failed to attract enough teacher candidates. Funded by the President's Committee on Juvenile Delinquency,
headed by Attorney-General Robert Kennedy, the experimental project, located in an all-black high school overlooking the Washington
Monument, recruited two master teachers of English and history and
ten Peace Corps volunteers who had returned from the Philippines,
Ethiopia, and Latin America. The Cardozo High School principal provided space and directed the first year of the program.

In the fall of 1963, I began to teach two U.S. history classes a day,
supervise four former volunteers who also taught two social studies
classes, develop new curriculum materials, and work in the community. Here were new roles for a teacher to enact and the possibilities
excited me. In those heady days of the Kennedy and Johnson adminis-
trations, when innocence and energy combined to make all things
seem possible, feelings of exhilaration, pessimism, and exhaustion al-
ternated for the next four years that I worked at Cardozo, two as
master teacher and two as director of the program.[1]

The ideology of the project asserted that low-income youth of
color dropped out of school because the teaching was unimaginative,
the texts were dull, and the people who taught had little contact with
students outside of the classroom. A project bringing in new teachers
who had worked in other cultures and new ideas would redirect the
school and save young people from a life of poverty.

In addition, the rationale for the program argued that the most
effective way to train college graduates who lacked certification for
inner-city schools was within the school itself. The university link
would be a collaborative effort creating a new curriculum of on-site
seminars anchored in what those preparing for inner-city teaching
would need to know about pedagogy, black culture, adolescents, and
the humanities. The teaching role that we constructed was tripartite:
instruction (e.g., two classes), curriculum development (e.g., writing
lessons and units for use in classrooms), community work (e.g., home
visits, community organizing, counseling outside of school, and so
forth).

Two years as master teacher taught me that the beliefs we held
about the nature of teaching in inner-city high schools were partly
accurate and partly naive (I write that with no apologies or anger). The
idea of a school-based, fifth-year master's program with a tripartite

teaching role nurtured by much collaboration and coaching seemed to work well. The interns and I could teach, create materials, and work with students outside of classrooms in both mundane and imaginative ways. Stress and tension over which of the three roles took precedence provoked debate, anxiety, and anger through the years, but the program and its subsequent adaptations flourished sufficiently to become the basis for National Teacher Corps legislation in 1965.

What was naive, and hopelessly so, was the expectation of altering a high school by training former Peace Corps volunteers. I learned first-hand about the awesome complexity of trying to change one high school nestled in a large district with a unique history and that simple solutions to entangled organizational problems were frequently either wrong or simple-minded.

After two years as master teacher, the soap-opera antics of federal funding and internal warring left me as the only experienced person within the program. In 1965 the principal had left and the talented, articulate master teacher of English who had initially conceived the idea for the program was pregnant. After drafting a proposal for an expanded project of twenty-five Peace Corps returnees to be placed at Cardozo and, for the first time, in a feeder junior high and elementary school, she, too, would leave.

The funding agency, the Office of Economic Opportunity, contacted me the day before school opened to say that our proposal, which had been buried on a program officer's desk for two months, had been approved. The head of an experimental subsystem in which Cardozo High School was located asked me to serve as director of the expanded project. Without pausing for a moment, I accepted and entered the world of school administration.

3

Principaling: Images and Roles

In the beginning there were teachers. Then there were principals. The first principals were teachers. Hence, the oldest form of public school administration was derived from the classroom.

Prior to 1800 most schools were ungraded, and had one or two teachers. The teacher did many tasks, from instruction to clerical, from cleaning to community work. But in cities, as early as the middle of the eighteenth century, schools were larger and the notion of a "master" in charge of a school, one who also spent time teaching, took hold. Boston, for example, had introduced grammar and writing masters in 1740.[1]

By the Civil War, city school boards would appoint a master, head, or principal-teacher to classify students, complete records, care for the furniture and school equipment, hire a janitor, make purchases, distribute supplies, handle the most difficult of the student disciplinary problems, and teach. Principal-teachers still taught three-quarters to fulltime, but they also received more money than teachers, assuring differences in social status. The job was created to give school trustees someone at the school site who would carry out their orders and insure that teachers did what the trustees asked. As one historian notes, "The principal was thus an administrator of routine and a clerk." Such arrangements would have persisted except for the growing numbers of students.[2]

The origins of the modern nonteaching principalship can be located in those mid-nineteenth century urban schools that had to wrestle with increasing student enrollments. Decades earlier, Lancastrian schools with one master (an early principal) and a cadre of monitors meeting in large rooms was one response to the expanding student population. As interest waned in monitorial schools, urban districts embraced another innovation, the graded school (begun in 1847 at the Quincy School in Boston), where students were classified by age or achievement (or both) and assigned to a room with one teacher. The Quincy School had twelve classrooms, each holding over fifty pupils; each student had a separate seat and desk, and the entire class spent the year with one teacher. The building housed twelve teachers and over 600 students.[3]

This novel approach, applied also to the growing number of high schools, combined order and efficiency in responding to ballooning enrollments. Graded schools also suggested to many that principals were more than clerks and low-level administrators; they needed time to supervise what was being taught in each room and to determine whether the teacher was doing a satisfactory job.

The wedge that pried principals out of classroom teaching was their superiors' growing expectations that they not only carry out orders, complete their reports on time, look after the building, maintain decent relations with adults and children, but that they also manage the curriculum and supervise instruction. To meet all of these expectations, they needed time. The less they taught, the more time they could spend managing and supervising. By the 1920s the notion of a principal as a professional also meant that the principal taught no classes.[4]

Embedded in the origins of the post, in arguments from practitioners determined to elevate the status of the job, and early books on the principalship are at least two dominant images: principal as bureaucrat and principal as instructional leader.[5]

COMPETING IMAGES OF THE PRINCIPAL[6]

Principal as Bureaucrat

Anchored in the origins of the principalship, the school board created the position of principal to place their agent at the school site to carry out orders while assisting teachers in their instructional duties. Lists of administrative duties, including numerous clerical and mainte-

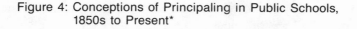

Figure 4: Conceptions of Principaling in Public Schools, 1850s to Present*

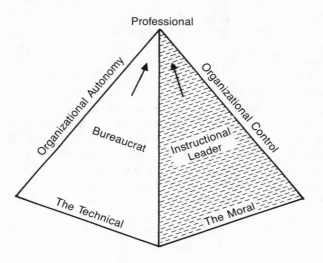

*This device tries to make sense of the available historical evidence. I use it to organize existing information about conceptions of teaching. I do *not* state that the figure is an accurate model of how all principals view the position past and present.

nance tasks, were common in mid-nineteenth century town and city schools with principals.[7]

The Boston School Committee's annual report for 1857, for example, listed the following duties for grammar and primary school masters:

- Admit individual pupils on examination.

- Give permission to classes to study the next textbooks when the year's assignment was completed prior to the regular promotion time.

- Require transfers and excuses for absences.

- Exclude unruly pupils.

- Make rules for the use of the school premises.[8]

Professor Frank McMurry, in one of the early works on the position, described the principal's work in the decades that followed:

> Every principal . . . is held directly responsible for the correctness of all reports that issue from his school. Even in signing the salary sheet, he must certify that none of the regulations, by-laws, etc. has been violated or that all violations have been reported. He must report on the condition of the building, on heating, ventilation, cleanliness, repairs, seating, lighting, fire drills; must make out estimates of supplies needed, must see to their distribution and adjustment; must interview parents; must know absentees and follow up cases of truancy, and attend to other cases of misconduct; besides all this, he must see to the execution of a large number of directions from higher school authorities. . . . Further, his efficiency as a principal, he believes, is likely to be judged by his superior officers primarily by his promptness and accuracy in regard to these more mechanical and tangible matters[9]

With the advent of "scientific management," spurred by the work of Frederick Taylor and his boosters among schoolmen, the corporate model of school management and "scientific efficiency" flourished in school districts during the decades bracketing World War I. Scientific management enhanced the image of the principal as bureaucrat with a grandeur heretofore missing.[10]

The passion for making schooling scientific produced an abundance of professor-led investigations of classrooms, schools, and districts. The results of these studies and expanded research contributed to a growing science of education that became equated with numbers. Study after study anchored conclusions in percentages, frequency distributions, and medians. Managerial efficiency, translated into dollars and cents, became the silver bullet that would improve schooling. The image of the principal as a scientifically trained professional who carried out the directives of a superintendent while expertly managing a complex operation gave practitioners in the early decades of this century the stature of corporate managers in a society entranced by industrial growth.[11]

In his textbook on the principalship published in 1923, Cubberley summarized the conventional wisdom of the day when he compared the relationship between the principal and the superintendent to relationships within corporate and military organizations.

The relationship is analogous in the business world to that of the manager of a town branch of a public utility to the general superintendent of the business; to that of the manager of a single department to the general manager of a department store; to that of the superintendent of a division of a railroad to the president of the company; or to that of the colonel of a regiment to the commanding general of an army.[12]

The image persists today because of the nature of the post. Positioned in the middle of the organization between the district office and teachers, principals scan new and revised regulations that will affect their schools. Job descriptions for principals invariably lean heavily upon managerial duties, which carry out the intentions of the school board and superintendent. When principals come together weekly or monthly in a district, the meetings often concentrate upon what new and revised directives need to be implemented. Policy manuals listing all the district's rules and procedures are seldom out of the reach of a principal's arm. If no one even heard about the image of principal as bureaucrat, it would have been invented.

The image of principal as bureaucrat, then, born out of the hierarchial demands of boards of education for school-site agents, nourished by the early twentieth century romance with the corporate manager, and weaned on the dream of scientific management, dominated for a century and a half the reported behavior of principals and persists today in the minds of both principals and nonprincipals. Many times image and performance merged. But other expectations generated a competing image of a principal improving instruction.

Principal as Instructional Leader

If the image of the principal as bureaucrat emerged simultaneously with the origin of the post, so, too, did the notion that the principal supervised the school's curriculum and instruction, leading the staff to improved schooling. In 1841 the Cincinnati public schools dismissed schools one hour early each Wednesday to "provide for practical improvement in the various studies, lessons, and qualifications appertaining to their professional duties." The principals of each school were directed to use that time to plan, organize, and implement a program.[13]

St. Louis Superintendent William Torrey Harris launched a plan to make principals into instructional supervisors. In 1871 he reported:

> Our principals are rapidly becoming supervisors as well as instructors and the schools under their charge are becoming uniform in their degree of excellence. Close daily supervision is the only method of securing desired results and one can scarcely believe how great a degree of efficiency may be reached in a corps of teachers of average ability, until he actually sees it as it exists in a large school under the management of a principal who knows how to perform his duty.[14]

Evidence of the competing images also can be inferred from Table 1, which summarizes the studies of what principals have done in their schools. While the dominant managerial pattern of principals as administrators is clear, not all principals fit the pattern. The range of reported percentages in these studies indicate that there was much variation in what principals did. Many reported spending larger chunks of time on supervision than administration.

Furthermore, instances of instructional leadership emerged early in the literature on principals. Descriptions of men and women who saw their primary obligations as supervising both curriculum and instruction, who saw themselves as a teacher of teachers, kept alive the image among academics and practitioners that principals could do more than make sure that pencils were in classrooms, that the heat was on in the winter, and that difficult pupils would have a place to go. Just before the turn of the century, for example, Kansas City, Missouri, principals submitted reports to their superintendents on how they conducted instruction in their schools, dismissed incompetent teachers, and advised others how to teach numbers in the primary grades.[15]

In 1922, at the request of the school board, a group of professors and practitioners investigated the Salt Lake City, Utah, public schools. Ellwood Cubberley led the group and compiled the findings. On the principals, he wrote:

> Usually the elementary school principalship is the weakest place in the entire school system, and one generally finds more dead wood in such positions than in any other place. In Salt Lake City this was not the case. On the contrary, with a few exceptions, the elementary school principals were a good body of supervisory officers, interested in their work and professionally awake. Some of them were among

the most efficient school principals members of the survey staff had ever seen, and their helpfulness to their teachers and their influence on both teachers and children seemed strong and good. One characteristic noted was that, if a member of the survey staff arrived at a school building after school had begun, he usually had to ring the hall bell to find the principal. He was somewhere in the rooms, busy with his work, instead of sitting on his chair in his office. In many school systems one seldom finds a school principal, during school hours, off his chair.[16]

Cubberley hardly concealed his eagerness to have principals perform as both instructional supervisors and efficient bureaucrats. In much of his writings, he forged the two conceptions into one: principal as professional. He urged making the principal into a scientifically trained manager who could make sound instructional decisions and, when necessary, wise administrative judgments while faithfully carrying out orders from the superintendent. The many dilemmas facing a professional in a bureaucracy, such as compliance or autonomy and conflicting demands from numerous constituencies, to name only two, seldom surfaced in what Cubberley and other advocates wrote and said. They wrote with a passion and certainty about what principals should be.

What Did Principals Do?

The earliest studies that I could locate describing what elementary and secondary principals did were in the early decades of this century. Earlier reports either cataloged the formal duties of principals or urged what they should do, not what they actually did. From academic studies, self-reports, diaries, and direct observations by professors and practitioners, I can provide a sketchy outline of what these men and women have done.[17]

The quality of these studies varies widely. For example, early researchers using questionnaires sent to principals often reported response rates of 50 percent or less; self-reports from principals differed because the categories used (e.g., clerical, managerial) were open to broad interpretation. Also, many research findings reported in professional journals were written by professors, principals, and superintendents deeply committed to making the principalship into a professional position. Professionalism was associated with teacher supervision, curricular involvement, and taking initiative—not writing reports, hiring janitors, or ordering toilet paper. These sentiments permeated much of the literature on principals in the early decades of this century.

Between 1911 and 1981, a number of studies of both elementary and secondary principals appeared that used similar categories in dividing up the principal's day between administration, supervision, clerical work, community work, and a catch-all category for other activities. What I have done is collapse clerical and other conventional managerial tasks into the category "Administration." Administration, therefore, includes all of those tasks aimed at maintaining the stability of the organization, from preparing reports, constructing class schedules, disciplining pupils, meeting with parents, solving noninstructional problems for teachers and students, to the common managerial duties of budgeting, making personnel decisions, and maintaining the building.

"Supervision" includes monitoring instruction through observing and evaluating teachers, coordinating and assessing curriculum, analyzing test results, reviewing report cards, teaching demonstration lessons, and leading teacher workshops. "Teaching" refers to that portion of time when principals teach classes formally, not as a substitute or to demonstrate a particular technique for other teachers. The category "Other" includes community contacts through parent-teacher associations, Rotary Club membership, writing articles for local newspapers, giving lunchtime talks, and participation in extracurricular school activities.

Over seven decades, using different instruments to extract information and drawing from different levels of school districts in various parts of the country, researchers compiled data for over 8,300 principals. Diaries, time-and-motion studies, self-reports, and survey responses converged to produce a striking uniformity in work patterns. Managerial tasks consumed most of a principal's time; instructional supervision was clearly secondary in proportion of time spent on it; some portion of the principal's time was devoted to cultivating community relations and other activities. Keep in mind, however, that reporting averages, as these studies do, masks a substantial variation among principals in each of the categories.

From time-and-motion studies and other detailed descriptions of individual principals, another picture of busy principals emerges: a picture of principals who skip from one task to another; who react to requests from others, yet maintain a large chunk of unscheduled time to pursue what they feel needs to be done; who vary in their styles insofar as working at their desks, using the phone, and scheduling meetings; and, finally, who spend between two-thirds to four-fifths of their time talking and listening to people of all ages in the school community.[18]

What becomes apparent from these studies and an awareness of the post's origins is a DNA of principaling. Positioned between their superiors who want orders followed and the teachers who do the actual work in the classrooms, principals are driven by imperatives over which they have little control. Their responsibility to act far exceeds their authority to command; their loyalties are dual: to their school and to headquarters; the professional and political expectations for what should occur in the school conflict; they are maintainers of stability and agents of change. In short, embedded within the principalship is genetic material, to extend the metaphor, that shapes to a large degree (but not totally) what principals do.

The evidence drawn from these and other studies documents that principals have spent most of their time on noninstructional tasks. Yet professional beliefs and training are (and have been since the 1920s) geared to the image of the principal as an instructional leader. The popular aphorism, "as is the principal, so is the school," signaled newcomers and veterans that what the principal did shaped how teachers and students performed.

As early as 1910 a professor who investigated the New York City elementary schools and their principals captured the hope of an emerging professionalism when he wrote:

> In brief, the principal, as a professional leader, is working for the same ends as the classroom teacher, but his pupils are the teachers themselves. His worth is to be judged, primarily, by his skill as a leader, as a teacher of teachers, just as theirs is to be judged by their skill as teachers of children. Thus, his first duty is to his teachers, to help them grow professionally.[19]

In the same decade. Stanford professor Ellwood P. Cubberley also criticized how too many principals "give their time almost entirely to administrative duties and do little supervisory work, though the latter ought to be their most important function." Since the turn of the century, motivating teachers to excel, harnessing their energies to improve classroom performance, and providing expert help to those in need framed the dream of principals as instructional supervisers.[20]

Table 1: HOW PRINCIPALS SPEND THEIR TIME IN SCHOOLS, 1911-1981

Year	School Level	ADM %	SUPERV % ——Total Time——	TEACH %	OTHER %	Place	Study Author	Instrument	N
1911	Elem.	67	33	NA	NA	New York	F.M. McMurry	Questionnaire	83
1920	Elem.	68	32	NA	NA	Seattle	Worth McClure	Self-Report	43
1921	High School	48	25	20	7	Midwest	C.O. Davis	Questionnaire	1350
1924	Elem.	53	34	NA	13	St. Louis	J.R. Benson	Self-Report	8
1925	Elem.	73	20	4	3	North Carolina	W.O. Hampton	Diaries	130
1928	Elem.	49	34	4	13	National	Elem. School Princ. Association	Questionnaire	614
1937	Elem.	42	40	10	8	New Jersey	Messinger	Questionnaire	217
1948	Elem.	44	39	2	14	National	Elem. School Prin. Association	Questionnaire	1413
1958	Elem.	44	35	3	18	National	Elem. School Prin. Association	Questionnaire	1905
1959	Elem.	57	14	NA	24	Texas	Goette	Questionnaire	576
1968	Elem.	44	38	4	13	National	Elem. School Prin. Association	Questionnaire	2318
1975	Elem.	58	17	0	17	Maryland	Montgomery County ((Maryland) Schools	Direct Observation	NA
1977	Elem.	87	5	0	7	Chicago	Peterson	Direct Observation	2
1979	High School	60	17	0	22	Northeast	Martin and Willower	Direct Observation	5
1981	Elem.	62	27	0	11	Northeast	Kmetz and Willower	Direct Observation	5

SOURCES FOR TABLE 1

F. M. McMurry, *Elementary School Students* (Yonkers, NY: World Book Co., 1913).

Worth McClure, "The Functions of the Elementary School Principal," *The Elementary School Journal*, 21, No. 7 (March, 1921).

Davis, C. O., "The Duties of High School Principals," *The School Review*, 29, (May, 1921).

J. R. Benson, "Division of the Principal's Time," *The Elementary School Journal*, 27, No. 2 (October, 1926).

W. O. Hampton, "How Public School Principals Use Their Time," cited in Bulletin of the Department of Elementary School Principals, "The Elementary School Principalship," Vol. 7, No. 3 (April, 1928).

Bulletin of the Department of Elementary School Principals, "The Elementary School Principalship," Vol. 7, No. 3 (April, 1928).

Mark Messenger, *The Non-Teaching Elementary School Principal in the State of New Jersey*, (Camden, New Jersey: No publisher listed, 1939).

Department of Elementary School Principals, "The Elementary School Principalship," (Washington, DC: National Education Association, 1948).

Department of Elementary School Principals, "The Elementary School Principalship," (Washington, DC: National Education Association, 1958).

Department of Elementary School Principals, "The Elementary School Principalship in 1968" (Washington, DC: National Education Association, 1968).

Roland Barth, *Run School Run* (Cambridge, MA: Harvard University Press, 1980).

Kent Peterson, "The Principal's Tasks," *Administrator's Notebook*, 26, No. 8 (1977–1978).

W. Martin and D. Willower, "The Managerial Behavior of High School Principals," *Educational Administration Quarterly*, 17, (1981).

J. Kmetz and D. Willower, "Elementary School Principals' Work Behavior," *Educational Administration Quarterly*, 18, (1982).

GAP BETWEEN IMAGES AND DESCRIPTIONS OF PERFORMANCE. But certainty and passion could scarcely hide the gap between what is and what should be. The gap must have produced much anguish among those who had recently left graduate school where they were inspired with images of instructional leadership and managerial efficiency, and gone to work in schools where they found themselves buried in administrative work. Both academics and practitioners have tried to close that gap. The formation of the Department of Elementary Principals within the NEA in 1920 added to the growing number of professors calling for higher standards in the training and selection of principals and accelerated the transformation of the post into a professional position. Still, embedded in that metamorphosis from a job to a profession was the stinging awareness of that seemingly unbridgeable gap between what is and what should be.[21]

Guilt among principals over spending far too much time on clerical tasks and noninstructional work rather than on supervision has surfaced repeatedly in self-reports since the 1920s. A common question asked of principals after they reported how much time they spent on administrative, supervisory, and other tasks was to list how they would prefer to spend their time. Four studies done in the 1920s, for example, asked principals what the *ideal* distribution of their time would be. In each case elementary principals wished to spend more time with supervision and less on administration.[22]

Because most descriptions of principals' work consistently depicted densely packed days geared toward maintaining organizational stability, with little time spent in classrooms and few exchanges with teachers, students, parents, or central office supervisors over either curriculum or instruction, some writers have seriously questioned whether principals *should be* instructional leaders. Proposals for principals to encourage others to provide instructional leadership in a school or even for the principalship to be divided up into separate posts for managerial and instructional functions have surfaced in literature repeatedly.[23]

Set against these occasional cries for splitting principals' functions, however, is an enormous body of literature exhorting and promoting principals to do everything. Entangled with the impulse toward professionalizing the principalship, instructional leadership emerged early as the vehicle for higher status. Acknowledging the administrative work and the awkward organizational position of being sandwiched between the central office and teachers, writers still urged principals to allocate their time differently in order to supervise the curriculum and classroom instruction. Be a leader, Cubberley and his descendants preached.[24]

The bind between the seemingly implacable realities of principaling and what it should be caused some writers to wrestle with the issue of autonomy and accountability within bureaucratic organizations. Exactly how much discretion should principals have within an organization where charts showed a hierarchial chain of command and specialization? To whom *should* the principal listen? To whom *should* the principal respond? For principals, orders from above compete with helping teachers do their jobs well and responding to students' needs. If the organizational metaphor is military or corporate (recall Cubberley's analogies), discretion narrows and opportunities for leadership shrink. It is a persistent, if not central, dilemma anchored in the predictable tension between the district office and the school site over independence and responsibility and whose expectations will emerge as dominant.

The image of the principal as bureaucrat, enmeshed in daily routines and driven by rules, competed with the one of principal as instructional leader, a mirage that seemingly danced beyond the reach of many, but not all, school heads as they went about their tasks. As times changed, as reform movements penetrated graduate programs on educational administration and public schools, these competing images came in and out of style, accounting for the confusing and shifting emphases in writing about the principalship.

Well over a half-century since Cubberley and other boosters of the principalship as a professional post exhorted both newcomers and old-timers to be both loyal bureaucrats and sterling supervisors, there are reformers who see few conflicts or dilemmas in principals now doing both—reaching to become Superman or Wonder Woman rather than a Clark Kent or Lois Lane.

Arising from the body of research findings on effective elementary schools that enroll large numbers of low-income, minority children, researchers and practitioners declare that principals who set goals, communicate them to teachers, supervise the curriculum and classroom instruction, evaluate teachers frequently, establish academic and behavioral expectations for both students and teachers a few notches higher than currently exist, are instructional leaders.[25]

Checklists of principal behaviors geared to improving the instructional program are common fare in textbooks, practitioner journals,

national conferences, and state-sponsored principal training programs.
Some superintendents judge principal performance by test score gains,
frequency and quality of teacher evaluations, and the school's academic climate as reported by parents and students. But in the midst of
this "born-again" instructional leadership, the image of the principal as
bureaucrat lurks uneasily.[26]

After all, most principals do spend their time engaged in administrative tasks that seemingly have few ties to instruction or curriculum.
Moreover, many principals have little inclination to supervise classrooms or develop curriculum since they believe that, by training and
experience, teachers are the specialists. Furthermore, constant monitoring of the classroom can cause tension with teachers and less classroom flexibility. Other principals define their central task as supporting
rather than hovering over teachers, which translates into buffering
them from parents and the district office, providing materials, and
taking care of disciplinary infractions. No Superman or Wonder
Woman here, instead a more mundane view of the principalship surfaces. But some superintendents, prodded by school boards, sensing
another change in educational fashion, or believing in the notion of
principals as instructional leaders, order their subordinates to get involved with curriculum, supervise teachers, evaluate instruction, and
monitor student performance. Thus, the dream of an earlier generation of reformers who saw the principal as both bureaucrat and instructional leader re-emerges.[27]

Merging the Two Images. An example will illustrate one uneasy
marriage of the principal as bureaucrat and principal as instructional
leader. Growing out of the research findings on effective schools and
effective teaching, Research for Better Schools (RBS), a federally
funded agency located in Philadelphia, has been working since 1981
with districts in Delaware, New Jersey, and Pennsylvania to improve
instruction in elementary schools. Researchers in collaboration with
practitioners have designed and tested a program called Achievement
Directed Leadership that concentrates upon improving student academic performance (i.e., achieve gains in standardized achievement
test scores). The program provides specific training materials and
workshops for teachers, principals, and district office staff.

Drawing heavily from teacher effective research findings, RBS isolated four variables as significantly linked to students' academic
achievement:

- students' prior knowledge of students

- the amount of time students spend on assigned tasks

- students' success with usual classroom academic tasks

- students' opportunity to absorb the knowledge on which they will be tested[28]

To manage these four variables, RBS trained practitioners to move through a four phase "improvement cycle" that consisted of the following: collecting information on what students are doing in classrooms; comparing what they collect with research findings to determine whether improvement should be made; selecting what changes should be made; and, finally, putting the changes into practice and monitoring them.

Since the improvement cycle aims to increase student performance on standardized tests, RBS fashioned a management strategy for teachers, principals, and district office staff to work together. "As a teacher uses the improvement cycle to plan changes in student behaviors," the training manual says, "the principal uses the improvement cycle to plan changes in teacher behaviors. . . . Similarly, central office staff can use information gained from conferences, classroom visits, and test data to plan training and supervision activities for principals." Thus, teachers "Plan, Manage, Instruct," principals "Plan, Train, Supervise," and district staff "Plan, Train, Supervise." These managerial functions that form the core of the program, according to the RBS manual, "appear to be leadership variables, or behaviors, at the building and central office levels of the school system which support instructional improvement."[29]

Training manuals for principals detail their role. Planning, training, and supervisory functions are spelled out explicitly. What tasks need to be done with teachers, when they are to be done, and how they are to be done are included in lists, handouts, timelines, and accompanying transparencies and videotapes. In some instances directions for the principal resemble a script. For example, in the manual the symbol * "indicates special directions to the leader. These directions may, for example, describe certain procedures to be followed, conclusions to be made, or potential problems to be avoided."[30]

In the districts cooperating with RBS, superintendents choose to initiate Achievement Directed Leadership. They mandate that

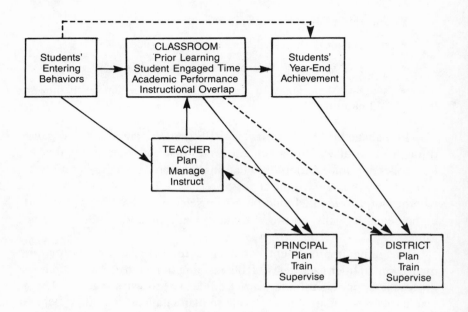

Figure 5: Relationship Among District Functions, Principal Functions,
          Teacher Functions, Student Entering Behavior, Student
          Classroom Behavior, and Student Year-End Achievement

Source: New Brunswick, (New Jersey), "Manual for Principals to
          Implement Improvement Program" (1984), p. 1–4

elementary principals and teachers be trained by RBS and use the materials. They bring together various elements of curriculum, instructional supervision, standardized tests, and materials into a tightly coupled system of improvement geared to producing higher test score results. Within this system, principals become both bureaucrats and instructional leaders. The two images blend, and Ellwood P. Cubberley's dream emerges anew in the invention of the instructional manager.

The example of RBS and school districts near Philadelphia, however, does *not* represent what most districts do with their principals. While there is a concerted push toward making principals behave as instructional managers, it is altogether unclear how many districts pursue the rigorously designed and scripted example cited above.[31]

Far more superintendents, it appears, press principals to get into classrooms, observe teachers, and help them improve aspects of their teaching that need bolstering. The spread of various commercial packages called "clinical supervision" documents the appeal of managerial approaches designed to make principals instructional supervisors. Superintendents who import commercial, prefabricated systems and train principals in their use merge (by fiat) the historic conceptions of principal as bureaucrat and principal as instructional leader into newly minted instructional managers.

Thus far I have sketched a broad outline of the history of the principalship, the dominant images of the post, and how these conceptions inspire and influence practice. At this point, let me explicitly describe what I see as the primary roles that principals discharge.[32]

THE CORE ROLES OF PRINCIPALING

Instructional

From the very origins of the post, principals taught both children and adults. Principals taught students for decades in rural and small town schools five to seven decades after the position was established. Furthermore, they were teachers of teachers. They were to be pedagogical experts, helping teachers improve their instruction. They were to know the formal curriculum and see that it was taught as intended.

In time, however, principals teaching children disappeared. Now only a few principals ever take over classes when a substitute fails to show, teach a demonstration lesson, or tutor individual students. It would be a "man-bites-dog" feature in a newspaper if a principal were to teach students today. Teaching adults slowly emerged as the primary instructional role for the principal.[33]

The conventional instructional role, however, shifts meaning for the principal once we move beyond classroom teaching or teaching teachers in a workshop. Principal as teacher refers to what principals do to persuade adults to alter their beliefs and behavior to achieve the goals the principal sets. At one level it incorporates common supervisory practices historically sought by principals: helping teachers improve their use of pedagogy, content, and classroom management; delivering the bad news to teachers who erred in entering classrooms; developing and monitoring the curriculum.

Beyond the familiar obligation to work with teachers, however, the principal's instructional role takes on a broader view. Through shaping the mission of the school, establishing a climate within the school that communicates a seriousness of purpose and a respect for the members of the school community, designing rituals and daily mechanisms that make tangible the mission and ethos, through communication skills, personal example, and numerous other informal means, the principal invents a personal curriculum of improvements for the school community and teachers. But it is the existence of purpose and intentions that determines the degree to which a principal wishes to teach that invented curriculum. In brief, then, the school community becomes a classroom. As a metaphor, teaching becomes persuading children, teachers, parents and superiors to learn a curriculum that the principal created and moving towards the principal's goals.

Few principals, however, come prepared to teach adults. Principals are recruited from the classroom where their formal authority to tell children what to do is legitimate and seldom gets challenged. Frequently they are chosen for their skills in working with children, not adults. The skills essential for observing classrooms, conferencing with teachers about their strengths and limitations, persuading teachers to support a program dear to the principal, negotiating with teachers which topics will have to be covered in the last six weeks of the school year, convening and running a curriculum committee, in short, the skills embedded in the supervision of instruction and curriculum seldom spring fully cultivated from courses in educational administration or from the mind of a new principal after a seven year stint in a third grade classroom. While coercion—DO IT OR ELSE—has been used frequently by principals over the last century, it has become increasingly less central to teaching adults in a culture where individual choice is prized among those who work in organizations and call themselves professionals.

There are many principals, of course, who master the skills of working with both adults and children in performing the instructional role. Consider Betty Belt, veteran principal of Oakridge Elementary School in Arlington, Virginia, who popped in and out of the thirty or so classrooms daily. Occasionally taking over a class or tutoring a child, Belt worked with children frequently. She knew most of the names of the 500 or so students that came to Oakridge each year. Her goal was straightforward: make Oakridge academically the number one school in the district.

In working with teachers, she asked staff to give her a sample of what their students wrote; on these papers she wrote comments. She reviewed report cards—their grades and written comments—every nine weeks before they were sent home. In her office she kept reading and math records for each child in the school, monitoring them periodically to see if there were any sudden changes in performance. She chaired school curriculum committees, often raising specific points about language arts or math items. She also taught. On classroom management, for example, she taught a lesson that was videotaped, and teachers critiqued her performance for the climate of the classroom, how she handled movement from one activity to another, and student participation.

Deeply interested in the development of reasoning in children, she read articles and circulated them among staff. When a new superintendent mandated that each school develop an improvement plan focused upon district goals and other goals the school staff proposed, Belt persuaded the staff to add reasoning skills to the list of goals. She did more. She wanted to find out at what grade teachers should use different approaches to teach various levels of reasoning. Using pre- and post-tests, Belt and a group teachers found that over a three year period teaching analogies at the fourth grade produced higher test score, while the same amount of time spent on this skill at the third grade was less productive. She found that the process of thinking through the entire effort with the cooperating teachers at those grade levels was as stimulating to teachers as the program was to students.

When it came to evaluating teachers, Belt met with teachers beforehand, did the classroom observation, and conferred with the teacher afterwards as the district policy prescribed. But she often went beyond that in helping teachers who displayed limited skills. She would diagnose what needed improvement and try to help the teacher herself. If that didn't work, she would reach out elsewhere in the district to find the appropriate person to aid the teacher. If the teacher failed to show sufficient improvement, Belt would figure out what else could be done to help the teacher. She was dogged, seldom brushing the problem aside. Teachers assigned to Oakridge knew that Betty Belt would monitor them, helping whenever appropriate. The school was no place for a tired teacher to hide.

Belt had taught thirteen years in the Washington, D.C., public schools, serving also as a demonstration teacher (that is, teaching lessons while colleagues around the system watched her) before taking time out to raise a family. She reentered teaching, crossing the Potomac River to Arlington. She had firm beliefs about how children learned (they need a clearly outlined set of structures within which they should be given choices), how teachers should teach (teacher-centered instruction), and how a school should be run (the principal, with the advice of the staff, makes major decisions). She saw that within a school, seemingly noninstructional decisions (e.g., whether or not to have a school-wide behavior code or honor roll) intersected very much with what happened in classrooms. She invested routine actions with instructional meaning.

There was, in effect, an Oakridge way of doing things, a climate of expectations for teachers and students, norms that were unfailingly monitored by Belt and that she came to embody. She asked teachers to make academic demands of students ranging from homework to research papers for the older, more talented students. She asked teachers to expect correct behavior from students; disruptions were simply unacceptable and punishment was both fair and swift. Middle-school teachers knew quickly which students—black or white—had come from Oakridge. As Oakridge's principal, Betty Belt taught both adults and children through her expectations, supervisory style, and personal behavior.[34]

High school principal Bob Eicholtz also taught adults and youth, but in a slightly different manner. Veteran teacher, coach, department head, assistant principal, and principal, whose thirty-five year career matured in the Whittier Union School District in California, Eicholtz came to Pioneer High School in 1979. At that time Pioneer had 2,100 students, mostly Hispanic and low-income; it was the basket-case of the district. Low daily attendance, truancy, littered grounds, graffiti, high suspension rate, gang activity on campus, and low teacher morale produced a tarnished image in Whittier. Add achievement test scores below the tenth percentile and the low reputation of the school becomes clear. His goal was to make the community proud of Pioneer High School.

Within three years, all of the reputed signs of a turnaround had occurred: attendance was up, no in-school gang activity, test scores had risen; the campus was litter-free; and teachers and students felt better about the school. While I am uncertain about what entangled variables explain the turnaround, Eicholtz played a significant part, especially in discharging his instructional role.[35]

Whatever factors explain the difference, one fact is evident: Eicholtz's instructional role clearly differed from Belt's. If she dealt directly with the instructional program and bent teacher behavior toward her vision, he concentrated on establishing the conditions for improved instruction. Eicholtz delegated to his staff duties for organizing Pioneer's instructional program. He recruited people who could build a better program and moved those who were inadequate.

Teachers, department heads, and his assistant principals developed ideas for his approval. He approved the Omega program, a college preparatory school-within-a-school, that included Advanced Placement offerings and yet permitted much mixing between these honors students and their classmates. He approved the total reorganization of the math curriculum (including the transfer of a department head), adding another year beyond the district's graduation requirement, and introducing courses to match student performance and level of instruction. He approved the incorporation of writing into social studies and other subject areas. He approved a flexible scheduling plan designed by a subordinate that permitted Omega students to take special and regular classes and other students to take electives before and after the reduced school day (a consequence of district fiscal retrenchment). He approved the intensive training of teachers for introducing computers, getting non-English teachers to teach writing in their classes, and helping students with limited reading skills.

While he visited classes twice each year to formally evaluate teachers and, on occasion, would pop into rooms to stay visible with both teachers and students, most of his time was spent in the corridors, elsewhere on the campus, and in the community.

From his first year as Pioneer's principal, he worked on first settling the school down, getting students back to classes and keeping them there. He established Boy's and Girl's Councils composed of current and ex-gang members that met with him weekly to discuss school activities that they could sponsor. A school-wide citizenship code, constructed jointly by staff, students, and parents, spelled out rights, responsibilities, and sanctions for violations and included the hiring of aides and broader visibility of staff. A no-litter campaign studded with incentives like an annual trip for the school to the amusement park, Knott's Berry Farm, produced swift changes in a once cluttered campus.

Eicholtz concentrated upon academic achievement while building self-esteem and pride among both teachers and students. He introduced the Principal's List for students who excelled in academics, sports, and extracurricular activities. Each semester, Eicholtz sent letters of commendation to such students. When substitute teachers left notes about how surprised they were about the warmth and quality of the students, Eicholtz shared these notes with all the students at assemblies. Special assemblies recognized student and teacher achievements. He received funds from parent booster clubs (they raised over $100,000 in one year) so the staff could distribute chits to those students who completed homework. The chits could be used at the school's snack shop for ice cream and other food. Also, for perfect attendance, students received a free yearbook; 127 annuals went to students in June 1985.

The principal knew most of the students by name. It was common for students to give him a hug when graduating or leaving school. Each December, a few days before the Christmas holidays, Eicholtz dressed up as Santa Claus to dispense small gifts to students and teachers. Yet he would act swiftly to punish a student if the larger school's purposes were abridged. When a college-bound Omega student threw a lit firecracker into a restroom he was suspended and transferred to another school.

For Eicholtz, the direct instructional role embodied by Belt is much less evident. His supervisory style differs from Belt, but he teaches, as she did, by personal example. To his subordinates and faculty he is the gatekeeper, permitting those programs and changes that nourish his aims for the school to pass. In building a school climate that prizes academic achievement and seriousness of purpose, he wants those norms to penetrate classrooms, reinforcing what his best teachers strive for and what he seeks for Pioneer. Furthermore, through his humaneness, humor, and seriousness, he teaches in a very personal sense all who come within the sound of his soft voice and the sight of his wry smile. There is a unity between what he believes, what he says, and what he does.

Managerial

The administrative tasks associated with carrying out district and school policies, such as planning, gathering and dispersing information, budgeting, hiring, scheduling classes, grouping of students, completing reports, dealing with conflict between varied participants, and maintaining the building, constitute this role. If the instructional role aims to alter existing teacher and student beliefs and behaviors to achieve larger aims, the overall direction to the managerial role is maintaining organizational stability. For those principals who imagine a direction for their schools, who wish to accomplish certain aims with students beyond those mandated by the district, the managerial and instructional roles intersect. However, for those principals whose orientation is to accomplish school district's goals, who see their job as primarily maintaining the existing arrangements, the managerial and instructional are largely separate roles.

Belt and Eicholtz represent those principals whose instructional roles dominate, although their styles differ. Thus, for both of them there is little distinction between managerial and instructional tasks. They merge; they are entangled. When Belt assigns fourth-grade children to a teacher, she assesses each teacher's strengths and weaknesses and wherever possible matches individual students strengths and limitations to those of the teacher. Eicholtz knows that a flexible schedule drives a substantial portion of the school day. Providing a broad array of electives for Pioneer's diverse students is essential to achieving his instructional goals. In both instances the principals take routine managerial tasks and invest them with instructional meaning, converting a rubber band into a coiled spring.

Most principals, however, have taken the instructional role and turned it into a routine managerial one, converting a coiled spring into a rubber band. Ed Bell, the pseudonym anthropologist Harry Wolcott gave to an Oregon elementary school principal who he observed during 1966–1967, illustrates the common display of the role.

Bell spent most of his time in scheduled and unscheduled meetings with his thirty teachers, other principals, parents, and the district office. Unscheduled meetings that took up a large chunk of his time invariably touched upon such matters as soothing an angry mother whose child was in a reading program scheduled at an awkward time for her, disciplining a child who had been sent to the office, discussing with the custodian a necessary repair, and the like. Returning phone calls, checking through the mail, and getting briefed by his secretary took up bits and pieces of time strung together between sporadic sweeps through the school or unexpected interruptions by teachers and students about matters that needed immediate attention.

On occasion Bell would leave the building to attend principal meetings, confer with his assistant superintendent, or meet with parents. For the most part, Bell saw these meetings as time-consuming and having little direct connection with his duties. But, in the manner of a soldier taking his turn at KP, Ed Bell would faithfully fulfill these obligations outside the school.

However, Wolcott also observed that very little of Bell's time was spent supervising the instructional program; Ed pursued managerial

tasks diligently and efficiently, fatigued at the end of a long day by the
amount of exchanges with adults and children yet unsure exactly of
how much he had accomplished that was worthwhile.[36]

Political

Since the birth of the position, principals have spent a portion of
their time organizing parent groups, speaking at weekly business club
luncheons, meeting with influential citizens to help subsidize a school
project and similar activities. Called "community relations" or, later,
public relations, these acts were implicitly political in their search in
the community for public support of the principal's authority. Many
principals simply recognized a central fact of American life: any public
organization, such as schools or hospitals in a democratic society will
not be left to the experts alone.

The classroom in which teachers perform their political roles is
unique in that it deals with minors compelled to attend school; however, the principal's political role is much more traditional, dealing with
adults in the school and community. The school, as a political setting,
is far more complex than a classroom both in the number of constituencies and in their contending purposes yet both remain intensely
political arenas.

For principals, *political* means to sense and transform public expectations (which is another way of saying *values*) into formal school
decisions and authoritative actions in order to achieve both organizational and personal goals. Principals are sandwiched between what
state and district policymakers intend, what the superintendent directs, what parents expect, what teachers need, and what students
want.

Many principals scan the terrain and determine what is possible,
and what can be done within their school given the existing parents,
teachers, students, and resources. Their position invites conflicts of
interest, competing expectations that produce resistance to what a
principal may seek to achieve. By their decisions and actions, by their
uses of formal and informal power, by their interpersonal skills, by
their core values, principals affect whether a policy is implemented
faithfully, converted to fit the school, or ignored.

Principals, therefore, engage in political acts when they persuade,
deflect, and enlist teachers, parents, or district officials to build support or overcome opposition to what administrators desire. Because

political action means striving to enact particular values embedded in goals, such action becomes moral behavior.[37]

This view, of course, assumes that principals consciously decide matters, that is, make judgments consistent with their beliefs and values that are directed at achieving both personal and organizational goals. Principals who, as a matter of habit, seldom consider whether managerial routines and instructional procedures are aligned with their values and beliefs and whose sense of organizational and personal goals are largely undefined or hidden would not be viewed as exercising an overt political role. Yet by enforcing district mandates and acting as agents of the superintendent, they would be engaging in tacit political activity through loyalty to existing arrangements.[38]

A principal, for example, who endorses the superintendent's directives to take clinical supervision courses and align school texts and district tests to the curriculum because such policies help children is acting politically; likewise, a colleague who believes that those same policies restrict both principal and teacher independence is acting politically in subverting and ignoring such policies. But another principal who sees these very same mandates as just another set of procedures similar to those for ordering supplies or handling personnel will approach the new orders in a routine fashion, lacking overt political content. In carrying out these organizational directives, however, consequences of the principal's actions are both political and moral in endorsing what the institution does. In short, there is no such phenomenon as nonpolitical behavior.

Some principals have always relished the political role. High school principal Norris Hogans is one such person. Appointed to head George Washington Carver in 1977 by Atlanta, Georgia, Superintendent Alonzo Crim, Hogans left his nearby elementary school to take over a building that had become a "dumping ground" for other schools that had ousted their truants and troublemakers. He concentrated initially upon enforcing rules for both students and teachers; restoring vigor and rigor to a decaying vocational curriculum, while instituting college preparatory courses; and attracting new resources from state, federal, and local agencies. Through the Interagency Council, which he established with the help of a corporate official, almost fifty community organizations (churches, volunteer groups, and corporations) gave money, people, and services to low-income, black students at Carver High School.

Hogans believes in black students working hard to succeed in the world beyond Carver's doors. He has firsthand knowledge of the wounds racism inflicts. He also believes that grit and push will produce successful blacks in a white world. Through the Explorers' program, for example, every tenth grader, wearing a white Explorer jacket, visits downtown corporations, businesses across town, and professionals in their offices. Hogans wants Carver students to see the possibilities and work hard to realize them. Contacts with influential whites and blacks throughout the city, cultivated tirelessly by Hogans and his associates, have opened doors. Hogans' mission for Carver grows from his vision of what poor, black students can achieve.

In accomplishing the turnaround of Carver High School and tying the community closely to the future of its one thousand students, Hogans has spent much time away from the school building coalitions negotiating grants and spreading the message of what can be done with inner-city high schools. He enjoys the visibility and sees every opportunity to speak as a chance to tell the "Carver Story" while gaining more support for the school.

Two observers, each separately spending three days at Carver in 1981, saw a principal who had indeed transformed a school from a dumping ground marked by teacher apathy and student hostility into a place where teachers and students largely took pride in the school. Carver was now orderly, free of graffiti, and its staff excited about what students could accomplish. However, the observers also saw an unimaginative curriculum that produce little intellectual engagement in classrooms. Hogans' concentration on managing the school efficiently and linking it to the larger community revealed how effective the astute playing of the managerial and political roles could be, but at the expense of instructional leadership. His political and managerial skills had brought dollars, people, and services into the school while building bridges for a two-way traffic between school and community. However Carver's success is defined, according to the observers, it will be due to the work of Norris Hogans.[39]

Betty Belt and Bob Eicholtz also acted politically. Getting the right teacher for Oakridge ranked high in Belt's priorities. Within a district where shrinking student enrollment led to reductions in the numbers of teachers each year, Belt, like her colleagues, wrestled annually with choosing a teacher from the long list of teachers whose positions had been abolished at schools with lower enrollments but whose seniority meant they had to be placed elsewhere in the district.

By using the district office and colleagues' grapevine, Belt determined which teachers on the list would best fit Oakridge vacancies. If she erred, then she would have to deal with the parental complaints for the entire school year.

Belt played the list like a symphony's first violinist. She assessed the strengths of each teacher, estimated when her turn would come to take the next person on the list, and did all she could to secure the best match for Oakridge. Sometimes, of course, little could be done and she would have to take whomever was available.

Within the school, Belt bargained with teachers to achieve better staff performance. For example, science instruction is seldom a strong suit among elementary teachers. Belt sought a better science program. She negotiated with her staff that if they would add a few more students to their classes, the school would be allocated a full-time science teacher and the staff would be relieved of preparing and teaching science. The staff agreed.

Why all the phone calls? Why all the meetings with the district administrators? Why all the negotiations with teachers? Why all the tactics? At Oakridge, Belt knew that her influence upon the instructional program came not only from the quality of the teaching staff and her own expertise, it also came from a cadre of active, informed parents who provided Belt the muscle needed within the school and the clout for Oakridge within the district. While Oakridge had a substantial minority and low-income population, parental involvement in the school through volunteers and fund raising came primarily from a group of affluent whites in the neighborhoods adjacent to the school. These parents expressed great confidence in Betty Belt.

For her part, Belt made sure that parents were informed about school programs, district policies that affected the school, and school needs. She responded swiftly to parental concerns, exercising restraint and tact in acceding to some and rejecting others since many requests had to be delicately handled when they concerned teacher assignments or complaints about staff performance. Parents viewed her as a strong, fair principal. Thus, when Belt expressed concern for those students who needed special help, the parent organization authorized Belt to use the money that they had raised through bake sales and other fund raisers to run a special summer school for Oakridge pupils who needed either help in basic skills or wanted enrichment.

If there were school issues that needed ventilation at the district office or with school board members, Belt kept parents informed.

Oakridge parents would make phone calls, visit the superintendent, speak at school board meetings, and do whatever else necessary to improve the school situation. Belt knew that her influence over the instructional program was enhanced, not threatened, by support from vocal, well-placed parents in the community. It was a narrow line that Belt trod between advocacy for the Oakridge program, keeping parents informed, retaining teacher confidence, pursuing district policies, and maintaining appropriate loyalty to the central office. A trapeze artist, working without a safety net, could not have done a better job.[40]

Bob Eicholtz also played the political role astutely. In his first year as principal at Pioneer, Proposition 13, which drastically cut school funding, damaged his program. This drove Eicholtz to find ways of generating new monies to keep a very troubled school, with a bad reputation within the community, out of educational bankruptcy.

Imagination, ingenuity, and determination certainly are important ingredients to political judgment. When the school board, for example, approved a twelve-foot chain-link fence to be placed around the school, giving it a prison-like appearance, Eicholtz organized parents, staff, and students to install instead a wrought-iron fence covered by fast growing ivy to give the exterior more of a campus-like appearance—for the same price as the chain-link fence.

Declining student enrollments led to further district retrenchment, spurring the new principal to lobby persistently the superintendent and school board for permission to run bingo games at the high school, with Pioneer taking a slice of the proceeds. He succeeded. Within a year over $40,000 flowed into the high school treasury from bingo receipts providing funds for school trips to amusement parks, supplies for teachers, new equipment, and dozens of items needed to lubricate a complex operation for a 2,100-student high school.

Eicholtz wanted the community to have pride in Pioneer. He knew that it would take some time to improve test scores, the coin of the educational realm in the 1980s. But he wanted to demonstrate that the largely Hispanic high school had high academic expectations for its students. He also wanted to generate a climate of academic excellence. Enter the Omega program.

With his assistants, an honors program complete with Advanced Placement courses (actual and symbolic markers of academic improvement) was established within a few years of his becoming principal. Concerned that Omega students not become an elite group segregated from their classmates, Eicholtz approved a scheduling arrangement, called the "scramble" which permitted Omega students to attend classes with other Pioneer classmates. Yet he wanted to make sure that the honors group also retained a sense of unity so a room was set aside, T-shirts were purchased, and other symbols of solidarity were nourished. What the Omega program did was move the possibility for academic success a few notches higher for the entire student body.

Another instance of political action was Eicholtz's effort to take those students who were either gang members or within their sphere of influence and make them part of the Pioneer community. He knew that the image of Pioneer as plagued by gang activity had to be erased. Within the first year, Eicholtz established a Boy's and a Girl's Council that included those students identified as active or peripheral gang members. Through incentives and personal lobbying, he began meeting with these groups weekly and initiated the slow process of transforming these groups into school social clubs. Within two years, gang-linked incidents had disappeared from campus. The Councils included students who ordinarily were suspicious of high school sponsored groups; many planned to work or enter the military after high school. When I met with representatives from the Councils, they expressed a kind of enthusiasm for the school and the principal uncommon for students thought to be troublemakers.

Both principals, Eicholtz and Belt, engage in political action because they see connections to the larger goals they seek. Both the process and the outcomes are political in the sense that policies negotiated in the crucible of the school board and community are mediated by the superintendent and, ultimately, by principals and teachers as they transform those decisions into managerial and instructional acts. They use formal authority and informal influence to nudge, lure, and drag the school staff toward those larger goals they prize. Thus, politics becomes, as was the case with teachers, morality in action. The instructional, managerial, and political roles form the core of principaling, although much variation exists among school heads in how the three roles are performed.

PATTERNS IN DISCHARGING THE CORE ROLES

In using Betty Belt, Bob Eicholtz, Ed Bell, and Norris Hogans as examples of principaling, I underscore the continuing potency of the images described earlier and the varied patterns and contexts in which principals discharge these roles. Distinguishing between the content of the three roles and style in which they are performed is important, if for no other reason than to stress that style, as an ineffable mix of personal behaviors and roles, takes infinite forms within the principal-ship. Styles vary. Settings differ. Two principals may perform the three roles similarly, but their personalities, experiences, values, behaviors, and work settings may differ sufficiently that the similarities are over-shadowed by stylistic contrasts. In exploring these core role patterns, I find it useful to visualize their differences without the distraction of style.[41]

Figure 6 suggests how these three principals enact their roles. By placing the display of these roles within the nested layers of a school district, the political role becomes clear. The degree of crossover that occurs depends, to be sure, on how principals view their jobs, on the leverage they have within their domains, and on the inevitable intru-siveness of the district office and community. The overlapping sec-tions of the roles for some principals suggest how instruction and management intersect and how political judgments and actions can infuse the core roles—as viewed by an observer such as myself.

Not all principals view their world in political terms, of course. Ed Bell and others pursue roles that either consciously divorce political concerns from instructional and managerial ones or are seemingly unaware of the political dimension. For example, an apparently apo-litical principal performs the three core roles as largely separate tasks. Teachers take care of teaching, and the principal's job is to help them do a better job in the classroom (i.e., provide resources, buffer teachers from parents and the central office, and so on). Managing the school is the principal's primary role; keeping parents and district offi-cials content constitutes administrative work. Although the prin-cipal would probably deny it, such work is fundamentally political in its consequences since its cumulative effect is loyalty to existing arrangements.[42]

The core roles, varied styles, and complexity of the work have not strayed far from the origins of the post a century and a half ago. With the swift advance of nonteaching principals and the professionalization of the post in the last half-century has come much cant from both practitioners and researchers about how principals *should* principal. The brass-band version of instructional leadership has deep roots in the split origins of the position. The "walk-on-water" rhetoric surfaces

Figure 6: Core Role Patterns Among Principals*

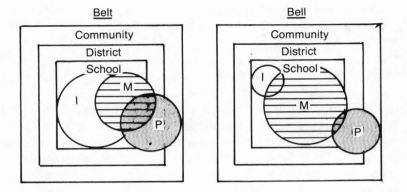

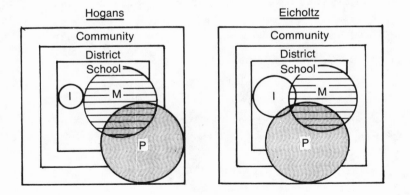

*These diagrams are devices to illustrate how each principal discharged their roles, as I view them. They are meant to show an array of different patterns; they are *not* empirically-derived diagrams.

sporadically to exhort another generation of candidates for the post to perform great deeds. They soon discover, however, that the bureaucratic work of principaling entangles them.

If anything, this chapter argues that the history of the post, the nature of the central tasks assigned to principals, the settings in which principals work, and the dominant images helped inspire and shape much of what these administrators practice. While styles differ, the managerial role, not instructional leadership, has dominated principals' behavior. But for some principals over the last century (what percentage I cannot estimate), the managerial and instructional roles have merged when they have envisioned what a school could possibly be. When visions are wedded to principals' beliefs and values, the political role comes into full play. Such principals transform their views of what can be into the mundane business of making a school work each day. When the principal's mission, however, is simply to maintain existing organizational patterns, the political role shrinks to reducing any static that might yield conflict.

For an administrative position that was taken from classrooms, both teachers and principals discharge similar core roles, becoming more comrades-in-arms than adversaries. That became part of my working knowledge when I served as both a teacher and an administrator of the Cardozo Project in the Urban Teaching Project.

4

Perverse Incentives: Moving Back and Forth Between Classroom and Administration, 1967–1972 [*]

I never served as a principal. The closest I came to the post was when I directed the Urban Teaching Project at Cardozo High School between 1965 and 1967 and acted as a quasi assistant principal. I say *quasi* because I did not have this title, but headed a separate program within a high school that trained teachers. I reported to the principal for such matters as scheduling our staff and interns to take over classes and other tasks. When the principal complained about interns or staff, he came to me.

Within the project, however, I was responsible for the recruiting, hiring, placing, training, and firing of interns, curriculum specialists, and teachers who helped supervise the newcomers. In addition, I negotiated with area universities for the awarding of master's degrees upon completion of the internship, course work on campus, and in-school seminars. Managerial tasks such as scheduling which teachers would teach high subjects, arranging seminars, locating speakers, allocating budgeted funds, securing a part-time psychiatrist to consult with us, and scheduling work for two secretaries went with the territory. Finally I continued to teach two classes of U.S. history and a seminar on the teaching of history for the four interns I supervised.

The principle was my in-school boss, who seldom intervened in project affairs except when they spilled over into the rest of the school; my other boss was the assistant superintendent who headed the

[*] David Tyack suggested the phrase *perverse incentives* as a title.

experimental Model School Division in which the Cardozo Project was one of over a dozen programs. Given a very long leash by the assistant superintendent to run the project within the high school, I nonetheless reported to him my progress, problems, and the like. Being in a subsystem of the District of Columbia schools that was federally funded and largely ignored by Superintendent Carl Hansen, the only times that I would hear from him was when interns were quoted in the newspapers on the outrageous conditions under which District teachers taught (inadequate texts, large classes, and so on) or on the inappropriate (selections that contained profanity) curriculum materials that we used. Phone calls from the superintendent would rattle underlings, and I would be called downtown.

Named director of the Cardozo project in Urban Teaching in September 1965, I had to administer by the seat of my pants. The only previous experience I had had was running a boys' camp, managing a classroom, and gradually taking on both supervisory and managerial tasks throughout 1964–1965 during the absence of the first director. Jockeying over the future of the project had pitted groups within the program against each other; the nasty elbowing that occurred left many tasks undone. I did the extra duties because I believed in what we were doing and wanted the project to continue. When word of the funding came and I was asked to serve, I took the job and never regretted it.

For the two years that I directed the program, I took daily roller-coaster rides—remember that this was in the midst of passionate concern for the disadvantaged in addition to a large flow of federal dollars (not seen before or since). Here was a pilot project that tested whether a new teaching role could be fashioned, within one year's time, with ex-Peace Corps volunteers while simultaneously offering a quality education for low-income minority youth and improving the entire school. It now seems an incredibly naive dream, yet innocent or not, we were constantly on display.

Visitors often swept through the large room where I, the entire staff, and interns had our desks, file cabinets, and ditto machines scattered about. Opportunities for additional funds and linkages with other programs were constantly presenting themselves. How seductive it was to believe that the media and national attention that we were receiving meant that we were being effective and making progress.

From the journals that I kept for those years, I have constructed a composite of the mundane tasks, routines, and activities that filled my day. The time that I've chosen is the winter of 1965–1966 when we (including interns who often provided the ideas and follow-through) expanded the central mission of teacher-education to include helping those high school students unserved by the District—those capable of going to college and those who would end up on the streets.

February 1966

7:00 A.M. Met with University of Maryland administrators and professors at College of Education about the Upward Bound proposal. The federal Office of Economic Opportunity (OEO) was funding programs that would move larger proportions of able low-income students into colleges. The program would put talented inner-city youth for a summer on a university campus and continue with a follow-up program during the school year. I had worked for OEO the previous summer evaluating pilot programs. As OEO now expanded the pilots into a national network, I had contacted Maryland to see if they were interested in joining Cardozo in submitting a proposal. They were.

Now we were in the midst of jointly writing a proposal that would take Cardozo students, project interns and staff, and blend university and school folks into a cohesive effort. We were successful in getting funded, and the project ran for a number of years.

9:45 A.M. Returned to Cardozo and taught my U.S. history class. I used lessons and units that I had developed at Glenville. We were in the midst of a unit on how slavery grew in America. Shifting gears from such widely different tasks as negotiating with Maryland people to figuring out which students in my class should get the tough questions and which the easier ones, I found difficult in the first five minutes, but once immersed into the lesson, the gears shifted smoothly.

Tardiness and absenteeism, especially on Fridays and Mondays, continually plagued my class, interns, and the entire school. I had hoped that project classrooms, including mine, because of new content, motivating pedagogy, and the high caliber of teachers, would somehow be insulated from the pervasive absenteeism and class-cutting. I was wrong. I discovered then that improving attendance could only be achieved with cooperation of the principal, staff, and all the teachers. During the four years that I was at Cardozo, attendance remained an unsolved problem other than through attrition from suspensions for truancy (yes, that is correct) and eventually drop-outs.

10:30 A.M. Went to office to work through the pile of telephone messages, mail, and forms and to hold quick conferences with secretaries, interns, and staff. I generally rifled through the telephone messages and divided them into two stacks: immediate and later. My criteria usually boiled down to responding first to messages from family and bosses or any marked "emergency." I handled my mail at work after everyone left the office, at home, or very early in the morning. "Larry, I gotta see you now," from anyone in the office or the school, received attention first.

On this particular day, I met with Roger Schneidewind, a history intern, to discuss how to handle a lesson he was going to do later that day. Conferred with interns Gerry Schwinn and Ash Hartwell about a proposal they were drafting for using thirty potential dropouts as teacher aides, nurses aides, recreational assistants, and other posts within the city government. Schwinn had gotten the idea from one of our afternoon seminars in which Bill Klein, from Howard University, had discussed with us how to prevent dropouts by training those who were likely to leave school how to help people. Learning through helping others is part of human wisdom; it struck many of us at the time as a very sensible way of motivating students who were uninterested in the academics to complete high school and to gain experience that might lead to further employment; they would also be paid for their services. OEO finally funded the Human Service Aide project. Howard University staff, former interns and I taught the academic portion of the program that was to be linked to their work while others supervised them on the job.

11:45 A.M. Went to United Planning Organization offices (UPO) to meet with deputy director about evaluating the project. UPO was the community action organization established by the city government to receive federal funds for a host of urban initiatives involving housing, health, schooling, and community development. Because all OEO funds for the Cardozo project came to UPO while I was director, I met periodically with their staff to keep them posted about what we were doing.

Before any renewal or expansion of funding, our project had to be evaluated. We were in the process of negotiating who would do it and the specifics of that evaluation. While UPO staff generally looked with favor upon the project (although with all the turnover they experienced, I eventually gave up trying to keep them posted), they were consistently hostile to Carl Hansen and central office officials. Their posture was that the public schools had messed up students for decades—the District desegregated formally in 1955—and that UPO was to be the gadfly on the system's flank.

1:30 P.M. Principal Randall Evans asked to see me. He had heard from a teacher that one of the interns was not following the senior English curriculum in using Richard Wright's *Black Boy*. I told him what the intern was doing in class with the book and that it was certainly within the general guidelines published by the District. Within a year, the District came out with a revised curriculum guide that encouraged teachers to use such works.

2:00 P.M. Observed Jay Mundstuk teach a lesson on the assassination of President Kennedy. Took notes and met with Mundstuk after class. He began by describing what he felt were the strengths and limitations to the lesson, including both content and management. I described what I saw and we measured that against what he wanted to happen in the class (his lesson plan) and what did happen. Because we both knew what the criteria were for effective lessons— something all of us had worked out the first two months of the internship—our discussion generally followed those criteria. We then talked about what he was planning to do the next day and how he could, if at all, build on what had been taught (and learned) today.

3:15 P.M. Returned to office to confer with secretary about which messages and people I needed to see before my next meeting. We went over the next day's schedule; I dictated some brief notes that I needed to get out quickly. A few students from my class came by to pick up assignments they had missed yesterday. Two junior high school interns came by to find out more about the paper they had to write for tomorrow's seminar on sociology taught by Howard University professor G. Franklin Edwards. Maxine Daly, English curriculum specialist in the project, a veteran Cardozo teacher who eventually headed the expanded Urban Teacher Corps for the District of Columbia schools when the system took over the funding of the project, and I met briefly to discuss exchanging interns to supervise. The previous year I had switched interns with my counterpart in English for a week and all of us found it useful. Daly wanted to do the same.

4:00 P.M. History Club met. A small group of students in my class wanted to start a History Club so I agreed to meet with them once every two weeks. About ten came to each meeting. Discussions would flow from issues the students raised, many of which were triggered by topics dealt with in class. For over two months, for example, we talked at great length about whether or not religion should be formally taught at Cardozo. Sober, restrained debate would erupt into emotional fervor when our discussions turned to the existence of heaven and hell, the teachings of the black Muslims (a temple was housed not too far from the school), and whether homosexuals are damned by God.

5:15 P.M. Returned to the office to clean off my desk, draft memos and the weekly schedule for interns. Neil Dickman and Judy Sheldon were in the office using the ditto machine. We talked for awhile, interrupted by phone calls since the secretary had already left. Maxine returned from her seminar with the English interns and we talked about what a proposal for next year's project might include.

6:30 P.M. Left for home.

This frenzy of teaching, administering, and politicking exhilarated me. Every day was an adventure; however, there were times when certain events would plunge me into a dark, opaque gloom: the alcoholic teacher who snored in the lounge during her daily nap; constant mindless announcements from the principal over the loudspeaker that would interrupt the lesson; a student stabbed at his locker; or word that a former student had died in Vietnam.

To avoid the hectic start of the previous year, I began planning in February for renewing OEO funding. Since decision making over expansion of the project had always involved interns, I began circulating proposal drafts to people inside and outside Cardozo. In record time we produced a document that touched every desk at OEO, UPO, and the District of Columbia offices. Funds for an extension were approved in April.

Because notice came early, we had planned a summer program at Howard University for new interns at Grimke Elementary, Banneker Junior High, and Cardozo High School. Another group of young men and women from the Peace Corps, Volunteers in Service to America (VISTA), and recent college graduates entered classrooms to teach, to create instructional materials, and to work in the community.

Early in the 1966–1967 school year I sensed that this would be my last year as director. The madcap pace had taken its toll on my wife, Barbara, and my daughters, Sondra and Janice (both under five years of age) creating tensions that I could no longer ignore. The juggling of my career, my family responsibilities, and my role as husband had left me fatigued and frustrated over not being able to spend time on the things I valued highly. Something had to give. I would leave the project, but not before the District of Columbia took over funding and a cadre of experienced staff were in place. Both became my goals for the year.

Through active lobbying with District officials, including members of the board of education, I began to build the framework for a locally funded program incorporating the best features of what we had learned over the last four years.

The local press had given us rave reviews, feature articles on particular ex-Peace Corps teachers who had a flair with students, and an occasional editorial about the contribution we made to the overall quality of the system. Such publicity sat well with some members of the board of education and professional reformers in Washington, but it annoyed Superintendent Hansen and other top school officials who viewed us as fly-by-night operators unfamiliar with the fundamental problems of the school district. What helped our effort to become part of the regular school system, I believe, was the teacher shortage and benign neglect.

Carl Hansen had come under increasing fire from a small but vocal group of activist blacks and politically liberal whites for resisting alterations to his Amidon Plan and Four-Track System in the secondary schools and bussing for purposes of desegregation. Hansen's concentration upon a traditional curriculum, with a healthy dose of character-building education—two areas a later generation of reformers would applaud, but were at the time seen as cruelly depriving poor children of an equitable education—kept him busy replying to critics who hammered at him through 1967.[1]

Letters to my boss and Hansen produced no response. Not until I drafted an evaluation proposal, secured a dean from a well-respected school of education, and sent to Hansen the glowing final report did we begin to receive official notice. This entire process took five months and active lobbying with two of the five members of the board of education. Finally the superintendent told his budget director to negotiate the incorporation of the Cardozo project into the District schools as the Urban Teacher Corps. Three months later Hansen resigned.

Board approval of the Urban Teacher Corps filled me with pride. Of the people who had founded the project four years earlier, I was the sole survivor. Far more important, veteran Cardozo teachers, former interns who remained at the high school, and a small band of regular teachers in nearby schools guaranteed that a continuity in leadership would guide the program in years to come.

What was I to do? During the year, two publishers had contacted me. One asked me to become general editor of an unconventional series of paperbacks on American history, world cultures, and urban life. Aimed at ninth through eleventh graders taking civics, world geography, and U.S. history, these paperbacks (rather than the usual one volume hardback) would use actual historical and contemporary accounts to encourage students to form ideas, analyze concepts, and apply them to situations. I was excited by the possibility of reaching a larger audience with the materials that I had written at Glenville and Cardozo, and believed they would be an improvement over unimaginative and uninteresting textbooks. My job would be to write the U.S. history with another teacher and edit the writings of others who would be hired to produce materials consistent with the conceptual framework that I laid out for the publisher. Former interns that I had trained to create instructional materials joined me for the project.

Also, an editor from another publisher had visited Cardozo and invited me to write a book on how to improve teaching in inner-city schools. While I began creating lessons and units at Glenville and enjoyed the game of writing, the only sustained writing I had done were articles for tiny professional journals and a few chapters of a dissertation on nineteenth and twentieth century black leadership in Cleveland. The thought of writing an entire book both intimidated and fascinated me.

By the middle of the year, I had signed contracts with both publishers. But I also wanted to teach. The deep pleasures that I gained from working with students on subjects I found interesting and encouraging them to think aloud and on paper continued to entice me.

Free from administrative demands and the frenzied life I previously led, the thought of teaching and writing led me to contact District personnel to seek a teaching position. An associate superintendent who had both criticized and supported what we were doing at Cardozo helped me through the bureaucratic maze to find a temporary half-time teaching position at Roosevelt High School, a few miles from Cardozo and just ten minutes by car from our home in northwest Washington. It was temporary because I did not meet fully the District of Columbia's teaching requirements (I have never taken courses on how to teach in secondary schools and on alcohol and tobacco abuse)—a fact that unflaggingly trailed my future.

That last summer I served as director I hired the interns, planned the training at Howard and Catholic Universities, and waited for the new director to arrive. When he did, I closed the door and returned to teaching and writing and my family.

TEACHING AT ROOSEVELT

I had asked the principal if I could teach lower track U.S. history classes. The "basic" track contained students who had performed poorly in school and had scored in the lower ranges on group intelligence tests. While a court decision the previous summer had supposedly ended tracking of students, it persisted at Roosevelt. He quickly accommodated my wishes. I was assigned two classes and a homeroom.

I asked for these classes to see if the materials I had created and was currently working on would fit these students. I believed that the critical thinking skills I sought to develop and strengthen were appropriate for all students. The content, pedagogy, and classroom organization were tailored to the strengths of the low-income, minority youth I had observed over the last decade: varied experience in life, an inherent interest in people, and an enthusiasm for verbal jousting.

The same problems of low motivation (after ten or so years of being categorized as "slow learners," high motivation would have been extraordinary), poorly developed skills in reading and writing, and absenteeism that were present at Cardozo were also present in my classes at Roosevelt. For absent students, calls home each week to those who had missed classes helped. I visited parents. Letters and frequent notes went out to both students who were sick or cut classes and those who were doing well. All of these devices helped somewhat to reduce the frequency and total number of school days missed for many of my students but not all. After all, there were circumstances over which I had no influence: Some students whose babies were cared for by their mothers or neighbors suddenly found these arrangements broken and therefore had to stay at home; other students couldn't get along with one or the other parent and left home; some students were seriously ill and had nowhere to turn. As a consequence, increasing the holding power of my class was a continual struggle the entire year.

For the academic problems, I pursued the general strategies developed at Cardozo and Glenville. No textbooks were provided. Instead, with purple-stained hands, I distributed dittoed materials. For students who could not read, I taped lessons and they worked on them individually. For each lesson, I would divide the period into large group discussions, small group tasks, and individual activities. One week I produced enough self-guided materials to hold a history laboratory: a set of activities on the Civil War where students would move from station to station, following the directions, and completing the tasks. I was so excited over how well it was working that I ran down to the principal's office and pulled him into the classroom to see what could be done with basic track classes.

Also, one of the counselors had asked me if I would be interested in starting a Negro history class—the label was still common in the mid–60s. When the new semester began, I had twenty students in the new course. The discussions were intense, highly emotional, often dominated by three students who had joined the local chapter of the Black Panthers. I was continually challenged on the readings I used, the facts I cited, and the directions that the discussions took. The class was split ideologically over the same issues dividing the civil rights movement in those years. After teaching basic classes the first semester that tended to have low-key, sporadic discussions, I found these classes emotionally draining and intellectually electrifying.

Those highs, however, were overshadowed by the frustration I would feel when, for example, three-quarters of a basic class would fail a test on the unit "The American Dream," or only one-quarter or one-half of the class would turn in their homework. Sometimes I would blame myself. I should do more, I said, but I was already reaching my limits. Then I would consider the situation in which I was working. Students came to class for 45 minutes; they went to five or more different classes a day; many had been certified by the school as dumb and believed it. How much could one expect from one teacher in one subject area, isolated from colleagues except at lunch time or before school? Again, the alternating pattern of hope and despair marked my thoughts and feelings during the year.

Over time, I could not muster the energy necessary to prepare all the materials needed every day for my classes, to mark all the papers, to visit the homes, and to write. I began to cut back. Teaching the materials I had developed did convince me that the average student, regardless of background, could grasp the content, engage in what educators today call "higher order thinking skills," and perform creditably on teacher-made tests. But it took an enormous amount of time and energy to overcome (as I came to see so clearly after a decade in classrooms) an organizational arrangement designed to make schools efficient in dealing with large numbers of students, rather than designed to help teachers teach or students learn.

The years 1967–1968 jolted the nation. Those were the months when Vietnam protests polarized Americans; Lyndon Johnson announced that he would not seek reelection. The civil rights movement split into warring factions. The murder of Martin Luther King Jr., occurred in April 1968 and the 14th St. corridor in Washington, D.C., went up in flames—just a few blocks from Roosevelt. The riots left racial feelings raw for months in the city. These events spilled over into my classroom.

Stokely Carmichael, a black activist who had worked for years in the South with the Students Non-Violent Coordinating Committee (SNCC), spoke to Roosevelt students on the importance of blacks respecting one another. The black history class spent a few days discussing his message. When my students wanted more information on the Vietnam protests, I organized an after-school forum, inviting a fellow history teacher to argue for American intervention in Vietnam and a black peace activist in the community to argue for unilateral withdrawal of American troops.

The principal told me I could not have the meeting because it would cause disruption during school or possible violence even if it were after school. I filed a grievance against the principal, and after the hearing, the forum was held. The principal, however, did ask the local precinct for two officers to patrol the school. Over forty students and eight teachers came and, of course, there were no disturbances.

As these events unfolded I continued to experience much internal conflict. Writing, teaching, and spending more time with my wife and children proved stimulating and satisfying except that I came to miss the action, the intensity, and the pressurized decision making of managerial life. Over the course of 1967–1968, I found myself yearning for more responsibility and leadership opportunities than were available to me within the classroom.

For a few months, I worked part-time at the U.S. Commission on Civil Rights as director of race and education. For a number of reasons, both within the Commission (it was undergoing an upheaval in personnel and philosophy) and within me (I was a practitioner trying to generate and administer a research program, an effort that ignored my strengths and illuminated my limitations), I erred in taking the job and left over the summer. Back home I continued to produce units for the textbook series and completed *To Make a Difference: Teaching in the Inner City*. When the District of Columbia public schools established a new Office of Staff Development to work with 8,000 teachers and almost a thousand administrators, a number of people asked me to apply to become its first director.

ADMINISTERING THE OFFICE OF STAFF DEVELOPMENT

Just a month before Superintendent Carl Hansen had resigned in 1967, a major, year-long study of the entire system was submitted to the board of education. They assigned the implementing of hundreds of recommendations about curriculum, instruction, organization, and staff development to acting superintendent Ben Henley (the first black to head the District schools).

The acting superintendent established numerous committees and by the end of 1968 these committees had submitted their recommendations to Henley who, in turn, endorsed most of them for board action.

A Division of Instruction was proposed under the direction of a deputy superintendent; within that division was to be created an Office of Staff Development (OSD) charged to establish a coherent and organized program of professional development for almost 9,000 District teachers and administrators. The board approved the recommendation and authorized a director with a small staff and an ample first year's budget. The new deputy superintendent for instruction wanted to fill the post quickly. I applied. In December 1968 I was appointed to direct the fledgling office.

The idea of creating some order out of the patchwork arrangements for professional development that existed and taking initiatives to help teachers and administrators appealed to me. Nor was it a trivial task. Over twenty-five school departments and eleven area colleges already conducted widely different programs for the professional staff and no one in the District had any grasp of what *was* happening, much less of what *should* happen. Responsible to the deputy superintendent, the number two person in the system, provided with a $100,000 budget, an assistant director, and a secretary, I jumped into the job with both feet. I almost drowned.

Within a few weeks I picked a former colleague from Roosevelt High School to be assistant director of OSD. While teaching at Roosevelt, I came to respect her organizational talents and compassionate understanding of people. In addition, a smart, technically competent, and ambitious woman who was attending college became my secretary. For one year the three of us were OSD, although we bootlegged staff and sympathetic colleagues (with a wink from my boss) to help us. In that first year, we accomplished a great deal:

- Developed a comprehensive plan for pre- and in-service education of teachers and administrators.

- Operated ten pilot programs that demonstrated alternative ways of training teachers, administrators, aides, and interns.

- Coordinated all pre-service programs with eleven local colleges by making over 2,000 placements of student teachers a year.

- Administered fourteen teacher-training programs funded through the U.S. Office of Education, which made it possible to implement portions of the comprehensive plan.

- Acquired over a million dollars in new federal and private funds to supplement the growing OSD budget authorized by the Board of Education.

Following are some of the programs that sparked great interest among teachers and principals in our first year:

Teacher Innovation Fund. Over 100 teachers received $200 grants for projects they designed for improvements in reading, math, and other identified areas.

School Innovation Fund. Grants of up to $4,000 were given to individual schools for installing innovative staff development programs. Teachers, administrators, students, and the community designed programs jointly.

Seminar in Analysis of Teaching. Over 500 teachers applied for a ten-week, tuition-free, late-afternoon course to learn more about understanding the process of teaching.

Even writing this almost two decades later, I shake my head in disbelief that we did all of the above in so brief a time and in the face of such enormous obstacles (a few of which I never overcame). Again, the context of OSD's rise and demise needs to be shared.

The District of Columbia's schools were in the midst of politically and racially turbulent times. Not only had Hansen been ousted in 1967, signaling an end to an era of schooling, but Congress, which had governed the District since 1906, had just authorized an elected school board, the first such board within the local government. Three appointed commissioners still headed the city government, although that would change shortly also. Under the amplified scrutiny of the public and the crescendo of national media interest, the first elected school board drew a mix of the serious, the civic-minded, the ambitious, the racially militant, and the quacks.

The traditional educational philosophy that Hansen represented and most of his programs were left in tact until federal Judge Skelly Wright ordered the dismantling of the entire ability-grouping scheme called the "Track System." In *Hobson v. Hansen* (plaintiff Julius Hobson served on the first elected Board of Education before moving to the elected City Council years later), Wright ruled that tracking discriminated against poor black children, and he mandated a number of remedies: the bussing of black children to a handful of white schools; equitable distribution of all resources, including teachers, to schools across the district; and instructional groupings that encouraged mixing students with varied abilities.

Amid this turmoil entered newly appointed William Manning, the last white superintendent to serve in the District. Completely unprepared to deal with the racial tensions in the schools, a divided central administration, a contentious teachers' union, and a fractious city government, he never took control. Without a dissenting vote, the board of education dismissed him in the summer of 1969.

Few mourned his departure; many welcomed the return of Acting Superintendent Ben Henley. I recall the first staff meeting for administrators that Henley addressed in August 1969. When Henley was introduced and approached the podium, the entire audience of administrators rose to their feet and applauded. I had never seen principals and central office staff, both black and white, who normally range from skeptical to cynical over changes in school chiefs, respond so enthusiastically to an acting superintendent.

Henley and the deputy superintendent were the top school leaders during 1969–1970, an interim period during which the Board of Education jockeyed over who should be the next superintendent. In such a situation, aggressive action or major decisions were unlikely. Uncertainty over whether Henley or his deputy would be asked to serve filtered down through all levels of the Presidential Building, the new downtown headquarters of the board of education. These new offices were just a block away from the building of the newly appointed city council and mayor. The city council (the president of the United States chose both the mayor and council members) was empowered to review the school system's budget and recommend to the Congress how much the public schools should receive.

Both contenders for the superintendency were in a fishbowl; their actions came under microscopic scrutiny from Congress, a new mayor and city council, a federal judge, and an elected Board of Education.

Within this agitated environment, OSD tried to carry out the charge to both coordinate and initiate professional development across the school district. I learned about leadership and large bureaucracies—their efficiencies and pathologies.

The tangled budgeting arrangements involving the Division of Instruction, the board of education, the city council, the mayor, the District subcommittees in the House of Representatives, and the Senate would bring a smile to the face of Rube Goldberg. In two years, not a week went by that one or more of the above did not ask me to justify the presence of OSD. Enormous amounts of time went into planning budgets, elbowing colleagues to grab available funds, and poker-faced bluffing of bosses over what could or could not be cut from existing programs. I learned each day in that organization that it is easier (and tactically smarter) to seek forgiveness than permission.

What proved to be far harder to overcome—and here my innocence shows—was the resilient opposition of the curriculum and supervision departments within the Division of Instruction (e.g., English, history and so on). While some of these veteran administrators viewed OSD's birth and growth as additional help, most of them viewed us as meddlesome intruders. *Their* job was staff development, and no new department was needed, thank you. All they needed was more money.

Supervisors' anger rose when they discovered that we would not automatically service their requests for consultants and workshops. When we (including the deputy superintendent) tried to get these independent barons to cooperate in programs jointly designed by teachers and principals, sabotage and resistance increased. Even primitive attempts to begin a clearinghouse of information for teachers on

available services were ignored. A directive from the deputy superintendent could not unplug information from the baronies. Even the
single attempt by the superintendent and deputy to end the self-
serving independence and move central office supervisors into schools
failed. By late 1969, Henley, the deputy superintendent, and I discovered that a group of curriculum supervisors had gone to city council
members and lobbied for the excision of OSD from the Board-
approved budget.

Secrecy was a joke at the Presidential Building, and some of the
supervisors bragged to colleagues of their meetings with council members. One city council member, chairman of the Education Committee
(and, incidentally, the brother of a curriculum supervisor), reportedly
had his eye on becoming superintendent. Observers said that he saw
an opportunity to gain city-wide recognition without attacking the
popular Henley. He concentrated upon abolishing OSD.

Also, race might have been an issue since I was one of the few
highly visible whites in the top administration, and I had just been
promoted to a rank above the curriculum supervisors. In short, in a
district that had been segregated since its birth and whose top officials
were now moving aggressively toward placing blacks in top positions
after decades of being excluded from these posts, I was an easy target.
By wiping out funds for OSD, the council member knew that the
Board of Education would define the issue not on race but on who is
running the school system: the city council or the Board of Education.

The board president responded to the council challenge and mo-
bilized board support for a showdown. The acting superintendent and
deputy, still campaigning for the top position, provided the kind of
support for OSD that a girlfriend shows a former beau whom she
discovers has a social disease. By the summer of 1970, it was clear to
me that OSD would be eviscerated, leaving a shadow office as an
appendage to the Division of Instruction. Through a series of frantic
last minute negotiations, one position was salvaged and a token appro-
priation, barely 10 percent of existing funds was restored.

My boss asked me to stay on as director. A new superintendent,
Hugh Scott, from Detroit had just been selected (Henley withdrew his
candidacy and the board passed over the deputy). More changes were
in store. I said "no" and resigned to return to the classroom.

I was terribly bruised by the bureaucratic and political battles.
The intimate look at how the top leadership of one of the largest
school districts in the nation worked convinced me that I could do as

well as the people who ran the District; I was sick of the backbiting, the rumors, and the racism (both black and white) that often clouded relationships, and the feverish pursuit of small victories that might, or might not, have anything to do with what teachers and children did in their classrooms. I had lost more of my innocence about how superintendents and top administrators work in the midst of political and racial turbulence. I needed time to recover. But I soon found out that the bureaucratic structures in this district contained perverse incentives against teaching; it was far easier for me to avoid the classroom and seek a comfortable nook and remain an administrator in the Presidential Building.

TEACHING WHILE MANAGING

After two years downtown, returning to teaching would be no shock. While I was at the Presidential Building, I continued to teach in either an elementary or secondary school. For one semester I was an instructional aide in a first-grade classroom at Thompson School, an elementary school about twelve blocks from my downtown office.

In that first-grade class, the teacher assigned me to the "slowest" reading group and asked me to help them learn the alphabet. Nine children (seven boys and two girls) and I worked together one morning a week with flash cards, games, and stories. I made up word cards from popular songs that they heard on the radio. I wanted each one to recognize, sound out, and print each letter of the alphabet. To those who could do all three, I promised prizes.

I learned that in the "slowest group" there were five children who, with some individual attention, swiftly identified the letters and sounds and could print the entire alphabet. These five moved into reading simple stories that they had created and I had written; the other four, however, never learned more than a third of the alphabet and had what I felt were severe problems with paying attention, sitting still, crying jags, and simple day-dreaming. Whether they were too young and unready for the formal school experience, or whether I was inadequate, I don't know.

In June I gave out books to the five and small things to the other four. Somehow, in the midst of the squabbles and bureaucratic Keystone Kops in which I participated for the other four-and-a-half days, this brief taste of teaching energized me, even when I got depressed over the four children who might never learn to read.

The pressures of the job, however, made it impossible to continue on a half-day basis the next school year. Since teaching remained so important in my life, I contacted the high school principal in our neighborhood and asked if I could teach an elective course on black history for three days a week at 7:30 A.M. He agreed and that is how I came to teach a class of ten at Coolidge High School three mornings a week before going downtown.

Teaching black history to seven or eight sleepy teenagers (the early hour kept the class small) was not my finest hour. I was so intent upon maintaining a personal sense of credibility as a teacher while serving as an administrator that I neglected to foresee such simple issues as my fatigue over doing both and the difficulties in building a relationship with a class when I was only around 45 minutes three mornings a week. Moreover, questions of a white teacher teaching black history arose immediately since I was a stranger to Coolidge students. The readings I gave them and a number of intense discussions diminished some of the difficulties, but I labored under many self-made burdens that entire semester.

I "bootlegged" both teaching assignments. I told no one at the Presidential Building how I spent my time, especially since I already put in long days and evenings on OSD business. So when the debacle of OSD's disappearance from the school budget occurred, the decision to go back to the classroom was only a major decision insofar as preparing for the inevitable salary reduction. Going from director of the Cardozo Project in Urban Teaching to teaching history at Roosevelt in 1967 hurt the wallet also, but advances from two publishers softened the financial pinch. I was prepared for receiving less money, but I was unprepared for the unintentional humiliation of going from a top-level district office position back to the classroom.

RETURNING TO THE CLASSROOM

To understand the bureaucratic slaps in the face I received, one must appreciate the perpetual guilt that many administrators have over leaving the classroom. Discuss the subject of teaching with central office administrators and you will inevitably hear from them how much they miss it: "Those were my happiest days. Working with kids, not pushing papers," a colleague reminisced before a meeting with the superintendent. "It's important to stay in touch with kids. That's where the action is"; adding quickly, "How I miss it." When I gently asked why he didn't return to the classroom, his eyes narrowed and his body stiffened. "I would like to, but, you know, the money, and, well, I like making decisions here and, well, I needed a change." "If salaries continue to go up," I asked, "would you then teach?"

"No," he replied.

Board of education members also felt that teaching was the core activity of the District schools. "Teaching," one board member said at a subcommittee meeting, "is the cutting edge of change in the school system." Another praised teachers as the guardians of morality, the keepers of tradition, and the innovators of reform. "No program," another said, "is better than the teachers who run it."

Nothing new here. Policymakers and administrators deeply believe that the classroom teacher is the backbone of schooling. Thus, when I decided to return to Roosevelt, I expected some encouragement from colleagues, perhaps a bit of support and an easy transition. How naive I was. Disbelief, punishment, and shame dogged each step of my return to teaching.

When word spread at the Presidential Building, no one believed me. A wink or smirk from someone in the corridor suggested that I was really waiting for a better offer. For the most part, however, I was ignored. I began to feel like a leper. I discovered that the administrators and board members who extolled teaching couldn't understand why anyone in their right mind would want to take a pay-cut and return to the classroom. If that wasn't bad enough, within the next two months a series of actions, unmalicious in intent, initiated and executed in a most efficient and impersonal manner, occurred that created within me a sense of shame and failure.

While I did know about a reduced salary, I was surprised to learn from the Board of Examiners (the department that certified credentials and established salary level) that none of the four years I had served as an administrator in the District schools counted for salary credit and only seven of the ten years I had taught met the standards of the District. Next came the official board action which transfers an employee from one position to another. I received a notice stating that I was "demoted without prejudice." The phrase, of course, was semantically correct. I was moving to a lower rung on the organizational ladder and being there was my choice. Still it made me feel uneasy; it was like being pushed back into a lower group because you are inadequate or you misbehave. The phrase comes from the vocabulary of failure.

Then the board of examiners informed me a week before school began that I would not receive a regular contract because I had never taken a college course in teaching in the secondary school. With over a decade of classroom experience in three cities, with four years experience in preparing teachers to work in the District's secondary schools, with a book and numerous articles on teacher education, I was told that unless I took a course on teaching in the secondary school within two years I would not be able to teach in the system. After a pay cut, a demotion, and then a threat, I felt that I had committed some crime. What had I done wrong?

What I had come face-to-face with were the perverse incentives that drive public schooling. The organizational rewards of more money, status, and control over one's time were, and still are, outside the classroom. As organized then (and still today), urban high school teaching was tough work: signing in every morning, teaching five classes a day, reading the papers of over 170 students, hall duty, a half-hour to gulp down a lunch, one period free to do preparation, seeing students after school, marking papers and preparing lessons at home, spending your money to buy what the school cannot give you or hasn't arrived in time. Under such working conditions, the gifted teacher either burns out just like a spent 100-watt bulb or makes a series of compromises to survive under such conditions. Some leave to work in administration, forever feeling guilty over deserting the classroom. The less gifted (the 25-watt bulbs) serve an apprenticeship in the classroom and stay, or, at the first chance, grab for the rung that hoists them onto the ladder leading to the principal's office or at least into small offices tucked away in some corner of the Presidential Building. Bureaucratic incentives simply ran in the wrong direction. I knew it in my head but experienced it in my heart in returning to Roosevelt in the fall of 1970.

If I needed some time to heal and to do work that I found both satisfying and worthwhile, teaching and writing would provide that opportunity. Just as the last time I taught at Roosevelt, I again began to write articles and plan a book on the Washington, D.C., public schools. I also knew that the inner turmoil that drove me to both treasure and reject teaching as my only career would reassert itself in time.

The first year came as a surprise. Two days after I began teaching my five classes of American history and government, the new director of the Urban Teacher Corps (a former Cardozo teacher) called. Now a District-funded venture that trained over 100 new teachers a year, she asked if I would be willing to take on a team of English interns at

Roosevelt since the person she had in mind had dropped out? I agreed on the condition that I would still teach two history classes; she spoke to the principal, and for 1970–1971 I was again a master teacher working with four interns similar to what I had done at Cardozo High School seven years earlier.

The second year I taught five classes a day. While I had learned to pace myself much better than when I was at Glenville years earlier, I still found that teaching five classes with three preparations (sociology, government, and U.S. history) forced me to make compromises in both the *what* and *how* of teaching. I simply could not prepare new materials for all five classes; one class was all I could manage. Nor could I assign essays twice a week in each class; once a week was all I could manage. I could see only a fraction of my 150 students before and after school and during my one preparation period. I saw only those who needed the most help; I practiced educational triage.

What drove me to do more, however, was the students' response to the history labs (learning centers or teaching stations, as some called them) that I set up monthly and the new units that I developed on reasoning skills. These units contained lessons on how to tell a fact from an opinion, how to determine what is a reliable source of information, how to judge the accuracy of eye-witness testimony, and so forth. I used these units for the first three weeks in each class. The rest of the semester, while using a textbook or my materials, I would repeatedly apply the half-dozen skills learned in the opening weeks of the class.

What enhanced these efforts was sharing with other like-minded teachers. My next-door neighbor, a new teacher, asked to use my materials and adapted them for his classes. We laughed over the joy of lessons that successed and knocked our heads in frustration over those that didn't. Carol Carstensten, a former Glenville student who had taken history from me a decade earlier, came to Washington, D.C., with her lawyer husband. She wanted to teach in the District and was assigned to Roosevelt. Bright, enthusiastic, and very savvy about teaching in inner-city schools, Carol and I joined forces on a number of student projects. We shared materials and ideas. The small group was not as cohesive or large as the Glenville cadre I had been part of, but at least I didn't feel isolated, the common workplace hazard for teachers.

A unique skirmish with another teacher during those two years distilled for me both the triumph and despair of inner-city teaching in the early 1970s. The prickly exchange between veteran teacher

Myrtle Davis and me occurred over a unit on the city in my U.S. history class. The class was divided into four groups to gather information about urban problems in the early twentieth century and in the 1970s; they would then report their findings to the entire class. One group decided to explore the prevalence of venereal diseases in cities then and now. As part of the information-gathering, they decided to construct a survey for both students and teachers on venereal diseases and means for reducing its spread. We worked together on how to construct questions and how to do a random sample. The one-page survey went out to selected teachers and students in the school.

Myrtle Davis, who had taught in District schools before desegregation and had a sterling reputation at Roosevelt for her no-nonsense approach to teaching, returned her survey with the attached note:

> To: Larry Cuban
> From: Myrtle Davis
> Subject: Survey Form from 5th Period U.S. History Class
>
> What justification is there for a survey of this kind under the banner of American History. These matters should, it seems to me, come within the province of the courses dealing with Health and Science.
>
> Moreover, the performance of our students in the social studies, American History, et al. have consistently fallen below acceptable standards. Could it be that each of us working in the field should make every moment of class time count in a concerted effort to bridge this no-information gap in American History?

I sent her a reply the same day.

> Dear Mrs. Davis:
>
> Our class is studying urban problems past and present. They are divided into four groups. The topics they chose to research were education, housing, venereal disease, and rats. Each group has to make an oral presentation and write a research paper with at least five sources of information.
>
> The group dealing with venereal disease researched history books, magazines, and films. They also decided to get knowledge from people. The form that you received was part of the effort.
>
> Since I believe that historical information can be a vehicle to learn skills and not only an end in itself, I feel that the skills students learn from researching, organizing, and presenting an issue they are

interested in is far more important than covering information in a textbook.

Thank you for your interest. Please feel free to visit the class, speak with students, or observe what is going on.

Before I sent the note to the teacher, I deleted the teacher's name and read her letter and my reply to my students. The class exploded in anger over the fact that another teacher had criticized what they were doing. A few suggested that the class write a response. By the next day, a few students had drafted a reply to accompany mine—again without knowing who the other teacher was. The reply was signed by seventeen of the nineteen students in class that day.

Dear _____

We the students of Mr. Cuban's class feel that we are obligated to write a response to your letter. We feel that your charges are not concrete; by this we mean that you do not have substantial evidence to say that we have fallen below acceptable standards. Your criticism is in the poorest taste, for we are learning. And before you criticize a teacher that is trying and has the interest of his class, check yourself. Feel free to visit any time!

Fifth Period

I gave the letter to Mrs. Davis that day. The next day she came to my room during my preparation period and asked if she could talk to the class. She wanted to read a reply to their letter. We arranged a time.

Mrs. Davis appeared and read the following letter:

Dear Mr. Cuban and Fifth Period Class:

In response to your letter dated May 10, I feel obligated to make the following comments.

1. I made no charge against anyone. My statement of fact concerning 'our students' referred to students of Roosevelt High School. Whether any of you as individuals were included in the numbers who have taken the various tests, I could not know because I did not know nor did I seek your names as individuals. The matter of fact which I cited was based upon information which had come to me through the counselors. In fact, in one meeting this year, the social studies teachers were admonished by one counselor to the extent

that she wondered if we were teaching U.S. History at any time or place in the curriculum. According to her records, the average score on the College Board Tests in U.S. History ranged in the mid–200s and the highest in the range of 350. The highest possible score is 800. A score from 550 to 750 is considered good to excellent. As late as last week, I learned that only one student at Roosevelt scored up to the cut-off point in the National Merit exams. These facts are on file in the counselor's offices.

2. I did not criticize Mr. Cuban. I am also a member of the "I Love Larry" club. I did raise what I considered a justifiable question. If to question is to criticize and to criticize is to oppose, then I plead guilty as charged. However, if this be so, the entire course of education and the concept of a free society are already lost.

3. Your suggestion that I check myself first before criticizing anyone suffers from the same shortcoming with which you so glibly charged me. What evidence do you have to indicate that I have or have not "checked" myself? You failed to cite any.

4. As to 'taste,' this is a matter of opinion. You surely are entitled to your opinion and I am entitled to mine.

Having carried this highly professional exchange to the illogical conclusion, I suggest that we continue to devote class time to basic learnings to help bridge the now developing non-information canyon. I am doing this at home—till 8 P.M. However, I do find it odd that a group of young people seem to resent having a question raised concerning a fundamental issue, when in this place and time in history the young are questioning all the time. A practice which I both welcome and encourage. Perhaps a real thorough examination of the basic rights of all people would reveal the truth of the old saying: 'What's good for the goose is good for the gander.'

Myrtle Davis
Chief Gander

After she read the letter, she asked if there were any questions. A few students again questioned her right to criticize another teacher. Another asked why she was making such a big deal out of learning facts from textbooks. She replied:

You have to learn these facts so you can do well on tests. If you do well on tests, you are going to get jobs, good jobs. All of us [Davis was black] have to play catch-up. We have been behind so long, we must learn all the skills and knowledge we can. By not getting facts and skills, your chances to do well on tests and get into college will be less. We have to catch up.

Davis was passionate in her words. Her voice rose in volume; she occasionally trembled. The high pitch of emotion in the room broke after she spoke. I asked for more questions but nothing was said. Davis left.

As soon as she left, the class exploded, hands were raised and students began calling out. Their emotional temperature zoomed. There was much yelling and anger, but it was mixed with respect for what she said and how she said it. The bell rang.

With only a few weeks before the end of school, the incident was soon forgotten in the rush to complete assignments, tests, and turn in work. What struck me then and even now as I write this, was the seriousness with which Myrtle Davis and I tangled over the subject matter of this class, even in the midst of the new reforms mandated in the late 1960s and early 1970s. Open classrooms, teacher accountability, community control, innovative reading programs, new curricula, and dozens of other schemes designed by nonteachers for classrooms were imposed upon elementary and secondary schools by boards of education and superintendents anxious to demonstrate their progressiveness.

In the midst of these feverish efforts to install "can't-miss" programs, two reasonably intelligent teachers (one annoyed by a colleague's departure from traditional content for an all-black class and the other amazed at her affection for test scores) debated old but crucial questions, ones that again surfaced in the 1980s when districts began wiring a traditional academic curriculum to standardized tests. Here were two independent, strong-willed individuals, who believed that the kind of class they created and the content they offered would help students, asking themselves: What is schooling for? What content is worth knowing? What role does a teacher play in learning? Which ways of teaching get students to learn what is important? Does an education for blacks differ from that given to whites? Not trivial questions by any means, yet few policymakers, researchers, or professional reformers ask them of teachers.

Myrtle Davis and I continued to teach at Roosevelt the following year, my last. We differed, but we respected one another's approach, recognizing that there is no one best way to teach history to students or to teach students history.

I left Roosevelt because I wanted to become a superintendent. Teaching gave me much pleasure, but five classes a day forced me to make compromises and drained me in such a way that the joy lessened as the months passed. Writing gave me the chance to stretch my mind. I wrote articles for the *D.C. Gazette,* a local alternative newspaper. I had completed a book *Youth As A Minority.* But it just wasn't enough. By 1972 the scars from OSD had healed. I wanted the action of administration, the decision making, the problem solving, and the chance to influence both adults and children beyond one classroom.

Becoming a superintendent, I discovered, was no easy leap from the classroom. Throughout 1971–1972, I applied for principalships and was turned down, ostensibly for lack of credentials and experience. Because I had administrative experience as director of the Cardozo Project and as director of OSD, I also applied for assistant superintendencies. Here my lack of a doctorate was mentioned repeatedly. Superintendents, friends, and colleagues advised me to get the doctorate, otherwise I would continue to be faced with closed doors.

After many discussions with Barbara and minute calculations of savings and expenses, we decided to make the plunge and apply to graduate schools. Going back to an academic setting after a decade's absence, and at the age of thirty-seven, made me anxious over how the family (daughters, ages ten and seven) would survive financially. To ease the dollar crunch, I applied for a research grant from the Office of Education to do a study of reform in the Washington, D.C., schools since desegregation. In February 1972 OE notified me that I received the grant, and a month later, I received word of my acceptance to Stanford's School of Education to study the history of education. In June 1972 we began the trek to California and graduate school.

5

Superintending: Images and Roles

The origins of the word *superintendent* as a label for the person the boards of education hired to oversee school affairs is uncertain. As early as 1804, Congress used the phrase *superintendence of public schools* in granting power to the District of Columbia city council to provide for local education. Newark, New Jersey, used the word in 1816 for the manager of the city's charity school. Not until the 1830s, when the first superintendents were appointed in cities along the eastern seaboard and the Ohio Valley, however, did the title become common. One opinion is that the title was borrowed from the factory; that is, managers of early nineteenth century mills were called *superintendents*. The admiration Americans felt for the economic benefits generated by factories may have best fit what they wanted from their schools: to produce children who were obedient, punctual, and hard-working.[1]

Another possibility is that the word derived from church history. As early as 1560 in Europe, *superintendent* referred to the official in charge of a group of parishes within the Lutheran Church. John Wesley, the British Methodist evangelist, named the men he ordained as bishops in the 1780s in the United States superintendents.

Whether the title of the post came from the factory or the church, was fed by a yearning for productivity or righteous fervor, has yet to be determined. Both origins, however, never strayed far from the expectations or the behavior of superintendents in the next century and a half.[2]

Either Buffalo, New York, Louisville, Kentucky, or Providence, Rhode Island, can claim the first appointment to the post of superintendent in 1837 or 1839; however, this fact is less important than establishing that the position became common in city school districts before the Civil War. School board members, frequently organized into standing committees (e.g., finance, course of study, board of examiners, and so on) were expected to not only oversee school operations but also to inspect the students' performance's and report to the community what occurred in the schools.

As city school districts grew in population and tiny schools blossomed helter-skelter in neighborhoods, even large school boards (the Boston School Committee had seventy-two members in 1856), organized into visiting committees, found that school inspection consumed inordinate amounts of time from members who had to work. Pressures to hire someone whose sole purpose was to carry out school board directions produced the post of superintendent.[3]

If the principalship emerged from the classroom, the first generation of superintendents were genuine bureaucrats hired to inspect and improve schooling for part-time boards of education. Just as a school board held a teacher responsible for a class and a principal for a school, now the board could hold someone accountable for district operations. Like the teacher and principal, the superintendent would wrestle with the inherent dilemmas linked to being both boss and bureaucrat. Unlike teachers and principals, however, the superintendent was the child of the school board and not the classroom. Over decades the superintendency would mature, struggle with its parent endlessly, but never escape its ancestry.[4]

IMAGES OF THE SUPERINTENDENCY

The origins of the superintendency produced expectations. From daily experiences of visiting schools, hiring janitors, lobbying school board members, writing reports, constructing statistical tables, and meeting with both corporate executives and parents, a number of "shoulds" concerning the tasks of the post emerged. The expectations formed by the origins, daily experiences, and advice in early textbooks on educational administration produced images of what superintendents ought to be and ought to do.

In an earlier study of the superintendency, I identified three dominant conceptions held by superintendents of what the position should be and what happened to those images over almost a century. To arrive at these images, I examined speeches made by urban superintendents at the annual meetings of the Department of Superintendence (a branch of the NEA) between 1870 and 1940 and the records of the American Association of School Administrators between 1940 and 1950. Next, I read articles written by 251 urban superintendents in the major educational journals between 1881 and 1950. Finally I identified frequently cited superintendents and read their speeches and articles. From these approaches, I extracted three dominant images of what a superintendent should be: instructional supervisor, administrative chief, and negotiator-statesman.[5]

Instructional Supervisor

The image of superintendent as a teacher of teachers arose early and flourished for years. When a group of teachers met in 1863 to organize the National Teachers' Association (NTA), renamed NEA in 1870, two superintendents were among the eleven founders. The first six presidents of the NTA were city superintendents.[6]

In 1899, for example, St. Louis superintendent W. T. Harris stated that the most important job of the superintendent was to make "good teachers out of poor ones." Kansas City school chief James W. Greenwood wrote: "I never trouble the members of the board. . . . They watch the business matters and I look after the schools." The bulk of his day was spent "visiting schools and inspecting the work." Horace Tarbell, superintendent for almost two decades in Providence, Rhode Island, feared that a city superintendent "might become a business man, a manager of affairs, rather than continue the attitude of the scholar and become more and more the teacher." Worse yet, he added, "he may become the politician." Indianapolis schoolman Lewis Jones felt that the proper function of supervisors and administrators was to study psychology, children, and pedagogy with teachers. "If the superintendent," he told fellow school chiefs, "can come to be the acknowledged leader in such broad consideration of . . . education he will have done much to enlarge the horizons of his teachers."[7]

Superintendents wrote frequently about philosophy, history, and pedagogy. In an 1890 report on the role of the superintendent, the central task was clear to readers:

> It must be made his recognized duty to train teachers and inspire
> them with high ideals; to revise the course of study when new light

shows that improvement is possible; to see that pupils and teachers
are supplied with needed appliances for the best possible work; to
devise rational methods of promoting pupils.[8]

Superintendents who held this conception of the post included Chicago's Ella Flagg Young. Young taught and principaled for many years
before being named general superintendent of the Chicago schools in
1909. The first woman to serve as a big city school chief, she also was
elected president of the NEA shortly afterwards.

While serving as a district superintendent, she interrupted her
career to study under John Dewey at the University of Chicago. Her
dissertation argued that teachers could never reach the full measure of
their strengths without the freedom to decide what was in the best
interests of students. How, she asked, could students be taught about
a democracy if their teachers took orders all the time and had little
autonomy to decide issues of instruction and curriculum? In that dissertation she recommended the formation of teachers' councils where
such decisions could be made.[9]

Appointed in 1909, she served (under annual contracts) a school
board separated into warring factions. In 1913, angered by board
squabbles, she resigned; however, the board bowed to public pressure
and reappointed her. She retired in 1915. In those difficult years when
the school population rose to over 300,000 children, she initiated
teachers' councils, expanded vocational courses, raised salaries for
teachers, and expanded other programs dear to her view of schooling.
But she was limited by the size of the district, annual contracts that
left little time for planning and stability, and a fractious board that
battled an aggressive teachers union led by her chief supporter, Margaret Haley.

Young recognized the issues of size and complexity in trying to
influence teachers' daily tasks. In 1916 she recalled:

> When I began teaching in the city of Chicago, the teaching force was
> so small that the superintendent, who had his institutes once a
> month, had in one schoolroom the teachers of the high school, the
> principal of the high school—there was then only one—the principal
> of the elementary schools, and all the grade teachers. There we met
> and discussed, on the same level, the subjects which were presented
> to us, or which were raised by persons present. But today it is simply
> impossible for the teachers in a great city or for even the principals

in a city like New York to meet and discuss freely the questions—a few do the talking, and they talk to the galleries.[10]

Young and the other school chiefs cited earlier imagined their central task to be leadership through the improvement of what occurs in classrooms.

Administrative Chief

If a teacher of teachers was at the core of the image of instructional supervisor, then the superintendent directing an organization devoted to productivity best conveyed the image of administrative chief. Themes of authority, control, instruction, curricular planning, and efficient management resonated in speeches and reports in the waning decades of the nineteenth century.

One model that many superintendents admired was the Cleveland Plan of 1892. Under this plan, a small elected city council named a director with complete executive authority. The school director appointed a superintendent of instruction who hired and fired all of his assistants and teachers without interference from the lay council or school director. Andrew Draper who served for two years within this arrangement fervently believed that the superintendent was the expert, the technocrat who directed, planned, and executed school affairs.[11]

Other urban superintendents were concerned over the frequent splitting of duties between a business manager responsible to the board and a school chief who concentrated upon instruction. These top administrators wanted both sets of duties centralized into one post, where the superintendent was "a man of affairs," efficiently managing buildings, fiscal affairs, and personnel. Veteran Columbus, Ohio, superintendent R. W. Stevenson wrote that "the superintendent is the best manager who can make his schools efficient in training the youth of his city . . . at the least possible expense."[12]

Aaron Gove who headed the Denver, Colorado, schools for three decades vigorously defined the school chief's job as being larger and more important than instructional supervision.

> It may be doubtless true that the professional efforts of superintendents directed only to the teaching side of his duties would result in a greater efficiency in and about the schoolroom, but these advances would be largely checked by neglect of the business side of a superintendent's duties.

> The construction and location of schoolhouses; the relations of the administration to the industrial and commercial communities, especially to expenditures . . . the too lavish or too niggardly appropriations for furniture, apparatus and supplies . . . are matters . . . within the direct duties of the superintendent.

Gove feared that an unqualified superintendent would be "incompetent . . . to participate in the business affairs of the corporation whose executive officer he is or should be."[13]

The impulse to gain broader authority from the school board often masked the insistent impulse among both lay people and superintendents towards efficient use of public funds. Also, booming urban school populations continually prodded administrators and school boards to search for shrewd ways of reducing what threatened to be runaway costs for expanded schooling. Recall that Lancastrian schools in the early 1800s were endorsed for, among other reasons, the cheap schooling of many poor children. In the 1840s, the innovative graded school (with the accompanying sequential course of study), which ultimately ended the ungraded one-room school, was embraced because it concentrated in one location a large number of children who could be schooled more efficiently than if they were dispersed to buildings and teachers in many locations.

Early concerns were voiced by both school boards and superintendents over the obvious inefficiencies linked to the repetition of grades by growing numbers of students. The introduction of specialized administrators (i.e., principals and superintendents) to supervise teachers in expanding school bureaucracies of pre- and post-Civil War cities led to curricular and instructional uniformity for both teachers and students; demographic changes prodded the search for efficiencies before and after the Civil War, a full half-century before the supposed introduction of scientific management to the public schools.[14]

The image, then, of the administrative Chief, a top technocrat in charge of the organization, competed with the one of instructional supervisor in the minds and hearts of superintendents.

Negotiator-Statesman

If the core of the image of the administrative chief was control and efficiency and the core of the instructional supervisor was teaching teachers, then the central image of the negotiator-statesman was one of politics. Within and outside the community, superintendents knew

Figure 7: Conceptions of Superintendents, 1870s to 1950s*

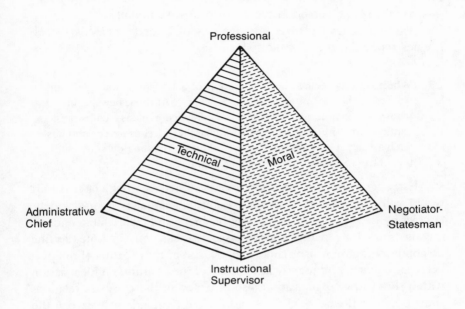

*These conceptions were drawn from superintendent speeches and articles. I display these dominant images in this manner as a device to illustrate the tripartite conception and to underscore how the political dimension (negotiator-statesman) was present in the minds of superintendents who wrote and spoke about the position.

that they faced varied groups, ranging in views from complete endorsement of the schools to undisguised hostility; they knew that the schools needed both financial and moral support of the majority; and they knew that with annual contract renewal their position was insecure. This knowledge was the seedbed for political behavior.

Prior to 1900, much was said about the political side of superintending, though it was cautiously worded and restrained by the taint of corrupt partisan politics, job-hungry teachers, and venal trustees. "While every year new men come upon the school board for the sake of keeping in employment certain teachers," said Baltimore superintendent William Creery in 1873, "it is the part of wisdom for us not to claim the power but to create a popular sentiment." Ten years later, a brother schoolman concluded that the "work of a superintendent is also political in its character. He ought to be a politician." But he quickly assured his audience that he was not recommending that a school chief engage in machine politics; he only meant the word *politician* to mean "one versed in the science of government."

A few decades later, yet another superintendent speaking to colleagues reminded them of the following:

> When we can secure the cooperation of a few influential men and women of the community, the support of two or three newspapers to whose opinion the public listens, the influence of clubs—clubs of the gentler sort—the endorsement of a chamber of commerce, perhaps we have taken a long step in the direction of making outside conditions favorable to successful management.[15]

Early generations of superintendents cultivated what a later cohort would call "community relations." Publishing annual reports widely, contacting local newspapers, joining business and civic clubs, endorsing the growth of parent-teacher associations, and, in time, letting neighborhood groups use school facilities, all of these forms of political behavior occurred frequently at the turn of the century. Political action within the district organization also emerged in the complex relationships between the school board and the superintendent; between the superintendent and principals; and between the superintendent and teachers. While nineteenth century norms of obedience to authority were more obvious and direct, still much happened within the organization, where persuasion, negotiation, and compromise blurred the boundaries of school affairs.

Superintendent William Chancellor recounts in his text published in 1904 a typical situation containing the generic political elements inherent to superintending.

> Monday morning with a heavy mail. There is no office secretary. Superintendent due to attend special exercises at a distant school at eleven o'clock. Unexpectedly the chairman of the board arrives for a consultation. A distinguished school superintendent from another community is due at one o'clock.
>
> • The other superintendent will help make or mar the local reputation as well as the general.
> • The exercises are public.
> • The board chairman is an important officer.

- The mail is important.
- The superintendent is new to the position.

If the superintendent excuses himself to open his mail and to dispose of it, the chairman may think that he is systematic; also, the chairman may think that he does not care much for board officers. The superintendent must not fail to be on hand at the exercises, for the parents are invited to hear and to meet him. He cannot return to his office for mail while the visitor is on hand.

To grip and hold the chairman may mean success: new and better schoolhouses, new and better teachers, new and better everything, and re-election (for the superintendent).

A man with the gift of an administrator will welcome the board chairman, calmly stow all the apparently important mail in his pocket, and sit down to consult the board chairman until the last minute before the time for leaving for the school exercises. When that time arrives, and not until then, he will invite the chairman to go with him. If the member cannot go, he will make an early engagement with him, as early as possible without breaking the appointment of the visiting superintendent. He will read his mail when he can, on the theory that matters of really imperative importance are very seldom transacted by mail.[16]

This political dimension, of course, became transparent where superintendents campaigned for election to the post. Los Angeles, Jersey City, and Cincinnati had elected superintendents for brief periods of time in the mid-nineteenth century. San Francisco and Buffalo retained their habit of electing school chiefs for almost a half-century until 1900. The election of county and state superintendents in various regions of the nation today is not only a vestige of the earlier pattern but also a recognition of the inherently political nature of the post—acknowledged in this image of superintending.[17]

Schoolmen such as Gove, Greenwood, and Harris seldom lost sight of this conception of superintending, even though they preferred other images of the post. "The superintendent," New York City's William Maxwell pointed out, "should be not merely a schoolmaster but a statesman who has a definite policy to carry out and who knows how to take advantage of time and opportunity to secure results." Here is politics as the art of the possible recast in terms that superintendents would applaud.[18]

There is evidence that these three images of the superintendency existed from the origins of the position in pre-Civil War America. Which dominated practitioners' thinking? Did they change over time? Using the speeches and writings of superintendents, I constructed the following tables, which suggest that these images shifted in importance.

These tables and the previous discussion suggest that the three images continued for over a century, shifting in importance among school chiefs in response to larger social and political changes in the culture. These images jostled one another within the person as he (seldom she) went about the business of superintending.[19]

The necessity of providing supervision to teachers and principals in the early decades of the superintendency produced the image of instructional supervisor. Improving classroom instruction and curriculum content inspired generations of administrators to see their task as central to the superintendency. As decades passed, the image of a teacher of teachers seemed to have waned as the image of administrative chief waxed, but for almost a century it nonetheless persisted.

The popularity of the administrative chief conception began with an aggressive drive by academics and practitioners in the turn- of-the-century progressive movement. They aimed to transform the job of a hired bureaucrat carrying out the orders of a lay school board into a profession of technocratic engineers. All the claims that education was a science were harnessed to elevate superintendents into educational engineers, nonpolitical experts who knew precisely where and when to apply knowledge, skill, and judgment. Schoolmen's passionate embrace of scientific expertise was as much an attempt to shield their occupational vulnerability from a rude firing as it was a sincere belief in scientific rationality. If so, then it would be neither the first nor the last time that fervent ideals and professional self-interest marched to the same drummer.

Regardless of how much control an expert could summon in applying technical solutions to school problems, the top executive was still hired by a lay school board who could (and often did) suddenly dismiss the most esteemed, nationally respected superintendent. Insecure tenure and a desire to serve both organizational and personal aims generated the image I call negotiator-statesman. No superintendent who wished to survive in the position could ignore for very long the political dimensions of the job.

Table 2. Percentages of Superintendents Holding Three Major Conceptions, as Drawn from Department of Superintendence and American Association of School Administrators, 1871-1950

	1871-1880	1881-1890	1891-1900	1901-1910	1911-1920	1921-1930	1931-1940	1941-1950
Teacher-scholar	60	46	53	63	32	32	28	27
curriculum	24	19	13	15	12	15	10	5
instruction	12	9	7	5	5	2	2	7
supervision	8	17	25	23	7	13	8	6
pupil services	16	1	8	20	8	8	8	9
Chief administrator	20	13	14	15	27	26	31	34
finance	0	0	0	2	5	7	11	6
school plant	4	0	4	2	2	4	1	6
district organization	4	2	3	5	7	5	1	3
management	12	11	7	6	15	10	18	15
Negotiator-statesman	12	14	13	11	26	19	25	27
school board	0	0	3	2	3	2	2	3
community	0	1	5	3	10	7	14	17
federal and state relations	12	13	5	6	13	10	9	7

Source: National Education Association, *Journal of Proceedings and Addresses*, 1871-1940; American Association of School Administrators, *Official Report*, 1940-1950.

From Cuban, *Urban School Chiefs Under Fire* (Chicago: University of Chicago Press, 1976), p. 123.

Table 3. Percentages of Superintendents Holding Three Major Conceptions,
As Drawn from the Writings of 251 Big-City Superintendents, 1881-1950

	1881-1890	1891-1900	1901-1910	1911-1920	1921-1930	1931-1940	1941-1950
Teacher-scholar	47 (46)	48 (53)	43 (63)	29 (32)	44 (32)	28 (28)	33 (27)
Chief administrator	5 (13)	18 (14)	19 (15)	31 (27)	37 (26)	33 (31)	34 (34)
Negotiator-statesman	0 (14)	15 (13)	11 (11)	12 (26)	7 (19)	10 (25)	15 (27)

Sources: Articles prior to 1928 come from *Education, Educational Review*, and the *American School Board Journal*, 1880-1910. After 1928, articles were compiled from *Education Index*.

Note: Percentages in parentheses come from Table 2.

From Cuban, *Urban School Chiefs Under Fire*, p. 125.

Over the last century, these three contending images rose and fell in popularity among superintendents, depending upon larger social and political forces, the districts in which they worked, and the particular experiences and values that they had.

What these conceptions suggest is that images may have a powerful influence on the practice of superintending. In short, the pictures help shape and guide behavior. But images are not truth; they fail to convey the total complexity, detail, and texture of what superintendents do.

If the history of these conceptions of superintending suggests something of the complexity of the occupation, what remains is describing what school executives do and the varied roles they play within a school district. The next sections explore each.

WHAT SUPERINTENDENTS DID

Reconstructing the duties of the earliest school chiefs begins initially with the explicit listing of their duties published by school boards in their public records. Of some help are the few narrative accounts that appear in superintendents' annual reports, in speeches, and in occasional recollections of those who served two or more decades, such as Boston's John Philbrick (1856–1878) and Denver's Aaron Gove (1874–1904). I could find no surveys or direct observations of superintendent activities before the 1920s.[20]

Two histories, both published in 1935 and drawing extensively from forty-three cities' published regulations, concurred that superintendents' primary formal duties before 1900 evolved from two central school board tasks: supervising teachers and principals and administering the diverse activities of an expanding organization. Neither study examined Syracuse, New York; so as an independent check on their central findings, I examined in detail a number of Syracuse annual reports prior to 1900, using the 1876 to illustrate that the previous studies were accurate in their rendering of the primary duties assigned to superintendents.

In 1876, Syracuse had slightly over 6,000 students attending eighteen schools (including one high school), employing 207 teachers (of whom 197 were women) and eighteen principals (of whom nine were women). The annual expenditures ran just over $155,000, of which two-thirds went for teachers' salaries.

Edward Smith served as superintendent to a school board of eight men; the board was elected by wards and organized into seven standing committees covering such matters as finance, teachers, and the course of study. From an office in the high school, Smith carried out his assigned duties (with a salary of $2000 a year) with the help of principals and teachers. No other staff was assigned to the superintendent except for a messenger.[21]

In the board's published rules, the listed duties began with the school chief's responsibility to be informed of "the nature and objects of common school education and the different branches taught." Specifically, the superintendent should know the "philosophy and practice of teaching" and what improvements were occurring elsewhere in order "to be able to give clear and specific directions to teachers concerning the classification and general arrangements of their schools."[22]

Board rules detailed the superintendent's duties in supervising teachers.

> He shall visit all schools as often as possible; observe the character of the instruction given, and the modes of discipline adopted; point out defects to teachers, and suggest remedies; and see that the regulations of the board are faithfully observed.[23]

In addition, the superintendent had to call principal and teacher meetings periodically, "as often as he shall find it necessary for the good of the schools," and he then had to "report the attendance and proceedings . . . to the board of education." Every July he was expected to examine not only teacher candidates but also students applying for admission to the high school. Moreover, the superintendent had to establish and regulate the "examination of all the schools of the city, and shall, as far as practicable, give these examinations his personal attention." Finally the board directed their agent to "furnish all teachers with blanks for school registers, and for all reports required by the regulations of the Board." He was charged to instruct teachers and principals in their use so as to "secure uniformity."[24]

The superintendent also served as clerk to the Board of Education. In that capacity, he notified members of all meetings; recorded minutes of each meeting; kept "the financial accounts of the school department," reporting annually to the board on the fiscal status of the district; made certain that a yearly census of all children between the ages of five and twenty-one occurred. Finally, he shall furnish to the schools a thermometer for each school room; the necessary amount of brooms, brushes, pails, and all furniture of a like temporary character; slates and pencils for the primary department; and he shall furnish each principal with school books for destitute and indigent children.[25]

Smith's duties were familiar to his colleagues across the nation, although details might differ due to the size of a district and its particular history. William Chancellor, who served as superintendent in small and large districts, published a text in 1904 on administration and supervision. In it he described a typical day for a small city superintendent at the turn of the century.

A SCHOOL SUPERINTENDENT'S DAY IN A SMALL CITY

1. Inspected school building. Sent messenger for painter to repair window glass. Notified chief of police to follow up street "hoodlums" who broke glass.

2. Read mail; business letters from places large and small: correspondence with colleges; teachers' applications; requests for subscriptions to help national charities; calls to give addresses here and there, generally gratis; answered mail.

3. Talked to mayor about next year's appropriations.

4. Looked into a new textbook.

5. Visited a school; sent one child home who had apparently an infectious disease; discussed salary with a discontented teacher.

6. Dictated circular letter to board of education regarding educational and financial matters.

7. Saw a textbook agent.

8. Ate lunch; interrupted by call from mother of sick child.

9. Read and signed letters of reply to morning mail.

10. Called at business place of board member; saw two politicians there; discussed three R's as usual.

11. Held grade meeting; gave sample lesson on mensuration.

12. Visited by Catholic sisters from parochial school, regarding truants.

13. Read afternoon mail; sent notes regretting absence from office to following callers: Presbyterian minister; carpenter to discuss repairs in a school building, mother of child suspended from school for misconduct.

14. Made a statistical table.

15. Ate dinner; caller on school matters came at seven o'clock.

16. Went to evening engagement and was called on to speak.

17. Read an hour and retired for the night.

Chancellor commented that this was an easy day. Were it a "hard day", one would need to "add a board or committee of the board meeting, a formal public address or the making of a test."[26]

The political dimension—missing from the earlier listing of duties—appears in Chancellor's typical day. Since *political* was considered to be a nasty nine-letter word by both academics and practitioners anxious to make school administration into a profession, portions of the activities in which superintendents engaged came to be called "public relations" or, in the grander terms of the professional associations, "community leadership."[27]

At the very core of the relationship between an elected lay school board, its superintendent, and the tax-paying community is the tacit understanding that effort must be expended in creating public favor for the community's schools. After all, a community indifferent or hostile to its schools will be less disposed to provide adequate funds. Nor can changes within schools be forced upon a reluctant community; if children must be schooled, the community must be educated. Whatever the vocabulary, superintendents failing to attend to such fundamental political tasks risked an early exit from the post.

Every superintendent had to juggle the various interests of board members while dealing with employees, parents, students, and citizens who differed with the policymakers. The board, for example, had to be kept fully informed of what occurred within the district, from whether there were sufficient spellers available to the current salaries for new teachers.

Chancellor's description of a typical day details a portion of the superintendent's political activity, including sensing which decisions and actions would be acceptable and which ones would require lobbying board members and circulating information, and in general attending to various constituencies within the schools and larger community.

From the origins of the superintendency until 1900, school chiefs' duties derived from the circumstances of the position's birth. Historians have documented the efforts to separate the instructional side from the business and financial sides, the drive to convert the superintendent into a chief executive officer, and other intramural struggles between lay boards and increasingly self-conscious superintendents who viewed themselves as educational experts. Nonetheless, the three tasks persisted.[28]

Since 1920, little systematically collected evidence has been available about what superintendents did in and out of their offices. What is available comes from a few studies drawn from self-reports, interviews, surveys, and occasional direct observations.

In 1928 one national survey of 663 principals and superintendents in various-sized districts reported on which tasks were performed and how frequently. Unfortunately the data on managerial, instructional, and community work are not reported in relation to one another. Four of five superintendents reported that they did the following:

- Go to the post office

- Deliver messages to teachers

- Draft special reports to state and U.S. Bureau of Education; prepare annual reports for school board

- Prepare letters of sympathy

- Conduct visitors through schools

- Examine school work sent to office

- Prevent salesmen from canvassing schools

- Answer questionnaires

- Gather school publicity data

- Adjust complaints of parents

- Consider applications, examine credentials, consult with principals in selecting teachers for district

- Secure substitute teachers

- Suggest professional books and articles for teachers

- Investigate criticism of teachers

- Assist teachers to find lodgings

- Attend summer school
- Visit schools elsewhere
- Talk before community groups
- Attend church social functions[29]

The following table summarizes the only studies I could locate that reported what superintendents said about their work. The patterns are similar to those of principals: more time is spent on administration than instructional supervision; public relations and teaching share a third level of priority.

Table 4: Distribution of Superintendents' Time Devoted to
Various Functions as Reported by City and Rural Chiefs, 1950

	CITY %	RURAL %
Administration	58	55
Instructional Supervision	31	35
Teaching	0	0
Community/Public Relations	11	10

Source: American Association of School Administrators, *The School Superintendent* (Washington, D.C.: American Association of School Administrators, 1952), pp. 452, 460.

Between 1950 and the mid–1970s, there were no comprehensive or systematic descriptions of what superintendents did on a daily or weekly basis. Apart from occasional individual accounts written by former or sitting superintendents and articles in professional journals, I could find no systematic investigations covering this period.

When I completed my research in 1973 on *Urban School Chiefs Under Fire*, a study of Chicago's Benjamin Willis, San Francisco's Harold Spears, and Washington D.C's Carl Hansen, I said: "While we know to the penny what salaries suburban administrators received, what degrees they earned, and where they were born, we know very little about what they, as executives, actually do each day." I cited Henry Mintzberg's study of five managers (including a suburban school chief) published in 1973 as a hopeful end to that ignorance.[30]

Mintzberg's structured observation approach, what used to be called shadowing or, in a slightly critical vein, neo-Taylorism, has since

1973 produced time-and-motion studies that recorded in minutes and hours how much time superintendents spent on various tasks each day for a week or more. While there are a number of strengths to this stopwatch, time-and-motion approach, particularly in offering a detailed, close-up view by an outside observer of how superintendents spend their time, there are also decided limitations.[31]

Although the data up to 1950, which is largely self-reports, and the surge of shadow studies since the early 1970s cannot be directly compared since the categories and methodologies used by the researchers differed, the two views provide at least a fuller, if not mildly contradictory, portrait of the post.

The self-reports showing superintendents spending most of their time in administration and less in instructional supervision, with brief moments squeezed into "community leadership," imply an orderly and prosaic routine; however, the superintendent-watching of the 1970s shows wide variation in behavior, but with some common patterns: superintending is a constant stream of brief encounters, mostly with school board members and subordinates in the central office; constant interruptions; little time spent at the desk or in the schools; and a decided concentration upon verbal exchanges with people (planned and spontaneous). In short, like principaling and teaching, superintending is a world of action. Unpredictability and uncertainty play larger roles than would have seemed readily apparent from the earlier set of data. A picture of superintendent behavior as planned and organized receives little support from these studies. The evidence paints the superintendent as no Superman; instead what we see is more like a frazzled Clark Kent struggling to get out of a phone booth.

Where the two sets of studies appear to converge is in the little time seemingly devoted to instructional supervision. The image of a superintendent in either small or large systems as an instructional supervisor trying to improve classroom teaching and the curriculum appears to have little credibility, given the few hours that superintendents spend in schools, much less classrooms.

The rebuttal to this point is that the methodologies employed in shadow studies seldom sought out superintendents' intentions. Most of these studies simply described and coded activities, counted the minutes engaged on each task, and calculated percentages. No interviews were conducted to determine *why* superintendents did what they did. A few researchers recorded what these executives did and then guessed at their motives; for example, a superintendent told one school board member certain information and told another nothing.

Table 5: A Comparison of School Superintendents' Activities and Contacts

| | STUDIES | | | | |
	Bussom	Pitner	Kurke	Mintzberg	Feilders
ACTIVITY					
Desk work					
% of time	31	20	20	16	4
Telephone calls					
% of time	11	8	3	6	2
Scheduled Meetings					
% of time	13	51	69	75	50
Unscheduled Meetings					
% of time	30	10	5	3	30
Tours					
% of time	5	2	0	1	3
CONTACTS					
with School Boards	4	19	28	17	26
with Subordinates	59	54	40	61	58
with Others	37	27	32	22	16

Sources for Table 5

Lars L. Larson, Robert Bussom, and William Vicars, "The Nature of a School Super-intendent's Work" (Carbondale, Illinois: Department of Administrative Sciences, College of Business, Southern Illinois University, 1981).

Henry Mintzberg, *The Nature of Managerial Work* (New York: Harkin and Rain, 1973).

John Feilders, "Action and Reaction: The Job of an Urban School Superintendent" (Stanford University: Unpublished doctoral dissertation, 1979).

Nancy Pitner, "Descriptive Study of the Everyday Activities of Suburban School Superintendents" (Ohio State University, Unpublished doctoral dissertation, 1978).

L. B. Kurke and H. E. Aldrich, "Mintzberg Was Right!: A Replication and Extension of *The Nature of Managerial Work* (Atlanta, Paper presented at meeting of Academy of Management, 1979).

So there is the possibility that apparently unconnected, mundane tasks (e.g., how to handle a teacher's grievance on not getting paid for an after-school workshop) may be importantly connected to a prized instructional aim in the mind of a superintendent (e.g., establishing a policy that directs all high school teachers regardless of subject matter to concentrate upon teaching critical thinking). Only a sustained famil-iarity with the superintendents' aspirations, style of working, view of how organizations work, and repeated interviews with various people would reveal any linkages between the prosaic and the intentional.[32]

Like principals, what evidence there is on performing administrative tasks suggests a fairly large gap between what is expected of superintendents (given the dominant images held by practitioners and lay folk) and what they do daily. Superintendents sense that gap, or at least have reported to their professional association that how they spend their time differs from how they would like to.[33] As with principals, the gap between the ideal and the real, with the accompanying sense of unfulfillment and nagging guilt, reveals again how the fundamental nature of the post is shaped by competing and conflicting expectations.

The DNA of superintending is embedded in these expectations. These expectations reflect the school board's historic desire for an efficient technocrat to carry out their orders; an effective manager whose procedures are organized and whose knowledge of the organization spans everything from the passenger-load on school buses to how much beef is in the hamburger patty; a professional whose technical expertise in instruction and curriculum will improve the district; a savvy, personable representative for schools who knows which relationships inside the district and within the community need to be cultivated for continuing public support (read: funding). Look at a superintendent's desk; it is cluttered with expectations: phone calls, memos for teachers, notes from principals, and a personal list of things to do. These demands are both constraints upon action and licenses to act; they are the equivalent of genetic material, the building blocks of the superintendency.

To understand what the position entails, begin with these expectations for what roles the school chief must play and recall the sparse historical evidence documenting what they have done. From this history of the dominant occupational images and a brief rendering of the work that superintendents do, I have extracted three core roles they have performed and now display in their work: instructional, managerial, and political.[34]

CORE ROLES OF SUPERINTENDING

Instructional

From the birth of the position in mid-nineteenth century America, superintendents taught both teachers and children. In small districts, superintendents taught one or more classes; in larger districts, superintendents would teach demonstration lessons for classroom teachers. School boards expected their appointed executive to be a pedagogical expert who could guide teachers and principals.

Boston superintendent John Philbrick offers an example common among the first few generations of top administrators in the mid-nineteenth century. In a district where 27,000 students were taught by 560 teachers in 200 primary, 20 grammar, and 3 high schools, Philbrick, who had served in the system as principal of the Quincy School, reputedly the first graded school in the nation, reported to a School Committee of 74 members. In his first annual report (1857), he described his lesson on the telescope.

> *Philbrick:* How many have seen a telescope? (Several hands are raised.)
>
> *Student:* My father has one.
>
> Philbrick asks a student to describe it and *tell* what he *knows* about it. The *word* is then pronounced in concert, several times, analysed phonetically, and spelled. Then, the first two syllables, *tele* pronounced.
>
> *Philbrick:* Has anyone seen a word that begins in the same way?
>
> Soon, a bright boy answers, *telegraph.* That is very curious. But there is a *reason* for beginning these *words, tele*scope and *tele*graph in the same way. Both the *things* these *words* stand for, have something to do with *distance*—what is far off.
>
> *Philbrick:* What did Charles do with the telescope?
>
> *Class:* Saw the steamboat away up the river.
>
> *Philbrick: Away* up! Yes, that is it. Or you might say, class, *far* up the river. Yes. Well, with the telegraph we *write afar off.* How many of you have *seen* the telegraph wire. (Several hands are raised.) These wires extend from Boston to cities hundreds of miles from us. A Man can stand in Boston and write in New York. How many have seen an instrument for observing very small objects? (Several hands are raised.) What is it called?
>
> *Student:* A microscope.
>
> *Philbrick:* Pronounce the word together. Analyse it. Spell it. What is the *last* syllable?
>
> *Class: Scope*

Philbrick: Yes. What is the last syllable of telescope?

Class: Scope

Philbrick: Well, now with both these instruments we do what?

Class: See something.

Philbrick: Right. And this syllable, *scope,* means *to see.* Can you think of some other word that has that syllable in it? [emphasis in original]

Philbrick ends this description by saying, "The teacher who understands his business will know when and how far to extend such exercises."[35]

By mid-twentieth century, although few superintendents (except in tiny districts) taught students regularly, the career path to the top post included a few years spent teaching. For example, in 1925, a survey reported that 73 percent of 1,100 superintendents reported that they had taught, ranging from almost three to just under seven years in classrooms for the middle half of those reporting. By the 1980s, becoming a superintendent *without* having taught was unusual.[36]

Nonetheless, having once taught seldom meant that incumbent superintendents sought out teaching again. While occasional superintendents would substitute for an absent teacher or teach a special lesson to illustrate particular approaches, they remained a rare breed. For those superintendents who still viewed themselves primarily as teachers, improving their staff emerged as their central instructional duty.

As with principals, the concept of an instructional role for superintendents shifts from the direct teaching of students and teachers to a concept of the superintendent as teacher of the school community. At one level, superintendent as teacher means the familiar instructional supervision historically sought by earlier generations of school executives: helping teachers improve their pedagogy; helping principals understand the curriculum; and teaching principals how to supervise and evaluate teachers.

At another level, the superintendent's instructional role is broader. Through shaping the mission of the district, establishing a district climate that signals a seriousness of purpose, designing rituals and structures that infuse life in both the mission and climate through communication skills and personal example, superintendents create a unique and personal curriculum from which they teach. In brief, the school board, the district organization, and the community become a classroom. Intentions and strategies become lesson plans. At this level, a superintendent who teaches is one who not only persuades children and adults, professionals and lay people, parents and non-parents to see schooling differently but also bends their efforts toward new goals through actively creating new organizational mechanisms or knitting together weakly connected structures.[37]

Many superintendents enact neither level of the instructional role directly. Many delegate the instructional role to a subordinate and through supervising that assistant superintendent or director of elementary education discharge the role. Some pursue only instructional supervision of principals with great passion; others embrace both levels.

For this latter group, a few illustrations may help convey concretely the two levels of teaching embodied in the instructional role. I offer Ella Flagg Young and Carl Hansen as examples.

Chicago superintendent Ella Flagg Young performed this instructional role between 1909 and 1915 in broadening the formal academic curriculum to include manual arts in all elementary schools and vocational courses at secondary schools—rather than separate vocational schools, which she saw as undemocratic. She introduced elements new to the curriculum (field trips, handicrafts, drama) that she and John Dewey had developed at the University of Chicago's Laboratory School and with students training to become teachers at Chicago Normal. Such innovations expanded children's experiences in public schools.[38]

She introduced teachers councils, an organizational mechanism for letting teachers give professional advice to the superintendent about curriculum, instruction, school organization, textbooks, and other topics at a time when the prevailing image of teachers was that of a bureaucrat, or public servant. Young's credibility as a teacher, principal, district superintendent, and top administrator of the second largest district in the nation was anchored in her prowess as a teacher of teachers.[39]

Carl Hansen, superintendent of the Washington, D.C., Schools for a turbulent decade (1958–1967), also displayed the instructional role clearly. Coming to the nation's capital from a high school principalship in Omaha, Nebraska, Hansen moved swiftly from executive assistant to the superintendent in 1947, to director of white elementary schools (the District of Columbia had a dual racial system of schools until 1955), to a similar position for secondary schools (where he gained national status as an advocate of desegregation), to the superintendency in 1958.[40]

While he offended many southern legislators who sat upon congressional committees overseeing the District's schools, he became a hero to the local and national liberal community. Within the system, however, Hansen's reputation as a superintendent originated from two instructional programs he designed for over 100,000 black and white schoolchildren.

The Amidon Plan (named after a new elementary school built in an urban renewal area southwest of the Capitol) was a "return to the sanity of order and logic in curriculum organization and to the wisdom of teaching subject matter to children in a direct and effective manner, using with judgment what is known about how we learn." Concentrating upon classroom order, the teaching of phonics was harnessed to what earlier and subsequent generations of reformers would cherish as a "traditional education." The Amidon Plan was mandated for all elementary schools. Courses of study were published so that for each scheduled period of instruction teachers would know what had to be taught. The curriculum was teacher-centered. Hansen stated his vision of the teacher:

> She returns to the front of the room with chalk in hand to explain, discuss, reinforce learning by immediate check on class responses. . . . From the wealth of her own scholarship she helps the class to see connections between the known and unknown, giving meaning to what otherwise may be missed by the pupil and taken for granted by the teacher.[41]

Also, Hansen introduced in 1956 the "variable curriculum," better known as tracking in senior high schools, during the first years of desegregation, and into junior high and elementary schools in 1958. Children were assigned to tracks (honors, college preparatory, general, basic) according to their ability as measured by tests and teacher recommendations. Such ability groupings attempted to tailor curriculum and instruction to individual differences. If tests masked a student's ability or if a student demonstrated marked improvement in one track, then, theoretically, movement into the next higher track was possible. Downward movement, of course, also occurred.[42]

Hansen was the moving force behind these instructional designs. His convictions about what was best for District of Columbia children were fired by a deep belief in professional educators possessing the training and experience to guide schools and classrooms. To reorganize the schools for curriculum and instruction as the Amidon Plan and tracking demanded, Hansen needed more than conviction. His style, authority as an education expert, and determination enlisted the appointed school board to provide the necessary staff and funds to underwrite these initiatives for the first five years of his tenure as school chief.

In the 1980s the instructional role of the superintendent has again reemerged as central to what superintendents *should* do. As read in the growing literature on "effective schools," an effort to increase the importance of the instructional role for teachers and principals has now expanded to district superintendents and in some instances state superintendents. Setting goals, establishing standards, selecting and supervising staff, insuring consistency in curricula and teaching approaches have become benchmarks of instructionally active superintendents.[43]

Managerial

The familiar administrative tasks associated with carrying out school board policies, such as planning, collecting and disbursing of information, budgeting, hiring and firing, supervising subordinates, and managing conflict across a broad array of activities constitute this role. Actions range from busing students and evaluating principals to allocating parking spaces at the district office and planning for a new building.

If the instructional role aims to alter existing beliefs and behaviors of members of the school community, the fundamental purpose of the managerial role is to maintain organizational stability. For those superintendents who envision a direction for the district, who aim to achieve certain purposes with students, teachers, and principals beyond preserving existing arrangements, the managerial and instructional roles merge. For those superintendents whose orientation is to accomplish no more than what the school board directs, the managerial and instructional roles are largely separate.

Previously I cited evidence that what superintendents do daily focuses much more on the administrative than the instructional. While this tilt toward managerial work may well be due to the nature of the post, how one becomes a superintendent may also account for what was reported.

Since the 1920s, the managerial role has been the "meat-and-potatoes" of graduate school training for administrators; few master's and doctoral programs for superintendents include substantial time devoted to curriculum and instruction. The impact of Cubberley and other academics who believed that administration is an applied science produced coursework in finance, budgeting, building maintenance, collecting and organizing data statistically, planning, and personnel practices. Pressure for professionalization led to state laws that required credentials, usually a set of courses taught in graduate schools.[44]

Among superintendents, either those who never saw the inside of a graduate seminar on educational administration or those who left universities with freshly minted doctorates, the managerial role was both familiar and important. The evidence cited earlier on duties assigned to the first generation of school chiefs and the limited data on what they did in their offices underscored the heavy administrative tilt of the position.

Aaron Gove, Denver's venerable superintendent who served the longest tenure in the district's history, lived the managerial role. After a decade in Denver, Gove told the National Council of Education in 1884 that a superintendent must do five tasks to be considered an expert adviser to the school board: First, "he must be familiar . . . with the financial affairs of the district. He must know about the assessment roll and about the tax collector's returns; he must be acquainted with the sources of income, and with the ratio of school expenses to other municipal expenses." Why? "Money," he explained, "is the greatest power in upbuilding school interests." Second, the superintendent should "be well informed in the arrangement and construction of schoolhouses."

Third, because school boards tend to overspend, the superintendent should advise the school board swiftly and in detail about the worth of their expenditures. He should also advise the school board on prudent investments of district funds. Fourth, he must keep the school board informed on what is happening in the schools since it is the board that reports to the community. On whose voice the board should hear, Gove was clear: "Pupils' and teachers' comments," he said, "upon the management are quite secondary to the utterances of him whom the people have selected to represent them on the board of management."

Finally, proper maintaining of school buildings is essential. "A broken pane, pencil, or chalk marks or whittlings in outhouses or on fences not only indicates weakness in supervision but are also a positive barrier to making desirable character among pupils." It is the superintendent who will "make visits of inspection and spur janitors and principals to eternal vigilance."

Gove, of course, did speak of instructional supervision and the importance of teaching teachers. His theme, however, was that the superintendent's managerial skills are paramount. The opening line of his talk captures the emphasis in both his speech and Denver superintendency: "The technical duties of a city superintendent are administrative."[45]

Both Young and Hansen also carried out the managerial role in their respective posts. In her first annual report (1909–1910) to the Chicago school Board, for example, Young reorganized the central administration. She appointed a first assistant superintendent who centralized the purchasing of school supplies, repairs, and building renovations into one office to eliminate the interminable delays and confusion that had existed earlier. Shifting responsibilities for evening schools and the securing of substitute teachers among her other assistants permitted her to visit schools and listen to staff.[46]

Concerned that just because she had taught and principaled in the Chicago schools, she would lean heavily on these prior experiences, she reorganized so that she could spend more time with teachers, principals, and students. "Truths and rules developed out of one's past are valuable," she told her school board, "but general principles must be reinterpreted and restated in the light of the present day, if affairs shall be administered for the best interests of the school and community." As a manager, Young acted to enhance her instructional role.[47]

Hansen performed in a like manner. In order to introduce the four-track system and the Amidon Plan, the reorganizing of the courses of study for both elementary and secondary schools, staff increases, in-service training of teachers and principals, and the expansion of testing and counseling services, to cite just a few instances, had to be planned and implemented.

Also, they needed to be funded. For these instructional designs to flourish and expand, they had to be structured into a budget, item by item, to receive stable annual funding. Intimate knowledge of an enormous budget, the appointing of a trusted professional whose knowledge of the budget was exceeded only by the superintendent's were primary requirements. Hansen met those requirements throughout his tenure. In short, managing a budget that had to survive the gauntlet of a school board and two separate congressional oversight committees requires extraordinary managerial, as well as political, skills in creating and sustaining the track system and the Amidon Plan. Here also, managerial and instructional roles merge.

Political

Since the first superintendent sat behind a desk, they spent time meeting with parents, businessmen, local officials, and others either to nourish public support for schools or offset criticism. Most superintendents recognized the fact that any public institution supported by taxes in this society will seldom be left to professionals alone to run.

As with teachers and principals, I use the term *political* to refer to activities beyond those that later generations of administrators, attempting to distance themselves from the taint of partisan politics, came to call "community leadership" and "public relations." The word refers to the goals held and the process superintendents used to determine and transform personal and public expectations into formal policies and official actions; it also refers to the authority, rules, and influence that superintendents exert in governing a school district.

Positioned between what state and local school boards direct, what parents expect, what teachers and principals need (and these differ), and what students want, superintendents live and breathe conflict. Their position is like a police officer directing traffic at a four-way intersection. The officer must know when to slow down and speed up traffic, and he also must know when to stop one line of cars in order to move another line through. Determining the ebb and flow of competing interests and expectations, while simultaneously handling the inevitable crash of conflicting interests, in order to avoid gridlock becomes a superintendent's major task. By their decisions and actions, by their exercise of formal and informal power, their display of interpersonal skills, their core values, and their perspectives on what is and is not possible, superintendents determine to what extent a policy is implemented as intended, converted to fit the particular contours of the district, or shelved.

School chiefs, then, act politically when they persuade, rebut, sell, and bargain with school board members, principals, teachers, students, taxpayer coalitions, parent activists, state department of education officials, and fired-up reverends of the local ministerial association. Because political action means working towards achieving particular values embedded in goals, such work is as intensely moral as the work of ministers on the other side of the street.[48]

Some superintendents have savored the political role. Frank Cody, veteran Detroit superintendent (1919–1942), relished the work. He was a joiner par excellence—from the Odd Fellows to the Chamber of Commerce, from churches to professional groups. He moved easily from the bar of the Saint Claire Hotel where he met frequently with school board members to the presidency of the NEA (1927).[49]

To Cody a superintendent has three major functions: administration, supervision, and "community relations." To him, "community relations are the contacts which are designed to discover the educational needs of the community and to interpret the schools to the community." In a large school district, the superintendent cannot do everything so functions must be delegated to staff. "He may delegate almost every other type of work," Cody wrote, "but not this one completely." The superintendent's "chief assignment is community relations."

> He must know his public in order to be able to sense its desires and its needs. Further, he must be able to "sell" the program of the schools to his local community.[50]

Ending her tenure just about the time Cody began his, Ella Flagg Young also performed the political role. In a city where the mayor appointed school board members, where an activist teachers' union demanded higher salaries and more classroom decision-making authority, where textbook agents lobbied individual board members to buy their company's books, and where the board created special committees to consider the superintendent's recommendations, Young tiptoed through an intensely political process. That she submitted a letter of resignation in 1913 (which the board of education ignored by reelecting her for another one-year contract) because she "was the victim of political intrigue among board members" only underscores the personal stakes involved.[51]

Young's ability to get the board to choose a new speller illustrates this political process well. Many teachers had complained to her about the inadequacies of the current speller and wanted a better one. On the superintendent's recommendation, the board chose a textbook. But the issue could not be resolved by choosing one that teachers wanted, not at least in 1912. Salesman James Plunkett had persuaded a number of board members that his speller was just what the Chicago schools needed. Young felt it was both inferior to other books and too expensive. Continued pressure on Young from two board members to recommend Plunkett's speller—one of whom supported the speller, according to Young, because it was union made—convinced her to urge the board president to refer the question to a committee, not a pleasant alternative. Threats from the two board members pushed Young to report the whole affair to a newspaper, which used the headline, "Mrs. Young Tells of Threats Made in Textbook War." In a public session of the board, under questioning from the president, she named the two members. Ultimately, the chair of the board subcommittee recommended that the board of education print its own speller. Relieved that she had averted the adoption of an inadequate speller that would have made teachers' work even more taxing, Young added to her work load by overseeing the writing of new spellers.[52]

Five decades later, Carl Hansen did not concern himself with the choice of textbooks; board members, by the 1960s, were largely insulated from agents' lobbying. What concerned Hansen far more in those years was the growing influence of federally funded reformers anxious to convert the District of Columbia schools into a national laboratory for their version of school improvement.

Hansen knew well the map of local politics. To negotiate a budget approval through the maze of a board of education review, the city bureaucracy, the three presidentially appointed commissioners, and two congressional committees whose sole jurisdiction was to oversee District affairs demanded a finely tuned radar system. Hansen had demonstrated already his political astuteness in mobilizing funds for the track system and the Amidon Plan.

When federal appointees of John F. and Robert Kennedy introduced in 1964 an independent Model School Division within the District schools, Hansen once again outmaneuvered opponents to protect his instructional programs. The struggle over whether a dozen schools located in slums north of the White House would be independent of the board of education (and Hansen) or under the aegis of the superintendent has been told elsewhere. The starkness of the political fight over control of schools, however, pitted Hansen, who sought federal dollars, against reformers with a large dollop of skepticism for tracking, lusty enthusiasm for better schools, and clout.[53]

Hansen survived each wave of reformers in the early to mid-1960s, yielding only to establishing a partially decentralized district within the Washington schools headed by a veteran administrator whom he appointed. The reforms undertaken in the Model School Division challenged both the Amidon Plan and tracking, but in a far milder manner than if the subsystem had been freed of District control. What Hansen had not counted on were the growing forces for change over which his sizable political skills had little influence. Desegregation, the black civil rights movement, local efforts to attain self-determination for the District of Columbia government and the schools, all became a tidal wave that swept Hansen out of the superintendency in 1967. In that year federal judge Skelly Wright ruled in *Hobson v. Hansen* that tracking was discriminatory and, therefore, unconstitutional. Hansen asked the board of education to appeal the decision. They said no. Hansen resigned. Within months the track system was formally dismantled; within a few years, the Amidon Plan became a collection of phonics charts stored in closets.

Cody, Young, and Hansen engaged in a political process because they saw a link between daily tasks and their larger goals. They used their formidable skills and influence to sell, lure, shove, and pull staff and citizens toward the goals they prized. Politics, then, became morality in action. Both the process and the outcomes were political in that policies negotiated in the crucible of the school board and community were initially sensed and formulated by the superintendent and then transformed into managerial and instructional decisions.

All three roles form the core of superintending. Much diversity exists, however, among school executives in how the three roles are enacted. I end this section with a vignette of a superintendent in 1987 who heads a school district between San Jose and San Francisco.

Paul Sakamoto

Superintendent of Mountainview-Los Altos Union High School District (MVLA) since 1975, Paul Sakamoto was born and raised in the San Jose area, adjacent to where he superintends. Sakamoto climbed the familiar career ladder for superintendents to the top post in the district. He began teaching science in 1956 at Sunnyvale High School in a nearby district, after five years, he moved into administration there as an assistant principal in charge of guidance and student activities, and then on to the principalship in 1966. After thirteen years at Sunnyvale (while picking up a master's degree in counseling and guidance), he left for Michigan State where he studied psychology and educational administration in completing a doctorate. Returning to the San Jose area, he was associate dean for students services briefly at San Jose State (his alma mater). In 1971 he decided to reenter school administration as deputy superintendent for curriculum and instruction in MVLA. Three years later, with the departure of his boss, the school board named the low-key Sakamoto superintendent.

What this capsule summary omits is that Sakamoto is also an artist. In his paintings, in his gardening, in the other hobbies he pursues, he proceeds with care, skill, and an artist's eye in choosing materials and producing a painting, a garden, or an office that is both business-like and restful to the eye.[54]

In his decade as superintendent, Sakamoto has seen student enrollment shrink by a third (from just under 4,600 to just over 3,000) and minority enrollment double (from 15 percent to almost 30 percent). He has presided over the closing of one of the three high schools and a fiscal retrenchment triggered by Proposition 13, which jolted high-income districts like MVLA.[55]

Through all of these changes, the district emerged with one less high school, a total budget only 5 percent higher than when he assumed the post, fewer teachers and administrators and the conventional indicators of academic achievement (test scores, percentage going to college, drop-out rate) at roughly the same level. Sakamoto has especially strong feelings on two issues: an equal schooling for minority students and instructional supervision.[56]

Along with the affluent, white population, an increasing number of low-income Hispanic and black students have presented issues for the predominantly white staff. Many of these students are reluctant to take college preparatory courses, either for fear of receiving low grades or because they lack the resources to attend college. Historically, parents of low-income minority students have less experience and time to press the case for their children with school officials. Also, many of these students are assigned to remedial courses because of previous low performance. Most high school teachers prefer to teach college-bound, highly motivated students. Thus, classes with students who have reading problems and who are less motivated tend to go to less experienced and less interested teachers. Unlike their more affluent peers whose parents and teachers push school boards and administrators to alter arrangements in order to accommodate students, these low-income students have few advocates. Sakamoto is one, however.

In 1981 he introduced the Parity Plan. Adopted by the school board, this plan calls for a proportionate number of minority students to be enrolled in college preparatory and honors courses, equal to the percentage of minority students in the school by 1987. To do this,

Sakamoto asked eighth grade teachers and counselors to identify minority students scoring above the fiftieth percentile on achievement tests. School counselors and administrators monitored these students and encouraged them to choose college preparatory courses. He scoured agencies to secure special funds for a teacher staff development program based on the instructional theories of Madeline Hunter at UCLA. Staff from MVLA went to Los Angeles, received training, and returned to lead workshops in the district. A voluntary program, teachers who participated received a $500 salary increment, costing the district over $90,000.[57]

Even in establishing a special tutorial center with a paid coordinator to help these students and the voluntary teacher in-service program, the Parity Plan has run into difficulties and may not achieve the goal set by Sakamoto. But his initiative has openly brought to his teachers' and administrators' attention an issue that touches the very core of most definitions of an equal schooling. In his weekly Administrative Council meetings, agenda items on improving instructional quality and remedial courses taken by many minority students have been discussed often. While department heads and senior faculty resist altering traditional ways of assigning classes, the superintendent keeps the issue front and center.[58]

Furthermore, he believes that having minority teachers is important not only for students but for the district. With the closure of one school, he worked diligently to even out the percentage of minority staff at both high schools by squeezing out of a dry budget sufficient funds to hire additional minority teachers. Sakamoto has spent a great deal of time explaining, cajoling, enlisting, and coercing teachers, administrators, parents, and school board members into implementing the Parity Plan.[59]

Instructional improvement ranks high on his list of values also. To make real the point of excellent teaching for all students, which he discusses in his memos, editorials in district newsletters, and speeches, Sakamoto visits classes. In 1983–1984 he set aside a few days each week to observe teachers. By April he had seen almost all (over 200) classes, spending twenty-five minutes or more with each. He wrote notes to each teacher, since he scheduled ten or more visits daily and could not individually confer with them.

Linked to this commitment for teacher improvement is the often volatile, often ignored process of teacher evaluation. Sakamoto has promoted a teacher evaluation plan that stresses teacher involvement, the accumulation of many sources of data to assess the performance of a teacher (including a portfolio of teacher and student work that includes student ratings), which finally concludes in a narrative written by the high school administrator. In his judgment,

> evaluation is the key to any comprehensive program of instructional improvement . . . the key to what goes on in schools. If high levels of student achievement are really our goal, then we should be focusing here. Teachers feel isolated, that no one cares, and just close the door. Evaluation opens the door.[60]

Sakamoto attends personally to the entire process. He reads every observation report written by school administrators. He insures that time is set aside in Administrative Council meetings for discussion of the process and that time is set aside at annual conferences for administrators to practice the skills necessary in collecting and reporting the data. Teacher complaints about insensitive principals or inept handling of certain portions of the process are often transformed into sessions for administrators. Language to support this approach to evaluation is contained within the contract between the teachers' union and the district. The superintendent, then, is very serious about the centrality of teacher, and administrative, evaluation to class and school improvement.

Blending instructional, managerial, and political roles becomes evident in this vignette of Superintendent Paul Sakamoto, who has served a changing district for over a decade.

PATTERNS IN DISCHARGING THE CORE ROLES

In using John Philbrick, Ella Flagg Young, Frank Cody, Carl Hansen, and Paul Sakamoto as examples of enacting the core roles of superintending, I stress the continuing power of the images described earlier, the varied patterns in which superintendents perform these roles, and the settings in which they worked. Distinguishing between the content of the core roles and the style in which they are enacted suggests a rich array of superintendent actions. Individual styles—that mysterious blend of personal traits and work tasks—will vary. Two superintendents may perform the three roles in a similar manner, but their personalities, experiences, work settings, and values may vary sufficiently that the similarities are blurred. In exploring these core role patterns, I find it helpful to imagine their differences without the distraction of style.

Figure 8 displays how these five superintendents performed their roles. By placing these roles within the various layers of a school district, the salience of the political role becomes evident in its bridging of organizational boundaries. The degree of bridging that occurs depends, of course, on how superintendents view their job, the influence they exert within the various sectors, and the degree of school board and community (including the state) intervention. The overlapping

Figure 8: Core Role Patterns Among Superintendents*

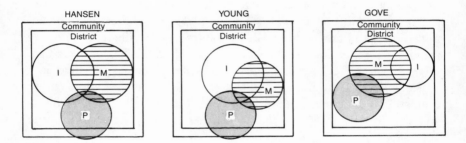

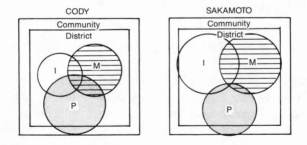

*These figures represent approximations of how I imagined these superintendents to have displayed the roles. They are meant as devices to show the array of ways that core roles converge and diverge.

roles suggest how instruction and management intersect and how political judgments spill over into other sectors.

As stated earlier, the core roles, varying styles, and complexity of the job have seldom strayed far from the origins of the position almost a century and a half ago. The swift conversion of a job into a professional career certified by the state, a process that took no more than three decades beginning at the turn of the century, also carried heavy baggage about what superintendents *should* do. The image of the Superintendent as a man for all seasons (only 1.2 percent are female, a figure unchanged since 1971) who concentrates on leading the instructional program, managing staff and teachers efficiently, practicing savvy community relations, handling conflict deftly, motivating teachers and principals, and being on call for twenty-four hours remains pretty well fixed in the minds of nonsuperintendents. One only has to read the brochures sent out by school boards advertising superintendent vacancies to see that only heroes need apply.[61]

This chapter argues that the history of the superintendency, the nature of the work assigned to school executives, dominant occupational images, personal values, and the work settings helped shape much of what these men and women have done in school districts. While styles differ, the managerial role, not instructional supervision, seemingly has dominated superintendents' behavior. For some school chiefs, however, (what percentage I cannot estimate) the managerial and instructional roles merge when they seek to achieve their particular goals. When superintendents try to achieve these goals, the political role comes into play. Such superintendents have vision and invest meaning into the daily routines of running a school district. When the superintendent's vision, however, aims to implement existing school board goals, the political role concentrates on conflict prevention and maintaining stability.

For a position born out of the lay school board's need for an agent to carry out its orders, the core roles of superintendents mirror those of principals and teachers. Yes, the patterns vary. Yes, the arenas in which they work differ. Yes, the political dimension grows larger and becomes more apparent the further one moves from the classroom. Still, the similarities in core roles for both teachers and administrators point to a similarity of purpose rather than incompatible interests. I discovered that in the years that I served as a superintendent.

6

From High School Teacher to Superintendent to Professor (1972–1981)

My palms were sweating. I could see out of the corner of my eye Barbara, Sondra, and Janice seated to my right among the 1,200 teachers and administrators spread out before me in the Thomas Jefferson Junior High School gymnasium. As I waited to be introduced by a school board member, I remembered that two months earlier I had been a graduate student finishing the final details on my dissertation. Twenty-six months earlier I had been teaching Roosevelt High School students American history in the District of Columbia.

I had already addressed Arlington administrators at the annual conference a few days earlier. My main message to the teachers would be the same as for the administrators, stating my beliefs, the problems I and the school board wanted to address, and the importance of setting goals to improve instruction. I knew clearly how I wanted to begin my talk given the two years of intense wrangling between the teachers and my predecessor, whom they viewed as indifferent to their concerns and classroom issues.

Finally the board member turned to me; the polite applause rippled toward the stage as I stepped forward to the microphone. "The last job I had before Arlington," I began, "was teaching high school across the river." The teachers let out a roar, and the mild handclapping that greeted my introduction erupted into shouts, stamping, and vigorous applause. I began my superintendency in Arlington with teacher applause ringing in my ears.

149

There had been little applause when we parked in front of 83B at Escondido Village, the housing provided for Stanford graduate students, in early September 1972. We were excited and scared. Each of us had so many questions about living on a campus, making friends, living within a tight budget, doing new things, and a dozen other concerns that flitted in and out of our minds. As it turned out, the two years that we lived at Stanford were ones that we recall with great affection, both as a family and individually. I remember it as being almost like an adolescent again, without the worry of acne.

But I did hear a clock ticking. I had told David Tyack, my adviser and ultimately my friend, that I wanted to get the doctorate swiftly and begin superintending. With an abiding interest in history, I not only pursued courses in the history of education with Tyack but also studied political science, organizational sociology, and the economics of education. It was a movable feast, an intellectual smorgasbord that immersed me in a community of like-minded practitioners and scholars, who differed among themselves about aspects of public schooling but possessed in common a passion for understanding.

If motivation and readiness are prerequisites for learning, I had them in excess. My experience in public schools were rich but specific. Discovering connections with the past, seeing theories at work in what I had done, and, most important for me, coming to understand the importance of seeing the world from many sides drove me to reexamine my classroom and administrative experiences. Lectures, long discussions with other students, close contact with a handful of professors, and work on a dissertation on three big-city superintendents made the two years an intensely satisfying experience.

David Tyack's patient but insightful prodding made the research and writing an intellectual high. Jim March opened up a world of organizational theory that meshed with my own experiences; I marvel to this day that even though March never spent a day in an inner-city school, he understood them so well. From March I learned the importance of looking at the world in multiple ways, of learning to live with uncertainty, of the tenacious hold that rationalism has upon both policymakers and practitioners, and of understanding that ambiguity and conflict are part of the natural terrain of organizational life.

So, whenever I read about superintendents or principals who found their graduate preparation either insufferable or inadequate, I recall how different my experience was. I earned a doctorate in the history of education, while taking a number of social science courses.

It was not a curricula designed for preparing educational administrators—and this at a school of education founded by Ellwood P. Cubberley. In pursuing history and social science, while investigating the superintendency, the two years at Stanford turned out to be a first-rate preparation for the next seven in Arlington.

But it was not easy getting a job, I discovered. Beginning in late 1973, I began applying for superintendencies around the country. The six months of job searching put me and the family on a roller-coaster ride of moods that is distasteful to recall. I had applied for fifty-three positions, forty-five superintendencies of mostly small cities, and eight principalships and deanships. By June 1974 I had been rejected by all of them, including a district that sent me a rejection letter for a position for which I had *not* applied. The closest I came to being selected was in the Harrisburg and York school districts in Pennsylvania, where I went through elaborate interviews only to be named the runner-up. (I was a finalist for Berkeley, California, but withdrew my candidacy.)

What became clear to me in this painful process was that my dream of serving as a superintendent was close to becoming a fantasy. Rejection letters and interviewers kept telling me that jumping into a superintendency from a high school teaching position (without ever having served as a principal), even with some administrative experience, was a grandiose leap of faith. To say that I was depressed in June was an understatement. The only application left was the one in Arlington, Virginia.

School board chairman Mike Timpane had written to me to say that I was a finalist and invited me to come for an interview. Of course I went, but my spirits were low; my self-confidence had hemorrhaged terribly. Arlington was the largest of the superintendencies I had applied for: It had 20,000 students, but was dropping in enrollment yearly. Across the river from Washington, D.C., Arlington's reputation as a politically conservative jurisdiction suggested there would be risks involved in choosing a superintendent whose prior service was across the bridge in the black, low-income schools of a city that a reactionary Arlingtonian called Sodom on the Potomac.

Interviews with school administrators, parents, students, and the school board raised my hopes somewhat, especially those interviews with the school board. This board was different from any that I had ever interviewed with or even studied. Four women, including the first black to serve on the school board, and one man, formed a politically liberal majority looking for their first superintendent.

The board had just forced the resignation of the previous superintendent; they wanted to take the school district in a different direction; they wanted someone who would address openly the teacher-administrator split, falling test scores, shrinking enrollment, and the growing presence of black, Hispanic, and Southeast Asian immigrants. One member had taught in the Arlington schools. All had children in the schools and were concerned about the lack of serious attention to these issues. They were enthusiastic. They had the endorsement of the then reigning political majority and they wanted to move now. The chemistry between Mike Timpane, Lou Deitrich, Ann Broder, Diane Henderson, and Eleanor Monroe during the interview, which was over dinner, was, for me, unusual. The questions and answers were punctuated by genuine conversation and raucous laughter. Afterwards in describing it to Barbara and my daughters I told them that it was closer to a family gathering than an interview. It was an extraordinary experience for me.

Two weeks later, Lou Deitrich, the new chairman of the school board called to ask if I would accept the superintendency. Without hesitation I said yes, but with two conditions: that I could spend the first six weeks visiting schools and classrooms before taking on the formal position of superintendent and hire one assistant. She called back immediately to say that the conditions were acceptable to the school board. Arlington had a new superintendent.

Let me describe Arlington briefly before dealing with the series of conflicts that were central to my seven year tenure. Once a middle-class, white suburb with segregated schools, by the early 1970s Arlington had become a city with an expanding multiethnic population. In those years Arlington got smaller, older, and culturally diverse. Demographics explain part of the transformation: The population dropped from almost 180,000 in 1966 to about 160,000 in 1980; there were fewer and smaller families with school age children; there were sharp jumps in the number of young singles and adults over fifty-five years of age. Coincident with these changes, scores of different nationalities moved into the county, swelling the minority population, but in insufficient numbers to counter the other shifts.[1]

These demographic changes altered schooling. Pupil enrollment dropped from a high of 26,000 in 1968 to 14,000 in 1982; from nearly forty schools in 1968, the number fell to thirty-one schools in 1982 (including three alternative schools). Also, from less than 15 percent minority students in 1970, the number of ethnic pupils doubled to over one-third in 1980. The jump came most sharply among non-

English speaking minorities, particularly Hispanic, Korean, and Vietnamese children.[2]

If population changes squeezed schools, so did the rising cost of schooling. When diminished revenues in the mid–1970s coincided with double-digit inflation, school costs and demands from employees for higher salaries squeezed the school board and superintendent from different directions.

Since the appointed five-member school board was fiscally dependent upon the elected five-member county board, state and federal revenue shortfalls plus inflation punctured school budgets badly in these years, precisely at the time that the effects of changing populations were being felt. What prevented the pinch from hurting Arlington schools too badly was that the county, because of family income and assessed valuation of property, was wealthy. That wealth somewhat eased the painful transition from suburb to city, especially during a recession. Arlington's prime location—across the Potomac from the nation's capital, improved further by a new subway system—and the county board's cautious fiscal policies gave it, in 1980, the lowest tax rate in the metropolitan area.

Nonetheless, the county board had to struggle with the politics of retrenchment. Irate property owners, most of whom no longer had children in school, wanted lower taxes as their property increased in value. Their demands competed with requests from other citizens who wanted higher school budgets to keep pace with inflation, subsidies for the elderly, improved police protection, and broader recreation and social services.

Caught like everyone else in the recession of the mid– and late–1970s, county officials retrenched. Schools, particularly, bore a major share of the cutbacks. The county emerged from the recession with most services intact, the lowest tax rate in the area, and a school system that had become an annual target for reducing expenditures.

Political change also occurred. There had been a gradual but persistent shift from a Republican county board in the 1960s to one consisting of a coalition of Democrats and independents. By 1971 this liberal bloc had taken over the five member elected county board. Consistent with the see-saw pattern of Arlington politics (reflecting the larger demographic changes beginning in the 1950s), the liberal domination of the county board gave way by 1978 to a three-member Republican majority. Since the county board appointed school board members, those who served on the school board throughout the 1970s had been appointed by the liberal majority. Due to the time lapse between Republicans reasserting their majority on the county board (1978) and making sufficient appointments on the school board to constitute a majority of like-minded members there, it was not until 1980 that the school board attained a three-member Republican majority. In the seven years that I served, I can only think of one or two school board members that had no formal ties to either political party.

As part of this political shift in the 1970s, the school board's relationship with its superintendent altered. While previous Republican-appointed school boards in the 1960s left operational decision making to its executive officer, appointees of the liberal majority intervened more actively in what many superintendents might have considered their territory. Inevitably, friction developed between the superintendent who had been appointed in 1969 by a school board content to let their hired expert run the district and the new, far more interventionist school board. In 1974, the first year of his renewed four-year contract, the superintendent resigned. I was appointed that year to complete the remaining three years.

The school board that appointed me in 1974 was troubled over the consequences of a shrinking enrollment, declining test scores, a growing dissatisfaction among parents over school quality, the rift between teachers and administrators, and what they viewed as an experienced instructional staff that was either unaware or resistant to the changes prompted by a diverse student population.

In deciding what to do and how to do it, I worked initially on establishing a reputation as a superintendent who would be accessible and who would listen to (but not necessarily agree with) anyone. The six weeks of visits to almost a thousand teachers in classrooms and in groups introduced me to an enormous amount of information about the quality of schooling available, the troubles that could not be ignored, and the dilemmas that I could do little about. Also, I began holding "Open Doors" at a different school each week, where I would listen to complaints and discover emerging issues. Parents, students, teachers, citizens, administrators came by. I found "Open Doors" to be a useful early warning system for problems and a clear signal to the entire school community that I was accessible.

The board's insistence on doing something about the shrinking numbers of students quickly translated into pursuing school mergers. While schools had been closed in Arlington because of desegregation or inadequate facilities, none had ever been closed because of too few students. The schools with the least number of students were in affluent parts of the county, where most of the school and county board members lived. The first two years my staff and I spent much time in establishing an orderly process by which the school board and the community could determine whether or not to close schools and, if necessary, which ones.

By 1975 the decision-making process for school consolidation was in place. The board and I agreed that I would provide the data, establish the process of sifting the data (through simulations of school candidates for closure), and examine each option through public work sessions and hearings. I would recommend criteria, but the board would decide which ones to use in making a decision. I would also recommend which school to close prior to public hearings so that the board would have the benefit of my thinking and could listen to the community's response to the superintendent's recommendation. Then the school board would decide.

Publicly and privately, I advised the board that if a decision to close a school was to appear as rational policy, it must be anchored in sufficient numbers. But there were other criteria and values that each person had to weigh and consider. The decision I and they reached would be, ultimately, a value-based decision. The shock surrounding the closing of the first elementary school reverberated throughout the affluent portion of the district. The board voted four to one to close Madison Elementary. It was a grueling year.

By 1980 five elementary schools and two junior highs had been merged with nearby schools. Moreover, the school board approved a secondary school reorganization that moved the ninth grade to the high school and retained four intermediate schools with seventh and eighth grades. The staff-built merger process appeared resilient enough to weather the controversy that erupted periodically over school closings.

The other central task that consumed much time was creating an organizational framework for improving instruction and student performance. By 1976–1977 the scaffolding had been put into place. The pieces to that framework were as follows:

1. The school board established a set of instructional goals for the district; for example, improving reading, math, writing, and thinking skills; improving students' understanding of humanities and human relations.

2. I and my staff constructed organizational mechanisms for con-

verting those goals into school and classroom priorities.

3. Each school staff, with advice from parents, drew up an Annual School Plan (ASP) for achieving the board's goals.

4. I reviewed each ASP, met with the principal at mid-year to discuss changes, and, at the end of the year, received an assessment of the plan's progress toward its goals.

5. With principals, I discussed the School Academic Profile which listed student outcomes for each school (e.g., test scores, survey results from students, teachers, and parents that were linked to the district's goals).

6. Administrator and teacher evaluation policies were revised to incorporate ASP objectives.

7. Curriculum objectives, kindergarten through twelfth grade in all subjects and skills, were aligned with school board goals. Instructional materials, including textbooks, were reviewed and modified to connect them to curriculum objectives. County-wide tests were constructed to assess the aims of the revised curriculum and to determine their fit with the materials in use. Item-by-item analysis on district and standardized achievement tests were conducted and shared with principals and teachers annually to determine areas for improvement and new goals for ASPs.

This managerial framework for instructional improvement tightened the generally loose connection between system goals, district curriculum, school goals, texts and materials, tests, and evaluation to allow the instructional staff to concentrate on fewer, more worthwhile targets. I wanted to construct a climate of seriousness regarding academic improvement. My personal involvement in reading each ASP, meeting with principals and teachers to discuss changes in plans, teaching workshops on goal-setting, and my written comments on the assessment submitted by the school staff and parents' advisory council established clearly, I believe, that this process was high on my agenda for school improvement.

I did discover, however, some disturbing trends toward the end of my tenure that caused me to temper my enthusiasm for the tight-coupling of district goals to curriculum, texts, and tests. I saw, for example, an increase in standardization. A strong, irresistible tug towards a uniform curriculum and adoption of single textbooks, workbooks, and other materials occurred. The use of supplementary materials tailored to individual differences in children declined. Grouping students within classrooms requires additional materials and far more teacher preparation. As a historian, I began to hear echoes of the previous century's reformers who sought a single, best curriculum for all students.

I also saw a press toward the use of those teaching practices cited in research findings as raising test scores: whole group instruction, active monitoring of student work, lecturing, recitation, seatwork, and so forth. I sensed that this drift might certify a set of practices as the single best way of teaching—something that, I, because of my experience as a teacher and my historical awareness of pedagogy, rejected.

This push for curricular and instructional uniformity is neither a strength nor a weakness; every school district strikes some balance between diversity and standardization. It could, however, go too far and I saw flashing red lights.

Linked to an improvement in school performance was establishing clearly the central importance of teaching. My visits to classrooms, not only in the first six weeks but one to two days a week for seven years, made it obvious to the staff where my priorities lay. I would come unannounced, watch, and, if possible, speak with the teacher about what had occurred while I was in the classroom. If I couldn't, I would write a note.

Within the first year, I located money in the budget that could be transferred to establish a Teachers Innovation Fund, similar to the one I had begun in the District of Columbia. In addition, I taught. I offered workshops for principals on constructing goals and assessing their ASPs; when we retooled the evaluation system for administrators and teachers, a few principals asked me to teach skills for conferencing and observing in classrooms. My particular favorite, however, was an annual series of workshops on developing thinking skills through questioning. I began these when the board adopted the goal of improving thinking skills. Each year I would offer it and anywhere from ten to fifteen teachers and principals would work together for four sessions. One summer I and twenty teachers constructed units for their classes on multicultural topics (e.g., contributions of Asian-Americans to the nation; understanding people different from ourselves, and so on). Finally, from time to time, I would teach students either as a substitute for an hour in an elementary school class or, in one occasion, for three days in a sophomore world history class. Not only did I find the direct contact with teachers, principals, and students invigorating but I also knew that I conveyed much more than the particular content of the lessons or workshops.

Did all of these goals, strategies, and tactics make a difference in school performance? I am not sure. I discovered that determining my influence upon the district, amidst shouts of acclaim and screams for dismissal, continually danced just beyond my reach.

I settled for proxies. The fact that my contract was renewed for four years and I received glowing annual evaluations merely demonstrated that the board was satisfied with my work—not a trivial achievement, but divorced from direct evidence of an influence on school performance. Biennial parent surveys recorded increasing satisfaction with the schools between 1972 and 1980. Administrators who annually assessed my performance moved from acute hostility to support in their ratings. While their perceptions became increasingly positive after an initial chill, such a message is a surrogate for effectiveness and quite removed from schools except as linked to a positive climate for academic performance. But what about test scores?

Test scores—the coin of the realm in Arlington—at the elementary level climbed consistently for seven straight years. The bar charts we presented in press conferences looked like a stairway to the stars and thrilled school board members. Even in the face of my repeated admonitions that these results were a very narrow part measure of what occurred in schools, that they could be used to identify problem areas, that they were largely inadequate as direct assessments of individual teachers or school performances, still reporters and board members hungered for the numbers. The next day's headlines and articles displayed the school-by-school results. School board members, like superintendents and other public officials, have so few concrete measures of effectiveness that they often seek surrogates—paste pearls for natural ones—which, with a wink of the eye, may pass for the real item.

This hunger for numbers left me very humble and even more skeptical about standardized test scores as indicators of effectiveness. The *Washington Post* annually published Scholastic Aptitude Test results for the metropolitan area districts. In 1979 I believe, Arlington edged out Fairfax County by one point (yes, one point) for the top SAT scores among the eight Washington-area school districts. I knew that the SAT results had nothing whatsoever to do with how our high schools performed. It was a standardized instrument used to predict college performance of individual students; it was not constructed to assess high school performance. I also knew that the test had little to do with what we taught in our curriculum, what texts or tests we used. Publicly, I told the board that. I told everyone within earshot of the Educational Testing Service's own claims denying its use for evaluating high school performance.

Nonetheless, the *Post* article with the boxscore of metropolitan test results produced more personal praise, more testimonials to my effectiveness as superintendent, and I believe, more acceptance for the board's policies than any single act during the seven years I served. The experience led me to cynically conclude that SAT's are ridiculous but politically potent indicators of a public craving any measurement of improvement. I still saw my primary task as achieving better numbers in order to reach other goals while explaining the tests' inherent limits and negative consequences.

Annual press conferences on test scores were a ritual that made as much sense to me as trying to find water using a divining rod. The school board became so used to my concern over excessive stress on standardized test scores that in public sessions, when I presented glowing annual results, they would repeat aloud and in chorus what I was about to say *before* I could say it—prompting great laughter from the audience.

Progress was less evident, however, at junior and senior high schools. We identified for the school board and community substantial gaps in academic achievement between minority and white students in 1978 and began to explore the complexities of closing those gaps. We broadened the performance indicators to include the numbers of students who volunteered for school activities and other nontest outcomes, but it was a constant struggle.

In short, a major effort was made over the initial four years to become personally accessible and responsive to instructional issues while directly wrestling with the powder keg of closing schools. Results were ambiguous. Effectiveness measures were uncertain. But this appears to be the lot of administrators—uncertainty over how well a job is done, except the feeling that you carry within yourself. This quick summary of the early years of my tenure in Arlington may suggest that events and decisions involving me, the school board, the staff, and interest groups in the community flowed smoothly. Far from it.

THE DNA OF THE SUPERINTENDENCY IN ARLINGTON: CONFLICT

From the very first week after I was appointed, challenges from the conservative wing of the local Republican party as to my credentials appeared in the press. Because I had not taken all the prescribed courses for superintendent eligibility in Virginia, I was called "unqualified." The issue of lacking formal course work that I faced a few years earlier in the District of Columbia still rang in my ears.

What course did I lack that made me "unqualified" to serve as Arlington's superintendent? Plant maintenance, or the care of school buildings, the State Department of Education said. So I quietly arranged to take a course at George Washington University from a professor I knew, who couldn't contain his laughter when I explained the situation. I attended no classes and wrote one paper on school mergers, which I later published as an article in a professional journal. The Virginia State Department of Education notified me in 1975 that I was fully credentialed as a superintendent.

However, the conflict continued. The essence of public schooling is the inexorability of competing goals, limited resources, and misperceptions. I knew it from my experience as a teacher and administrator; it was confirmed at Stanford by researchers. I lived it in Arlington.

Consider the fallout from a court decision. In 1976 the governor of Virginia sued the Arlington county and school boards for unconstitutionally carrying on collective bargaining since 1967. The governor lost in the local court, but won on appeal the next year in the state supreme court. After a decade of bargaining and establishing personnel procedures with four different unions (including administrators), the school board found that it was illegal to sit down with employee representatives to negotiate salaries, hours, and working conditions.

Coincident with the supreme court's decision there occurred a number of retrenchment measures forced upon the schools by the county board, itself coping with a reduced revenue flow. The school board and I worked out a series of cuts that reduced instructional and support staff and eliminated certain programs. With 85 percent of the budget invested in salaries and with inflation soaking up existing funds, teachers saw their salaries lag behind an unrelenting inflationary upward spiral.

After the collapse of collective bargaining and under excessive pressure from the county board to make further cuts in our budget, in

1977 the board approved my recommendation for a 2 percent salary increase; angry teachers likened the decision to a slap in the face. The resentment over this 2 percent increase smoldered in subsequent years, erupting in 1979 with a union call for a work-to-the-rule action and a majority vote of the membership asking for my resignation.

By that time, though, I had served five years and my contract had already been renewed (but not without a flurry of attacks from those who continued to argue that I was unqualified and bringing the schools to rack and ruin). My relationship with the school board was solid. We saw ourselves as a team; actually "marriage" was a common metaphor used by all of us to describe how closely we worked together and the frankness that characterized both our public and private exchanges. Even though board members came and went, the norms established by the five that hired me persisted: When you have a rumor or complaint, check with the superintendent first; keep board members informed of any breaking news that may have serious consequences for the district—don't surprise board members; everyone has a responsibility to air disagreements prior to a vote being taken, including the superintendent.

I worked hard at cultivating those norms, and especially openness on sticky issues, through biweekly lunches on executive matters, weekly conferences with the board chair to discuss agendas for the bimonthly sessions of the board, and our annual retreat to set the next year's goals. Moreover, we evaluated one another. They prepared an assessment based upon my goals and information from others who evaluated me; I shared with them my views of their strengths and limitations. The mutual trust that marked our formal and informal relationship for six of my seven years permitted me to implement a jointly constructed agenda of school improvement without looking back over my shoulder.

The first year I served, however, produced a barrel-full of controversy that sorely tested that growing trust.

After five months on the job, I recommended to the school board the transfer of a veteran principal from the mother high school, Washington-Lee, to the central office. I made the decision based upon what I saw in the school, what I heard from a number of teachers, students, and parents, and what I learned from months of dealing directly with the principal.

Within the first two months of my arrival, I had discovered that this principal had hunkered down and was just waiting to retire five years hence, yet we faced a deteriorating academic program and a million-dollar renovation of the building. A large portion of the veteran teaching staff, who recalled a "golden age" when few changes occurred in the student population, confused academic excellence with just doing business as usual. These staff members exerted great influence on the principal. Here was a school coasting on a tattered reputation. Complaints from veteran teachers and school administrators about declining student quality constituted the primary response to a changing school. I could find no initiative for beginning a process of improvement, no energy to overhaul a declining program in a school about to undergo construction of a new wing. If anything, the principal saw the school as being in excellent condition and wanted me to disappear. Delegating a large part of managing the school to an assertive assistant principal, he also distanced himself from facing issues of improvement.

I wanted someone in that building who could work with students, teachers, and parents in imagining, constructing, and carrying through new instructional programs, matched to the emerging needs of a different school population, without sacrificing standards of academic excellence. It was a tightrope walk, but it had to be done. The school board unanimously approved the recommendation. No one saw anything unusual in transferring a principal from one post to another.

Within forty-eight hours of my speaking with the principal, he had leaked the order for a transfer to teachers and parents, and the fires were lit. Within two months, a public protest had been organized by the Republicans (who had lost their majority on the county board) and his lawyer filed an age-discrimination suit. I had taken a tired administrator waiting to retire, hardly admired by his staff, students, or parent community and created a *cause celebre*. Local Republicans saw a fat curve served up by a school board and new superintendent, and they smacked the ball as hard as they could. Finally a settlement was reached between the board lawyer and their lawyer that kept the principal at Washington-Lee for another year to aid the transition of his successor. He would move to the central office at the end of that year.

The incident dogged our heels throughout the seven years. It provided political ammunition for Republicans to attack the superintendent and the school board on a variety of issues. It provided a rallying point for those citizens frustrated by the liberal majority on the county board and school board. The principal's loyalty to his newly found political party was rewarded in 1979 when he (just recently retired) was appointed to the school board, and he became my boss in

1980 when a three member majority on the school board appointed by the Republicans named him chairman.

The affair got a lot of local press coverage and helped at least one Republican get elected to the county board, and the reverberations continued for some time. While it claimed the attention of the board and myself temporarily, we eventually focused our attention on more significant matters, such as school closings, securing additional funds, and collective bargaining. What is often overlooked, however, is the fact that in the daily whirl of events this was a minor conflict compared to the dozens of other matters that I and the school board had to deal with. What was a day like during my first year?[3]

OCTOBER 24, 1975

Scheduled Appointments

Henry Gardner, director of personnel (15 minutes): discussed proposed Corrective Action procedure for use with all employees; reviewed workshop for administrators on the new process of evaluating them.

Todd Endo, executive assistant (35 minutes): in an effort to begin coordinating all locally and federally funded multicultural programs, Endo had taken the initiative to determine where the problems were and which people were needed. His judgments on bilingual programs and negotiations with the federal Office of Civil Rights' position were weekly matters that we discussed. He developed proposals to plug the holes we encountered in dealing with underserved populations in the district. We discussed a broad range of issues and how we should move ahead to bring order to unconnected programs.

Ed Oliver, director of employee relations and collective bargaining, (15 minutes): Oliver reported the grievances that had been filed that week, his estimate of the legitimacy of the complaint, and recommendations on what to do if they went unresolved, that is, should we go to arbitration. On those issues that were clear losers for the school board, I had to decide whether or not the principle embedded within the grievance was worth going to arbitration given the board's and superintendent's goals.

Joe Ringers, assistant superintendent for business and facilities (25 minutes): Ringers briefed me on the renovation plans for

Washington-Lee high school; the last meeting of the school's citizen-staff advisory commission to the board on their views of the renovation; some glitches in busing special education students; and more complaints from the district office staff on parking.

Hal Wilson, associated superintendent for instruction (25 minutes): discussed where we should go with the Teacher Innovation Fund next year; two problems with teachers at Washington-Lee that he wanted me to be aware of; told me of his plans to keep an orchestra in the high schools by trying to have the offering at the centrally located new Career Center. We went over his recommendations for budget cuts mandated by the county board because of shortfalls in state and federal revenues announced last week. We both knew that the county board would not pick up the lost revenues and that we would have to make mid-year program and staffing reductions. I wanted to be ready when the board asked for recommendations. I deleted two items that he had on the list and suggested one that he balked at. We compromised on another.

Tom Weber, principal of Stratford Junior High (25 minutes): was still having trouble doing his ASP and wanted to see if he was on the right track. We went over the guidelines and compared them to what he had been doing with a few members of his faculty. We discussed at length the importance of his broadening teacher involvement in the ASP. I asked him to tell me what he would like to see Stratford become and discussed how he might take a piece of his vision for the school and make an ASP goal out of it.

Allan Norris, director of Planning, Management, and Budget (15 minutes): brought the most recent simulations for closing Madison, Taylor, and Woodmont elementary schools. We reviewed the data to make sure what the board wanted and the criteria that they had approved were included in the printouts. I made some minor points and told him to get it ready for next week's public work session with the board.

School visit to Tuckahoe Elementary (three hours). Visited seven classrooms that I had missed on my last visit in the spring. Talked with John Willis, the principal, before and after about how things were going and issues of importance to him.

Unscheduled Appointments

My office had three doors. One door connected from inside the office to my associate superintendent for instruction and one to the clerk of the school board. The third door was to the outside area where Bettye Dudley, my secretary, had her desk and where visitors checked in. Since that door was left open (except for confidential meetings) staff members, including principals and teachers, knew that they could see me if the door was open. On this particular day, I spent about an hour with eight drop-ins on a variety of topics: construction problems at Washington-Lee, which Hal Wilson and Joe Ringers brought in; Judy Gillies, public information officer, sensed that the questions a *Washington Post* reporter was asking about an incident at a school might be more serious than the principal had told us and that I might wish to tell the board; and Adele Pennifull, clerk to the school board, reviewed items for next week's agenda.

Phone Calls and Desk Work

On this day I spent over an hour and a half on the following:
- Drafting a speech I would give to teachers who had been awarded Innovation grants.
- Drafting a Dear Colleague letter on my views about staff development for teachers and principals.
- Spoke with board members Ann Broder and Diane Henderson, who had called about a variety of complaints they had received from parents and teachers; discussed what the district was planning to do about the surge in Vietnamese students arriving in Arlington; and discussed the memorial service that we were to attend that evening for Floyd Gravitt.
- Took two phone calls from parents about their special education children and the long time that they were spending on the buses in the morning—afternoons were alright. I listened and took notes for Joe Ringers to respond. Put a reminder in my tickler file under Ringers' name to check later.
- Wrote short notes to seven teachers I had visited at Tuckahoe.
- Reviewed letters to two principals about their ASPs. Ralph Stone, a principal on assignment to me (funded by state monies that Endo had discovered), reviewed and assessed ASPs that I had already read. We discussed each and talked through the main points to be included in the letter that he would draft.
- Took a phone call from a former Glenville student who lived in Washington, D.C., and wanted to get together.
- Read draft of Newscheck, important information Gillies had prepared for all employees about the district that was enclosed with paychecks.
- Signed letters I had dictated to Dudley yesterday and documents (retirement papers for teachers, award certificates,

special payroll vouchers for employees that had missed their checks, and so forth).

Evening

After going home at 5:30 for dinner, I left at about 7:30 to attend a memorial service for Floyd Gravitt, our director of human relations, who had been found murdered in his Washington, D.C., apartment the previous week. Hank Gardner and I had gone to his funeral a few days earlier in a small town in southside Virginia. The service brought together hundreds of friends and admirers—adults and students—of the popular Gravitt who had been the first black to serve in a top position in the district office and had worked hard to bridge the large differences that still existed in a school system that had formally desegregated its last all-black elementary school in 1971. I arrived home at 10:00 P.M.

The work day was just over nine hours long and packed with constant movement, action, and verbal exchanges with staff, parents, board members, students—a kaleidoscope of activity, everchanging and unpredictable.

The conflicts that I faced were transitory, occasionally grave, and sometimes trivial. Keeping in mind, amid this frenzied activity, why I was superintending was a constant struggle. My goals, aspirations for students, teachers, and the community could easily get lost in trying to manage the queues outside my office, the mail, phone calls, and requests for favors, disturbances, and angry parents. Struggling with the cumulative effects of superintending, the three to four evenings out, the editorials criticizing a decision that I or the board had made, and the occasional hate mail had inevitable impact on me and my family.

THE PERSONAL SIDE OF SUPERINTENDING

The superintendency was both exhilarating and exhausting. As a line from a song put it: "Some days were diamonds; some days were stones." What values I prized about public service and helping people were enacted daily; what skills I had were tapped frequently; and the post pushed me into learning new skills and plumbing hidden reserves of energy. In short, being superintendent stretched me in ways I keenly felt were worthwhile. I enjoyed the job immensely. But—there has to be a *but*—there were a number of job-related issues that arose over the years, softening my rosy assessment, forcing me to face the inevitable trade-offs that accompany the top executive post in a school district.

What initially turned our lives topsy-turvy was the time I had to spend on the job after two years as a graduate student and, before that, as a teacher. The days usually began at 8:00 A.M. in the office and ended at 11:00 P.M. about two to three nights a week (and even more nights out during budget season). On those long days, I would race home for dinner at 5:00 P.M. and leave two hours later for a board meeting, work session, or some other community event. During the week, I saw my family for a few minutes in the morning and at dinner. Fatigue tracked me relentlessly the first few years; I'd fall asleep watching the evening news and take long afternoon naps on weekends. Adjusting to new time demands proved difficult for all of us.

While we had not given too much thought to the issue of privacy, Barbara and I had made a few decisions about our family time. We had agreed that Friday evening dinners to celebrate the Sabbath were a high priority. I had asked the school board to be excused from obligations on Friday evenings, and they honored my request for the seven years, except for those few instances when I decided that I had to attend a meeting or event. Apart from critical county board meetings on Saturday, my bosses made few demands upon me during the weekends, apart from phone calls.

A listed telephone number proved to be less of an issue than we had anticipated. I rarely received more than a half-dozen calls a week from parents, students, or citizens, except during snow storms or when I made a controversial recommendation to the school board. Surprisingly, we received few crank or obscene phone calls.

Buffering the family from the job was tough enough. Deciding what to do about those social invitations, where much business was transacted informally, without reducing time spent with my family troubled me. The first week on the job, for example, a principal who then headed the administrators' union invited me to join a poker game with a number of principals and district office administrators that met twice a month. My predecessor, he said, had been a regular player for the five years that he was superintendent. Moreover, it would offer me a splendid chance to meet some of the veteran staff away from the office in relaxed surroundings. Aware of the advantage in joining and the costs to my family, I thanked the principal for the generous invitation but said no. It had also occurred to me that I would be making personnel changes and a certain amount of social distance from people I supervised might be best.

Dinner invitations proved troublesome as well. Invariably at these affairs, conversations would center on school matters and juicy political gossip. These evenings became work for me and difficult for Barbara who was immersed in completing her undergraduate degree. The last thing both of us wanted to hear on a Saturday night out was more about the Arlington schools. Except for socializing with the few friends that we had made in the county whom we could relax with and not be concerned about what we said—mainly members of the school board—we turned down most invitations after our second year in town.

We remained, however, part of the ceremonial life in Arlington. I ate chicken at boy scout dinners; sampled hors d'oeurves at chamber of commerce affairs (until I dropped out from the organization because of its persistent attacks upon the school budgets); spoke at church suppers; and represented the school board at civic meetings.

We were fortunate to have had a network of close friends in the Washington area since 1963. I could see now, in ways that I could not have seen earlier, that by entering the community as an outsider and remaining separate from existing social networks, that there would be certain costs. That was, I believe, one price we paid for being outsiders and for trying to prevent the superintendency from completely invading our home.

But, of course, the shadow of the superintendency, with all of its pluses and minuses, fell over the family nonetheless. For example, our daughters (ages ten and thirteen in 1974) were not only singled out, both positively and negatively, by teachers, they also had to deal with all of the complications of being teenagers, losing old friends and gaining new ones, and coping with schoolwork and family issues. The desire to be accepted and just like the others put a constant strain on both girls; from early on they were singled out as being different because of their father's position in the community and their religion. Active, smart, and friendly, Sondra and Janice both enjoyed and hated the attention. While some teachers were especially sensitive to the awkward position the girls were in, others were callous. Principals of the schools they attended were very understanding and tried to help, but little could be done with the occasionally insensitive teacher.

When salary negotiations heated up, for example, two of their teachers (in two separate schools) made caustic remarks to each girl about her father's lack of concern for the teachers' economic welfare. The pressures were such that our eldest daughter wanted to try another school. It proved to be the hardest decision that Barbara and I made while I was superintendent. For us, her welfare was more important than concerns over what others might think of a superintendent pulling his daughter out of the public schools. We transferred her to a private school in Washington, D.C., where she began to thrive academically and socially. Of course, the local newspaper carried an article about it. Our other daughter went to a private school for one year but wanted very much to return to the Arlington schools and did so for her high school years.

Barbara was clear on what she wanted. She did not wish to be "the superintendent's wife." She wanted to complete her undergraduate degree and enter a profession. In seven years, she finished her degree at George Washington University and earned a master's in social work from Catholic University while completing the necessary internships for a career in clinical social work. Between caring for a family, doing coursework, research papers, tests, and coping with a tired husband, Barbara had little time or concern for meeting others' expectations of how a superintendent's wife should act.

Yet, try as we might, it was difficult to insulate ourselves from the fact that I was a superintendent in a small city. My efforts, for example, to keep my family and my job separate when serious decisions had to be made often did not work. Firing a teacher, determining the size of a pay raise, recommending which schools to close, and dozens of other decisions had to be made. After listening to many individuals and groups, receiving advice from my staff, and hearing all the pros and cons from my closest advisers, I still had to make the decision. At these times, I might discuss the situation with Barbara. Often, however, there were family concerns that required our attention instead. Yet I would still come home with the arguments richoceting in my mind; and I would carry on an internal dialogue while I was eating dinner, raking leaves, playing with the girls, or on a weekend trip with the family. I was home, but I was distant.

Over the years I became more skilled at telling my family that something from the job was bothering me and that if I seemed distracted it had nothing to do with them. But I never acquired the knack of leaving serious issues on the doorstep when I came home. Some-times, escaping the job was impossible. Newspaper articles or the 11:00 P.M. television news reports on the schools entered our home whether we liked it or not.

What did stun me, however, was the lengths that some people would go for political advantage, including destroying someone's repu-tation. Elected officials, accustomed to the political in-fighting, might find such back-biting trivial; however. It jolted me and my family. I'll give one example. Shortly before the school board reappointed me for another four years, a board member called to ask if I had ever been arrested in Washington, D.C., on a drug charge. No, I hadn't, I told her. She said that there was a story that would appear in the next day's newspaper stating that I had been arrested and put in jail for posses-sion of heroin. Within the next hour, I received a dozen calls from county officials, parents, friends of school board members, and the head of the teachers' union asking me if the newspaper story were true and if there was anything they could do to help. Finally a newspaper reporter called to say that they were printing the story and did I have any comments to make. I told the reporter that there was no basis for the allegation and that before printing such a lie they would do well to get a record of the alleged arrest and other documentation. The news-paper did not print the story.

What shocked me most was the fragility of a professional reputa-tion, the willingness of people to believe the worst (this occurred a few years after Watergate), and the lengths some people would go to de-stroy someone they disliked politically.

The seven years as superintendent taught me a great deal about the mixing of public and private lives for officials like myself. More prosaic than senators who party or congressmen who resign for disclo-sure of sexual jaunts, or corrupt governors our experiences still map an unfamiliar terrain for a superintendent and family who tried to maintain privacy.

LEAVING THE SUPERINTENDENCY AND RETURNING TO TEACHING

By early 1980, two years before my contract was up and the year when my slim three-two majority on the school board would disappear with the appointment of two more Republicans, I decided that it was time to leave. While there was a chance that I could make a public battle over seeking reappointment for another term, I would ultimately lose. After all, a school board should have someone who reflects their values. The board I now served would have a majority of political conservatives whose appointments were aimed at a set of policies different than the ones I and earlier boards represented. Moreover, the county board wanted a low-profile, fiscally cautious superintendent who could keep a self-imposed ceiling on school costs, rather than one who continually asked the county board to fund expanded programs and higher teacher salaries. I came to Arlington because a new school board wanted someone who mirrored their values; now that those who were out had gotten back in, the familiar pattern reasserted itself. That was the game. No superintendent was a man for all seasons. In any case, seven years was the most time I had spent in any job in my lifetime. The shuttling I had previously done between teaching and administration was again an option.

Also, I wanted to write, think, and teach. So, in making plans for leaving the post, I applied for a research grant from the National Institute of Education (NIE) to study how teachers had taught over the last century. NIE awarded the grant in the summer of 1980 and I announced that I would not seek renewal of my contract.

In trying to recapture the meaning of the seven years I served, I reexamined the major issues in 1974 and what had occurred by 1981. Admittedly a highly personal estimate, what I wrote in my final statement to the school board concentrated on how a district, in the midst of getting smaller and culturally diverse, closing schools and fiscal retrenchment, and controversies over collective bargaining, transfers and firings, proved that they could maintain academic excellence and increase parental satisfaction as measured by conventional indicators of success. I count that as a major victory for a school board and superintendent in hard times. Of course others, particularly long-time critics, would see the 1970s in a different light.

After announcing the research grant and my departure, I was asked to apply for a number of other superintendencies. I refused. Far more attractive to me were the universities that contacted me. The idea of having time to teach, write, and think was like serving ambrosia to a starved traveler. When Stanford began its search for a professor in educational administration, the chair of the search committee called to ask if I would be interested. The answer was yes. Stanford was my first choice among the offers. In 1981 we moved (one daughter was already away at college) to California for the second time in our lives. The hope of returning to administration again, however, was still there.

A career of moving back and forth between teaching and administration is one that few can negotiate today because of restrictions on the transfer of retirement benefits, few job incentives to do so, and other barriers. For example, no reciprocity between states exists for administrators' and teachers' retirement systems. Certification to teach and administer across the states comes begrudgingly, if at all. I withdrew funds whenever I left a post and constructed my own investments for retirement. Educators who have one foot planted in the classroom and the other in the office, or those who have one foot in the university and one in the public school, remain a rare breed.

However, like fragile flowers, I believe they should be cultivated. If cultivated they can become (and I shamelessly switch metaphors) sturdy bridges between boards and instructional staff, between scholars and practitioners, between research-produced and experience-generated knowledge. They can transform issues of classroom complexities into administrative understanding. They can convert issues of professional practice into researchable questions. They can take research findings and apply them to policy issues within schools. I have found it to be the most exciting blend of thought and action, of working with adults and youth, of what can be and what is. But rigid credentialism and few career incentives hinder the growth of such paths for both teachers and administrators.

I believe in the worth of such a career path not because I and others have done it and, therefore, recommend it for all. The letters that I receive and the people who ask me how to do what I have done have convinced me that there are many teachers, administrators, and college professors who are talented, skilled, and motivated, but who are trapped by circumstances. They would seek out such opportunities if available, if such movement back and forth would produce rewards rather than penalties.

What they see in the two-way traffic between classrooms and administrative offices is the potential for extending themselves intellectually while serving others. The mix captures the sense of personal fulfillment and the hope for making a contribution to scholars, practitioners, and children. This book with its alternating chapters, on teaching and administering, on scholarship and practice, mirror the intersection between them at different levels.

REFLECTIONS ON A CAREER

In 1985 I tried to return to a superintendency. I applied for those city and state posts that I felt would stretch me while offering me the chance to contribute to the education of children. While I was on the list of finalists for five vacancies, no offer was made. I was very disappointed. The effect of applying, interviewing, waiting and waiting erodes the self-confidence and the spirit. With my contract expiring at Stanford, I decided to seek a renewal. That occurred in 1986.

Moving from the professoriate to an administrative post in a school district remains possible, but diminishes with time; however, I moved into university administration for a few years when a new dean asked me to serve as associate dean for academic and student affairs and I will return to teaching both in public schools and the university again.

This chapter and chapters 2 and 4 outline stages of my intellectual and social development which were spurred by unfocused ambition and followed by plateaus of contentment and calm, only to be interrupted by an urge to pursue something else that would stretch me. Within this erratic and episodic pattern, luck entered my professional and personal development also.

Teaching at Glenville for seven years was the longest time I held a job until I served as superintendent. In those two positions of teacher and administrator, I experienced two phases of development.[4] The first phase is survival. It asks the question, how adequate am I? I experienced this stage as a teacher at McKeesport Tech and Glenville. Can I control my classes? Do I understand the subjects I have to teach? What do I do when students ask questions for which I lack answers? Will I pass inspection when the principal visits my classes? Concerns over meeting others' expectations emerged as primary. But my major concern was: am I capable of doing this job? Concerns about whether or not students were learning were peripheral.

As I recall my experience as a superintendent, I vividly remember my first year as a survival test in which similar questions surfaced. Can I do all that the school board expects of me? The expectations seemed impossible to meet and here I was ready to take the first step. Can I understand the budget much less construct one that has my thumbprints on it? Who can I, an outsider, an agent of an activist board determined to shake the district's complacency, trust on my immediate staff? How can I juggle my drive to excel in the job with my strong desire to be a decent father and husband? I remember well those moments, particularly on frenetic days during my first year, of feeling hopelessly overwhelmed by details and expectations.

With experience comes the second phase, where issues of survival and personal adequacy give way to ones that focus on mastery and outcomes. By the third year at Glenville, I was more concerned about the ethnic content, writing and using materials, what students were learning, and assessing what contributions, if any, I was making. When the principal came into class, I no longer panicked. I urged him to speak with students or to contribute to the discussion. I felt confident enough to get involved in numerous student and faculty matters.

Similarly, by the third year of my superintendency, I had mastered the daily routines, developed responses in my mind, a repertoire for handling the inexorable crises that arose; I had placed my mark on two budgets and had taken enough initiatives in personnel, curriculum, and school improvement to last me a lifetime. By the third year, we had begun to issue an annual performance report on student achievement on the five goals chosen by the school board. My speeches and articles now incorporated issues of program impact upon students.

In my quest for intellectual survival, there was a burst of energy that was often a mix of radical and conservative practices driven by the image of the craftsman/artist and my constellation of the instructional, managerial, and political roles. Once mastery occurs (and, of course, for some it does not happen), then a period of consolidation, of polishing what works, ensues. A clearer sense of one's identity as a teacher or superintendent emerges. My hunch is that in this period of consolidation, the managerial role becomes dominant.

For some teachers and administrators, the repertoire remains untouched for years. Initiatives become routines. Why change what works? For others, unease and boredom intrude. Somewhere between five and ten years of teaching or administering in the same job, all hidden corners have been explored and the person asks, is this all there is? Is this what I will do for the rest of my working days?

Sabbaticals (where they exist in public schools) is a practical response to this early career restiveness that touches so many. To reduce the familiar and the tedious, some teachers will switch schools or grades, dump out all of their materials, go back to a university, take a year off to work in another job, or numerous other efforts of injecting iron into tired blood. They see themselves as teachers for life and treasure that identity, but they want to remain alive intellectually. Others, and I include myself, seek special teaching positions or "promotions" into administration.

Both kinds of teachers and administrators seek personal renewal. They want freshness and vitality in their lives. They, too, search for new insights and meanings. For them, a career is not a logical step-by-step progression it is a series of risks taken in forging an identity out of the raw material of new experiences. My identity as a scholar/ practitioner is one that I have created.

Sometimes one's personal life spill's over into the job. A turbulent divorce leaves a teacher little emotional energy to experiment with a different course of study; simply continuing the familiar is barely manageable. A fiftieth birthday awakes a sense of impending death and spurs an administrator to begin a project or introduce an old idea stored away in her mind: somehow she wants to leave a legacy in her school. Another burst of energy punctuates what had been a period of managerial tranquillity.

I see such uneven shifting between constancy and change in my career. Such a career as mine, however, may be atypical. Does it occur with others? I believe that it does, at least, from my experience with friends and those I have worked with. The problem is that we have so few life histories that document the images and role patterns, the spurts of energy and the periods of calm, the intersection between life-cycle events and job performance of a typical—much less atypical—teacher, principal, and superintendent. Describing my years as an educator is a start at examining the twists and turns of what social scientists call organizational socialization and adult development, but what I have come to call my life and career. It is also a beginning in wrestling with the mysteries of leadership in schools.

II

Meanings

7

From Images and Roles to Leadership

Teachers and administrators have much in common. Beyond the obvious purpose of helping children learn, a bond that attracted many into education, both teachers and administrators perform surprisingly similar roles and pursue similar images. Surprisingly, because amidst the forces that pit one against the other, that accentuate the differences between teachers and administrators, such as collective bargaining and school reforms, we often miss the glue that binds the two occupations together.

I have argued that teachers, principals, and superintendents in serving children perform the same core roles: instructional, managerial, and political. Kindergarten teacher Thelma Katz in Pittsburgh, Pennsylvania, Principal Bob Eicholtz in Whittier, California, and Ella Flagg Young in Chicago, Illinois, shared crucial likenesses in the three roles even though they worked on very different stages at different times. These different settings (classroom, school office, and district headquarters) account for why teaching in room 235 seems so different from a superintendent reviewing an agenda with the school board president, or why a principal's political decision to work with three senior faculty in securing agreement upon a new science textbook seems so different from the superintendent's having lunch with the chamber of commerce executive director prior to city council hearings on the budget. Indeed, the immediate environment of teachers differs substantially from that of principals, whose setting varies from that of superintendents. Yes, the stages are different but the processes are common across settings.

Settings vary, but teachers and administrators perform the same roles. These core roles have persisted regardless of organizational size, the district's socioeconomic status, or a person's experience or training. The particular pattern of roles for any one teacher or administrator, derives, in part, from the history of that occupation; what the various interest groups expect; that person's intentions, values, and experiences; and the target audiences within the specific setting (i.e., for teachers, students, principals, or teachers). But different role patterns, overlaid with stylistic variety and played out in sharply different settings, should not obscure the fundamental commonality that fuse teaching and administering.

Similarly, the images that dominated each occupation's history and permeated each teacher's and administrator's ideology and training share much in common. The teacher as bureaucrat/technocrat and craftsman/artist, for example, roughly overlaps the principal as bureaucrat and instructional leader; both approximate the superintendent as administrative chief and instructional supervisor.[1] These images promoted both satisfaction and guilt; they inspired and frustrated. Sometimes they merged with what occurred in a teacher's or administrator's life; sometimes they helped create realities. And sometimes they danced just beyond the reach of both occupations. Thus, between images and roles, a commonality in direction and performance emerged.

Because so much has been written by policymakers, practitioners, and scholars on the differences between teachers and administrators, the constraints that limit each, and the incompatible interests that divide them from one another, I want to concentrate on the workplace bonds that merge the two occupations. They share the same purpose, and the same yearning for good work from young people; this binds teachers and administrators together. In late May or early June, stand in the back of an elementary school's auditorium or multi-purpose room crowded with parents, brothers and sisters, friends, teachers and administrators. Feel the sense of unity when students receive awards and recognition for academic, artistic, and athletic achievements. There are no divisions, no splits into warring factions. The unity can be felt, almost touched. First and foremost, then, teachers and administrators are educators committed to a common purpose anchored in student growth and achievement. Consider further what other similarities bind teachers and administrators together.

Figure 9: Organizational Commonalities Bonding Teachers and Administrators*

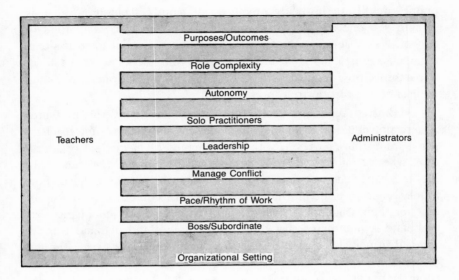

- Both occupations live in bureaucratic organizations where members are simultaneously subordinates and superiors. To the student, for example, teachers are the chief executive officers in the classroom. They assign homework, discipline students, organize lessons, and determine what is taught and when. Outside of the classroom, teachers may be required to sign in when they arrive at school, complete forms for the district office, and obey school regulations. School-master inside the classroom, and civil servant outside. Superintendents, district CEOs, who can close schools when a snow storm hits, who can reprimand employees, who can spell the difference between a promotion or demotion of a subordinate, must carry out school board orders, however distasteful, or leave their post.

Arising from this common bond are similar organizational tasks that teachers and administrators perform. Both, for instance, must supervise subordinates to determine whether the goals for the classroom, school, and district are pursued; they must evaluate subordinates to determine whether those goals are achieved.[2]

- Both teachers and administrators are solo practitioners. Classrooms are arranged both physically and organizationally to isolate teachers. Teachers, as C. B. Silver observed, have peers but no colleagues. they work alone for most of the day. Contact is minimal and frequently deals with nonpractice issues. Principals assigned to separate buildings are also isolated from their colleagues. Except by phone, weekly or biweekly meetings, or simply accident, principals seldom see one another on a sustained basis to discuss matters of concern. The same is true for superintendents. Except for occasional regional, state, or national meetings, superintendents seldom talk to one another on a regular basis. All are organizational loners, pursuing their craft in isolation from one another.[3]

• Both occupations seek professional autonomy, the pleasures and responsibilities of making independent judgments. Yet teachers and administrators wrestle with the demands of hierarchial organizations where conformity is rewarded. If teachers believe that their training and experience equip them to choose which tests to give, how much weight to place on those tests, and what content is more important for their students, they must also contend with school, district, and state requirements that limit those choices and demand compliance. If principals pride themselves on having served as teachers and having been trained as administrators, they must also contend with superintendents who possess other visions for their schools and rules that constrain their manueverability.

Furthermore, loyalties conflict. To whom does a principal, for example, owe allegiance? To the superintendent, teachers, parents, children, or their professional beliefs? Principals, for example, represent a school. They are advocates, cheerleaders for that school. Yet their duties, listed explicitly in formal job descriptions, demand that they judge subordinates' performance—a task designed to incite anxiety among teachers, the very people who determine how effective principals are. The tension caused by trying to find a satisfactory mix of being a public servant and a professional is a persistent dilemma for both teachers and administrators.

Linked to this dilemma is another tension arising from lay citizens determining policies for professionals. The governance of public schools established lay control over professional judgment. Doctors in Veterans Administration hospitals, city lawyers, and the joint chiefs of staff all cope with the dilemma of experts being told by nonexperts what policies to pursue. For teachers and administrators, they also grind teeth while trying to accomodate policies and regulations that challenge their expertise.[4]

- Both occupations are caught in a net of contradictory expectations and incompatible demands that produce conflict. Among the crosscutting expectations of the school board, superintendent, principal, and parents concerning what should happen in classrooms, teachers must also insure student compliance to achieve classroom goals, while motivating them to learn. In doing so, students' aspirations and needs enter into the tacit bargaining that teachers and students engage in to maintain tolerable levels of interest, free of disruptive tension.

Similarly, for principals to manage, amidst the conflicting demands of the district office staff, superintendent, school board, and parents, they must juggle those expectations while insuring that teachers' opinions are heard. The risk of conflict confusing daily routines is everpresent. The stability is so fragile that bargaining with subordinates, juggling demands, and balancing incompatible interests occur continually to keep the external noise within acceptable limits for those that do the work.[5]

- Both occupations enjoy considerable similarity in the pace, volume, quality, and nature of daily work. Teachers, principals, and superintendents experience a workday marked by brief exchanges, disjointed and unfinished activities, unpredictability, varied tasks, and constant talk. They are busy people who rush through a day of intense activity with both children and adults. Time available for reflection is rare. Establishing routines brings a semblance of order to the day, but teachers and administrators know that those routines will be interrupted by the unexpected.[6]

Finally, both teachers and administrators share the magic of leadership. The word *magic* is intentional because it refers to the mysterious, the unknown and that which has magnetic appeal. To take the argument to where I can make the case that leadership is inherent to the act of teaching, principaling, and superintending even though a managerial imperative embedded in schooling depresses its potential, I need to outline the steps that initially led me to make the claim.

ROLE COMPLEXITY, CHOICE, AND AUTONOMY

The following argument that both teachers and administrators are potential leaders is constructed from a series of propositions, some theoretically derived, some empirically produced, and some drawn from both. The propositions are as follows:

1. School district organizations, characterized by a high degree of loose and tight coupling, adapt their structures and processes to a changing, turbulent environment in order to maintain stability; these adaptive organizations contain formal structures and processes that are both connected to and disconnected from what happens daily in schools and classrooms.[7]

2. Within these organizations, teaching and administering are marked by a high degree of role complexity.[8]

3. From role complexity arises conflict and choice.[9]

4. Choice is the "seedbed of autonomy"; autonomy is an essential prior condition for leadership to occur.[10]

Each proposition deserves elaboration. What follows is a brief summary including examples.

School District Organizations, Characterized by a High Degree of Loose and Tight Coupling, Adapt to Their Environments

Budgetary uncertainties, demographic changes, the entrance and exit of key actors into school affairs, shifting state policies suggest an unpredictable environment that districts cope with through organizational adaptations. Placing contingency funds in a budget, embracing current innovations in order to appear modern, establishing school improvement committees enlisting vocal critics, leasing or selling closed schools when enrollments shrink are instances of school districts and schools trying to introduce certainty to unstable situations.

The organizational adaptations, however, spread unevenly. Amidst the stretched links, there exist some formal structures and processes that are tightly connected. For example, constructing bus schedules or doing certain business tasks, such as purchasing, making bids, paying vendors, or hiring staff, are instances of where standard operating procedures produce visible outcomes with a fair degree of reliability. At the school level, principals *do* respond to district controls governing budget, personnel, and pupil behavior. For such rule-driven functions, there is a high positive correlation between intentions and actions.[11]

But these are support functions for the central tasks of a school district: teachers teaching and students learning. Are these tasks tightly linked? Not very much. In instructional supervision, for example, few superintendents have a fairly clear picture of how any one principal is performing as a manager or instructional supervisor based upon direct observation or verifiable information. Within a high school faculty of 75 to 125 teachers, few principals know what happens in either a physics teacher's or remedial reading teacher's class. Many teachers go unobserved by administrators for an entire year. Supervision (i.e., observations, conferences) is largely perfunctory and divorced from improving daily practice. If ties are stretched thinly between supervision and inspection of schools and classrooms, imagine what few connections there are between a principal's formal evaluation of teachers and superintendent's assessment of a principal's performance.

The connections between the district curriculum and what occurs in classrooms are similarly attenuated. A tightly coupled curriculum and instructional program directed from a central office may appear in directives and brochures closely tied to classrooms, but this seldom occurs in practice. Unobserved and seldom evaluated on such matters, teachers exercise discretion by default in making curricular choices.

Still, such distinctions fail to capture the complete mix of tight and loose couplings that occur in school districts. Within a school system, for example, there may be a school or a central office in which the shared values, rituals, and informal norms produce a subculture that ties janitors, teachers, secretaries, and administrators into a tightly knit work group, quite different from an adjacent school or department.

School district organizations characterized by a mix of tight and loose coupling (particularly around the central functions of schooling) nonetheless adapt to their settings and thereby maintain a roughly hewn stability amidst changing conditions.[12]

WITHIN SUCH ORGANIZATIONS, TEACHING AND ADMINISTERING ARE MARKED BY A HIGH DEGREE OF ROLE COMPLEXITY. Performing the three core roles makes teaching and administering complicated. Each role contains behaviors that range from the obvious to the subtle. Veteran practitioners develop repertoires for each role; neophytes wrestle with tough instructional, managerial, and political decisions daily. What further magnifies this complexity is the silent (and, on occasion, noisy) partners that teachers have in carrying out their work. Children, colleagues, principals, central office staff, superintendents, parents, and citizens all contribute either tangibly or indirectly to what teachers should and actually do. Their material support, their opinions, their perceptions count in varying degrees. None can be ignored.

The teacher is in charge of the classroom, for example, but without the cooperation of students, little can be accomplished. While teachers are isolated from colleagues most of the workday, their opinions of each other are important. For the teacher, the principal is a critical partner in terms of supplies, support in disciplining students, and buffering from parents. The teacher may never see the superintendent in the school, but that influence, however weak or strong, highly or lowly regarded, is still noticed.[13]

Similarly, for the principal and superintendent, beyond the three core roles they discharge, each has a set of partners that influence what they do daily and to whom attention must be paid, even though these partners are seldom visible. For principals, what complicates their work are such partners as children, teachers, custodians, secretaries, central office staff, the superintendent, parents, board members, and colleagues. For superintendents, the circle encompasses an even larger set of partners, including district office staff, noninstructional staff, teachers, principals, citizen interest groups, and state and federal officials.

What entangles the set of expectations further is that among teachers, principals, and superintendents are professional norms, derived from training and experience, that generate additional obligations. A teacher, for example, faces district regulations that specify the number of units and lessons that must be completed by the end of the semester. Yet that teacher may be sorely troubled by a sense of professional duty to the half of the class that will never complete the content. Should the teacher simply plow ahead with the prescribed units? Slow down and reteach the content? Develop new materials so slower students can catch up? Principals and superintendents also must finesse organizational directives that hinder their sense of professional obligation. All of these expectations, generated by subordinates, professional obligations, and organizational demands permeate the concept of role complexity.[14]

From Role Complexity Arises Conflict and Choice. Because each partner occupies a different niche in the organization, the perspectives differ and expectations for what the teacher or administrator should do vary. A teacher, for example, sees thirty very different individuals; the mother sees only her daughter, Alice, who has a mild handicap and needs special attention. The superintendent sees a computer-generated bus schedule that picks up and delivers 7,000 students twice daily; the bus driver sees a tightly scheduled daily run that prevents her from getting the contractually agreed afternoon break. The principal listens to a student who claims that the teacher turns back homework that is unmarked or barely commented upon. The teacher explains that the school's new homework policy, instituted by the principal in response to the new superintendent's concerns about the academic excellence, requires that he grade so many papers each week that he cannot keep up with it.

Disturbances result. Each partner believes that his perspective is correct, and his expectations of the teacher or administrator are legitimate. Alice's mother complains to the teacher that her child receives inadequate attention. If nothing is done, she will go to the principal. The bus driver files a grievance against the superintendent. Students circulate a petition to alter the principal's policy on homework. Incompatible obligations emerge daily from the very structure of schooling. These conflicts within each post are inevitable; they are the genetic material of schooling.

The inexorability of conflict arising from so many role partners and the performance of three complex roles also offers each teacher and administrator choices. No one can satisfy all or even most of the expectations. Choices must be made to cope with the disturbances that arise daily. While such crosscutting obligations can paralyze action, teachers and administrators who endure in the occupations have learned to choose.[15]

Consider the teacher who tells the student who has just come to him for help to come back another time since he has to finish a report that the principal wants immediately. Or a principal who shows up late for a meeting with the superintendent because she had a conference with a teacher about a student, which, she says, came first. Or the superintendent who chooses to give a plaque at a high school assembly honoring a veteran teacher rather than chair the Kiwanis meeting where the mayor will be speaking. Thus, what at first glance appears as an impossible set of obligations for any teacher and administrator to meet becomes, at second glance, a set of choices—some rational, some intuitive, some planned, and some spontaneous—each involving trade-offs and producing a "seedbed of autonomy."[16]

CHOICE IS THE "SEEDBED OF AUTONOMY." Creating room to make independent decisions from the impossibility of satisfying all demands—external and internal—constitutes what I call a marginal autonomy. How does a narrow zone of independence emerge?

Initially it arises from the inescapable fact that no teacher or administrator can satisfy the multiple and incompatible demands placed upon them. Thus, choices must be made as to which expectations will be satisfied. But the freedom to act also arises from other organizational facts; all the partners of the teacher, for example, have different degrees of interest in what occurs (i.e., the student's interest is immediate; the superintendent's is distant). Moreover, each partner is more or less influential in affecting what the teacher and administrator does. The superintendent knows that the school board, not the local taxpayer association, evaluates his performance for contract renewal. A principal may listen more carefully to what the PTA president says about a teacher than what a student says.

Finally, not all the partners are in a position to directly observe what teachers and administrators do each day. Aside from occasional visits from a principal, few adults voluntarily enter a teacher's classroom; principals will see the director of special education, or the chief custodian, or a district office curriculum supervisor on occasion. An infrequent school visit from the superintendent usually is a whirlwind tour that lasts a half-hour.

Thus, the divergent interests that each partner has in the performances of either teachers or administrators, the varied influence that each has, and the insulation from direct observation all accumulate to yield discretion for determining which obligations to meet and which expectations to ignore. Even within conflicting expectations and organizational constraints that limit what teachers and administrators can do, a marginal autonomy emerges.[17]

To use the independence they construct out of conflicting expectations, teachers and administrators basically have four choices available (with infinite variations among them):

1. Conform to some expectations and not to others: that is, teachers and administrators choose which expectations are legitimate obligations to be met and which ones are illegitimate or can be safely ignored, although the cost will need to be calculated. Determine the source of the expectation and the level of influence associated with it. Calculate which have penalties attached or missing that would require some action or none. In brief, discriminate among expectations.

2. Construct some compromises that try to conform to as many of the expectations as possible. Go to the least common denominator: placate many; offend few.

3. Avoid conforming to as many of the expectations as possible.

Resist expectations that run counter to one's dominant beliefs, values, and experience.

4. Do nothing.[18]

A small district superintendent, for example, entangled in salary negotiations with ninety-seven teachers in a three-school system faces the competing expectations of his school board, teachers, principals, parents, the taxpayer's association, and what he believes is best for the children's and the district's welfare. He could adopt the school board's expectations (and those of the taxpayers' association) to hold the line on salaries and use the funds elsewhere; or the superintendent could align with the teachers (and a faction of parents anxious to avoid a strike) who expect him to fight for higher salaries; or he could try to negotiate a salary settlement that would be less than what the teachers ask and more than the school board wants to give; or, finally, the superintendent could go to the board, declare an impasse and ask the board to negotiate directly or hire someone else to do it for them.[19]

This example, of course, is relatively simple in the array of incompatible expectations. However simple, choices must be made. The superintendent, constrained as he is by state and district laws, the local culture, available funds and what beliefs, experience, and values he brings to bear on the decision, nonetheless has a marginal autonomy to act.

On what grounds does a teacher or administrator choose? To those conscious of such choices, they begin by determining which expectations and obligations are legitimate, which have sanctions tied to them, and which they believe would advance their personal and organizational goals. Much, however, depends on the perspective that each teacher or administrator has about the organizational world within which they work. Their perceptions and beliefs crystalize to form a view of what can or cannot be done. Within this perspective, calculations are made. Consider a principal who is expected by the district office to execute the contract with the union just as it is written. The principal, caught between dependence upon teacher good will and district office requirements, seeks flexibility. So a principal in this situation who sees the work world as a set of unbendable rules that must be complied with, rules that provide little or no margin for give and take, will deal with teachers who wish to grieve a clause in the contract differently than a principal who looks upon the contract as a set of opportunities to achieve what is desirable for both teachers and students.[20]

Decisions blend facts, values, beliefs, perceptions, and experiences. Those decisions and the actions taken in their wake become the marginal autonomy available to teachers and administrators, which is a necessary (but not sufficient) condition for leadership.

LEADERSHIP

What is organizational leadership? Defining the ineffable—love, jazz, leadership—intimidates many. Turning to scholarship is little help. If Eskimos have seven different names for snow because of their familiarity with it, social scientists have given many more than seven names to *leadership*. As Warren Bennis said, decades of analysis and thousands of studies in this century have produced more than 350 definitions of leadership but no "clear and unequivocal understanding as to what distinguishes leaders from non-leaders." Elsewhere he offers a clever but cryptic distinction between a manager and a leader: a manager does the thing right; a leader does the right thing.[21] Football player Red Grange spoke of the elusiveness of defining the undefineable when he was asked to explain how he evaded tacklers as he threaded his way toward the goal line.

> I can't explain it or take credit for it. You can teach a man how to block or tackle, run or pass, but you can't teach a man how to run so tacklers can't tackle him. No one ever taught me and I can't teach anyone. If you can't explain it, how can you take credit for it.[22]

I do not wish to contribute further to the confusion. How, then, do we, in spite of the conceptual anarchy that infuses the notion of leadership, apply something clear and plausible to teaching and administering? Acknowledging the complexity in the range of meanings attached to the concept is a beginning. Leadership in organizations is considered to be associated with but not confined to managerial functions (e.g., a corporate executive officer; the commander of a bomber; a bishop in the church; a nursing supervisor on a hospital floor). This view has encouraged researchers to explore a broad range of issues such as personal traits of those designated as organizational leaders, styles of managerial behavior, the clusters of roles they play, perceptions of followers, and the tools that managers use to initiate and execute change.[23]

Research results and practitioner enthusiasm for this direction have encouraged the view that there is a science of management; that leaders can be identified, selected, and trained; that leadership is central to organizational work and essential to shaping events and outcomes.[24]

Leadership is also viewed as a relationship within a process of getting things done; that is, a way of organizing followers and manipulating settings to produce desired results. In this view, having a vision, harnessing the energies of followers to that vision, and using language and symbols to cultivate commitment among followers are essentials in a process that is far closer to an art than a managerial science. (Such diverse people as Martin Luther King, Jr., John F. Kennedy, Green Bay Packer's Vince Lombardi, IBM's Tom Watson have all worked magic on their followers.)[25]

To some social science researchers, leadership is also viewed as an exaggerated phenomenon that is largely ineffectual in the face of the turbulent, unpredictable environments that ultimately shape an organization's structures, processes, and outcomes. In such organizations, where goals are ambiguous, where power is distributed widely within the organization—not located in the boss's office—decision making seldom follows chapters in management texts. In such a perspective, leadership is at best a minor activity, closer to theatrics than scoring touchdowns or getting machines out the door into the salesroom. Such researchers label the ideal of controlling both organizational resources and subordinates' behavior as superstition. In a vivid metaphor coined by Jim March, such a leader is a driver of a skidding automobile.[26]

Related to this view is one in which some argue that leadership is how participants and observers connect managerial actions to organizational outcomes; what is called leadership, then, is a perception constructed by others to make sense and give meaning to what occurs. For example, what turned Chrysler around was *not* Lee Iacocca; it was the policies of Lee Iacocca's predecessor, a set of economic conditions that convinced legislators to bail out the automaker, and an economy that improved shortly after the federal government rescued the corporation. These factors more than the individual actions of a corporate executive who had a knack for self-promotion created the results for which Iacocca has taken credit. To make sense of the Chrysler "miracle," observers and media forged links between the actions of the chief executive officer and the increased auto sales and the swift payoff of federal loans. They concluded that the top executive made the difference.[27]

Such social science views have yet to penetrate the larger culture. The shared view among lay people and practitioners is that leadership means individual action, controlling the unpredictable, and bringing certainty to uncertain conditions. Heroic rather than prosaic images—John Wayne not Gomer Pyle—lend a romantic aura to the concept. Including this value-laden, heroically endowed view of leadership, helps to further map the intricate topography of the concept but gives little guidance in selecting from diverse views, views that describe leadership in scientific and artistic terms, deny its potency in organizations, or suggest that it is merely an artifact created by observers.[28]

While I hold no heroic view of organizational leadership, leadership often comes about by chance, accident, or unanticipated events, I nonetheless believe the phenomenon called leadership can play a small but significant part in influencing organizational direction and outcomes. In the interest of full disclosure, I label this belief as faith, not fact.

How, then, to construct a plausible concept from among the competing views in order to apply the concept of leadership to teachers, principals, and superintendents? Findings from empirical research offer little guidance. Researchers, in their quest to understand the complexities of leadership, have splintered the notion into fragments to be isolated, studied, quantified, and made more objective but have yet, like Humpty-Dumpty, to be put back together again into a concept recognizable to both practitioners and researchers.

What helps somewhat is the simple cultural fact that leadership is widely believed to exist. Organizations exist with formal positions steeped in the expectations of leadership. People who aspire to these organizational positions believe in their hearts that they can lead. More important, followers expect those who serve in such posts to lead. The bond between shared beliefs and expectations, then, becomes real; it exists in the minds of both the leaders and the led, regardless of what some researchers claim. It may be heroic; it may be exaggerated; but it is part of the social reality surrounding organizations. Dismissing the perception as romantic, embellished, or even unscientific ignores the power that such beliefs exert in motivating individuals to achieve personal and organizational goals.[29]

Hence, the prevailing cultural beliefs that organizations must have leaders and that such leadership accounts for the victories and defeats form a concept understood by practitioners and policymakers, although some researchers may wince. The phrase *organizational leadership*, then, refers to people who bend the motivations and actions of others to achieving certain goals; it implies taking initiatives and risks.

This familiar restatement of common beliefs is holistic, consistent with dominant perceptions and broad enough to suggest that leaders exist at all levels in an organization and that many people are capable of leadership. Whether the terms are empirically true or even testable as hypotheses is less important to practitioners and policymakers (but infinitely crucial to researchers) than the pervasiveness of shared beliefs that come to make "organizational leadership" true in its existence as a shared perception.

Are teachers, principals, and superintendents who have a marginal autonomy and who make choices potential leaders? Yes, because they occupy organizational positions in which others expect them to lead. But to answer the question fully, I need to elaborate further on the familiar perception and apply it specifically to each occupation in its unique setting. What helps is that a number of organizational theorists have conceptualized leadership in terms akin to the shared cultural perception.

Chester Barnard, a New Jersey Bell Telephone executive in the 1920s and 1930s, Philip Selznick, organizational researcher, in the 1950s, and James McGregor Burns, political scientist, in the 1970s, argued that the following must be accomplished by those who would act as organizational leaders:

- Imagine what the organization can become; define a mission and set goals that embody that vision.[30]

- Motivate and harness followers' energies toward achieving goals.[31]

- Link the mission to organizational routines.[32]

- Promote and protect certain values that give an organization a distinctive character.[33]

- Produce desired outcomes.[34]

This synthesis of cultural beliefs and particular elements of social science research into arguable propositions is the basis for my applying a concept of leadership to teaching and administering. The leader improvises and routinizes, creates and disrupts, imagines and plods, sets fires and puts them out, aggressively acts and docilely follows. Leaders, then, judge when to maintain the status quo, when to enhance the bureaucratic, when to invent, and when to improvise. They combine the technical and the moral.

I will argue that common leadership expectations and behaviors create a bond between teachers, principals, and superintendents and their classrooms, schools, and districts. Many teachers and administrators use their narrow zone of discretion to act as leaders at different points in their careers; others do so to lesser degrees, and many not at all. Moreover, among teachers and administrators who act as leaders, no single style captures what they do. A variety of personal styles and strategies mark what occurs in classrooms, schools, and districts.

I will argue that the context (organizational and environmental) exercises substantial influence on the degree of success that teachers and administrators have in both the execution of their duties and whether or not they achieve desirable outcomes.

I will argue that teachers and administrators who lead may alter existing arrangements or strengthen current ones. Those who induce change may be just as much leaders as preservers. The teacher or administrator who fights doggedly to maintain what is believed to be precious and imperiled is as much a leader as those who try to alter the organizational landscape.

I will argue that leadership at one level in a district organization affects what occurs at other levels. Many big city superintendents in the 1980s, for example, anxious to demonstrate their high regard for students' academic performances on standardized achievement tests, used the organizational levers at their fingertips to influence principals. Instances of competency-based curricula, harnessing test results to student promotion and failure, and linking principal evaluation to achieving district goals for instructional performance suggest that those in the middle of the hierarchy (i.e., principals) are closely monitored. Their discretion shrank. These principals, in turn, frequently narrowed the zone of independence available to their teachers through a constant presence in classrooms, monitoring measures of student performance in each class, and close supervision. The constriction of autonomy in districts such as I have described affects what principals, teachers, and students can and cannot do. Also note that teachers may limit a principal's actions, and principals may, in turn, limit a superin-

Figure 10: Organizational Leadership: Elements, Relationships, Settings, and Outcomes*

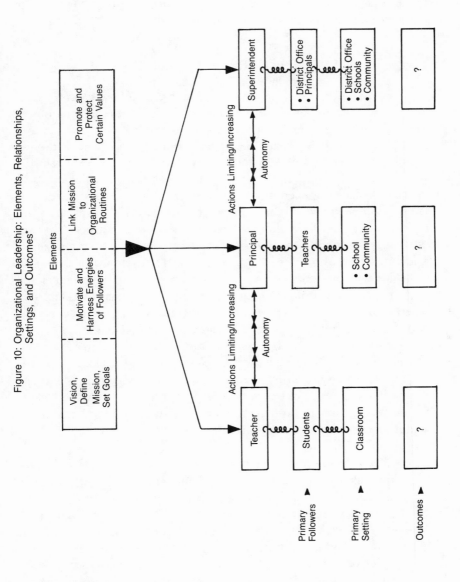

tendent's actions. I offer this example only to illustrate the cumulative and interactive effects of how leadership actions at one organizational level constrain or expand the actions of those at another level.[35]

But all of this seems so general and disconnected. In an attempt to tie images and roles to leadership tangibly, I turn to vignettes of teachers and administrators who have led.

TEACHERS AS LEADERS

The descriptions of particular teachers that follow capture many but not all of the elements of leadership. I offer these illustrations as examples of how a few teachers weave the three core roles into a verbal tapestry that reveals in the foreground a class and a teacher against a background of role complexity, autonomy, and leadership.

These are, however, far from complete portraits of teachers as leaders. What happened to these teachers three years or a decade later, I do not know. I do not know whether career changes, personal trauma, or tedium have altered these teachers or whether they persist in what is described here. Hence, they only present a brief glimpse of a few teachers who infuse the elements of leadership into their relationships with students and seek chosen outcomes in a particular setting at a specific time. Whether they achieved these outcomes or whether what was achieved can be attributed to what the teachers did is beyond what either I or these illustrations can conclude.

Finally, I offer them because so little has been written of teachers as leaders. Many more references to classroom leadership appeared in the mid-nineteenth century than a century later. If Horace Mann and Henry Barnard spoke of teachers as leaders, Ellwood P. Cubberley and James B. Conant (and other prominent twentieth century educators) seldom mentioned leadership and classroom teaching in the same sentence. But a few did.

Willard Waller had a chapter in *The Sociology of Teaching* called "Teaching as Institutionalized Leadership" in which he examined teachers' authority and power when dealing with students. More recently, in a journal for practitioners, David Berliner described such "executive functions" of teaching as setting objectives, communicating expectations, and structuring work. He likened a teacher to a corporate executive practicing the art and science of management. Never using the word *leadership*, Berliner listed many of the elements that I included above.[36]

For whatever reasons, the link in the early decades of public schooling between teaching and leadership and the unabashed use of the word *leadership* eroded and the closest connection between teaching and leadership seemed to be high-level managerial skills.

Thus, I wish to resurrect a forgotten vocabulary of teachers as leaders that existed well over a century ago. In losing those notions, we may have lost the capacity to imagine teachers as classroom leaders, especially for the 1980s when the deficits of teachers are noted and improvement efforts seldom employ the language of imagination, innovation, and initiative. To reconnect the notion of leadership to teaching revives a vital tradition. These vignettes begin that task.

Eugene Cain, 1970

From a class composed of mostly black students studying Afro-American history taught by Eugene Cain, a black teacher at Cooley High School in Detroit, Michigan, comes a transcript of a discussion on nineteenth century slave revolts.

> *Cain:* If we look at the classical definitions, we would have to say the revolts led by Denmark Vesey, Gabriel Prosser, Nat Turner turned out to be failures. But we're gonna have to look beyond that. These revolts demonstrated—what?
>
> *Student:* That black people were not going to accept being slaves without some kind of resistance, you know. . . .
>
> *Cain:* Let's bring it on home to 1970. Are there things you all think about? Is everything just okay with you; everything breezin' along? What is it you're uptight about?
>
> *Various Students:* The educational system. Checking ID cards. Law enforcement, primarily the police department. The war in Vietnam.
>
> *Cain:* Now I've asked you all this because what's involved historically as well as now is the question of authority, the question of who determines who is gonna do this, that and the other. That's what you're telling me. Now, as a group of students, what power do you have [to change what you are dissatisfied with]?
>
> *Students:* None. The power to protest. We can think about it and figure out something to do, etc.
>
> *Cain:* Do you think these persons, Prosser, Vesey, used their power effectively? Or did they have any power? Remember, the slaves were in the majority in Virginia at the time of Nat's revolt, and in Charleston

at the time of Vesey's. Now let's go back to what Charles said before
that in order to take effective steps you must be organized. Now
when ol' Tom [slave informers who alerted whites to the various
rebellions] came and spilled the beans on these other guys, Tom was
not dedicated. In terms of his makeup, he was consistent. He didn't
feel he needed an organization. This dude could see how he was
getting along. And he was gonna use this primarily as an opportunity
to get closer to his master and say, "Well, look at them out there. I
don't have to undergo the same kind of punishment that these other
guys. . . . If I'm close to the master, what's affecting them won't
affect me. . . ."

Now, Vesey's solution to the problem was armed revolution. Carl,
what's your solution to the war in Vietnam? [No answer]. Del, what
is your solution to the educational hang-ups? [Del's answer is vague
and general]. Now, Charles said before that organization is necessary. He comes to you and me, Shirley, and says we got to organize
some pickets, do this, do that, come up with some political demands or what-have-you. Would you be game to go along with him?

Student: Yes, if I could be sure that a lot of other people would too.
[Laughter in class]. What can I do by myself?

Cain: Say! That's a good question. I can't answer that by myself.
And I also want to raise the question: Should you be concerned
about overall numbers or dedication to the cause?

[The discussion shifts back and forth between the police, poor
schools, white and black heroes in history books. As time for the
class to end approaches, the teacher gives the assignment.]

Cain: Now, the paper we're taking home, will you kindly read it?
We'll be discussing, primarily, the methods used by Nat Turner to
liberate his people.

And I don't think any of you should go out satisfied and feeling as
though we've solved any problems or what-have-you, but these are
things in which you should constantly use your reason. You should
constantly question the things you are subjected to, and not only
question but come up with some sort of reasonable and rational
manner of solving problems.[37]

Author Philip Sterling interviewed Cain and his wife at their
home. In their living room, where poster-size portraits of black heroes
adorned walls, Cain described growing up in Birmingham, Alabama,
and his college years at nearby Talladega College during the early years

of the civil rights movement. He participated in sit-ins at the local pharmacy and the Trailways bus station, and helped organize a boycott of the white merchants who supplied the college. He attributed his interest in black history to a college adviser, a Nigerian, who prodded him to examine his history. His great-grandmother, still alive at the time, was an exslave. Sterling asked Cain about his views on teaching and education.

> The word "education" implies change. To be educated is to be more or less reborn. My job as a social studies teacher is to look at our society with complete emphasis on the need for change. I care less for what-in-the-hell they did fifty, sixty, seventy years ago. Although I do believe that kids need historical references to relate present to past ideas, to see how archaic they were and are. . . .

> We shouldn't tell them about the Constitution: "Man, the thing is beautiful." In an ordinary civics class, when they say that, they're talking about structure. I care *less* about structure. I'm concerned about *process*. This is why I go to no end to find my material and present it in my classroom. . . . We've had to argue back and forth on some of these issues. I've read them some case histories of the use of police power and some of the white kids didn't believe this stuff actually happened. So I took the kids downtown to [police court]. They came back and said: "Gosh, there's no justice down there, Mr. Cain. It's just like you were telling us." I said, "Okay, I was showing you what the deal is. Now, what are you going to do about it?" I wasn't expecting an answer, but I didn't want those kids to forget the *question* I was raising. I believe that their role should be to realize the need for social changes, you see.

Sterling asked about his relationships with students. Cain went on to explain his views of teacher-student relationships.

> The kids—these are my friends. They call up: "Hey, what are you doing?" and come over. . . . They come by for constructive things. And if they want to hear Blood, Sweat, and Tears, the Beatles, or James Brown, fine . . . and we can sit in the classroom, too, and talk about that. Yet and still, we can learn regardless.

> I feel as though teaching goes beyond the classroom. The wife (who teaches at a junior high school) and I have had a little campaign for about two years. Anywhere some kids want to go on the weekend, if we aren't busy, we take them. We've been to basketball games, baseball games, concerts. They got to go out and get the ticket money.

We supply the gas and the chaperones. She'll try to borrow a station wagon and I'll get my car.

Cain took out a drawerful of student photographs with inscriptions to Cain on the reverse side.

- "You are one person who isn't afraid to commit himself. Many students will remember you for that."

- "If all the teachers were like you, there wouldn't be any drop-outs."

- "One of the hardest but nicest teachers a person could have."[38]

Vera Milz, 1980s

Milz teaches first grade in a Bloomfield Hills, Michigan, elementary school. She began teaching in the early 1960s in a school district using a Dick, Jane, and Sally reader: "Look, look! Run, run! See, see!" In the assigned workbooks, students had to search each page for words beginning with a certain letter. By the end of the third year of teaching she saw that she was not helping all the children and was falling short of what she wanted to achieve. She felt frustration for the students who could not master the look-say approach and annoyed with the limits of the materials for those students who already knew how to read.

On her own she took courses on reading at nearby universities, visited schools, and educated herself on different approaches to teaching primary students how to read. When she visited British schools during the height of the open school movement, she was intrigued with how five and six year olds wrote in notebooks and the relationship between writing, reading, and thinking. Slowly she began to develop a view of how first graders could become readers, thinkers, and doers through writing. By this time she had taken a position in the Bloomfield Hills District, a Detroit suburb. She told Ken Macrorie how she began this connection between writing and reading in the first few days of school.

> I usually put out a lot of books as I'm getting the room unpacked. I'll show them some of the books we're going to be using and some of my favorite stories. I'll also point out the mailbox in the room where they'll be able to get mail from me. And I tell them that I have a

mailbox and when they want to send notes to me they can put them in there, and I'll read them by the next day.

Not every child is going to bring me in a note. I never say to them, "You must write me something." However, usually by the first day of school I can say that my children are already writing to me. Several will come in clutching little notes they've written to me. Some have asked their parents, "How do you write this? How do you spell this?" The notes may be very conventional: "Dear Miss Milz. It was nice to meet you. Love, Caroline." One child will come in with a picture with a name written at the bottom, while another may say, "DEER MISS MILZ, I LK U, LV, TED.

At the end of each school day I clean out the mailbox and then the children get notes back from me the next morning. These notes provide a personalized reading text for each child. We both write to suit our own needs and purposes. If they need a menu for meals in the lunchroom, or something like that, they'll put notes in the box for me. If I have to be away from the classroom or if I'm out sick, I'll come back to many notes saying that they've missed me. This letter writing often continues beyond the school year. Some children now in high school I still communicate with.

Usually, during the first week of school I give each child a notebook and ask them for a dated entry. If it comes in at the end of the day, I can read it after school or that evening. Some children will draw pictures, and others will write quite a bit. They'll use Invented Spelling, so that they may write the word *car* and spell it *kr* yet they are already beginning to draw relationships with the conventional print in books.

Macrorie wanted to know more about her approach, which she called "Whole Language Learning" or learning within a social context.

This is different from teaching children first a letter, then a sound, then a word, and expecting they'll put all the words together to make meaning. I want my students to read the whole world around them. Reading is not just connecting a number of words. As a reader, I don't take a bunch of words and string them together into something that makes sense. As I talk to you, I say things to create a *meaning* so you understand my message. I want to help children do this from the beginning.

To make this point, Milz told Macrorie of the nine year old boy who transferred to her class with a record that stated he could not read at all. He had failed repeatedly in the other class.

> I asked him to write me about things that he liked. "Tell me about
> your house. What is your bedroom like? What's your favorite toy?"
> One story he wrote was about his dog. Up until then he had showed
> no progress on any reading test. By the end of the year he showed
> six month's growth in reading. He had been considered a total non-
> reader. People who came to my class were floored at the changes in
> that second-grade boy. He had been so negative. He felt really bad
> about himself. How he's a child who's excited about reading.

Milz felt strongly about the importance of not only writing from
children's experience in order to learn to read but she also stressed the
importance of reading aloud.

> Too many teachers fail to read aloud regularly to their students. With
> my first graders I read picture books that carry few words and also
> thick books that are all words. I'll read maybe for five or ten minutes
> and then put the book aside or go back to later. . . . Some of the
> books I choose, the kids can't read by themselves and others they
> can. I introduce them to books they never would hear of otherwise.
> When I begin a school year I read stories by one author. By the end
> of the first week my first graders have appeared in the media center
> or public library and said, "I want the books by so and so"—the same
> author they've heard me read in class.

Milz uses reading and writing across her entire first grade curriculum. In trips to nature centers or for science experiments, the content
becomes a tool for further reading and writing. Similarly, for math,
history, geography, and the array of ethnic and national holidays that
first graders experience, each become opportunities Milz exploits to
integrate reading and writing. When asked by Macrorie about the
standardized tests that her first graders have to take and whether her
students are learning, Milz answered:

> How are my children doing in reading? Standardized tests can't show
> that fully. For one thing, they fail to take children's logic into consid-
> eration. Standardized tests don't recognize such things. And in them
> there's no place for one of the girls in my class to put down that in
> one year she has read three of the Laura Ingalls Wilder books at an
> age when many children in conventionally taught classes are reading
> nothing but primers. Likewise a child who loves books but may be
> at a point of struggling to learn to read may be labeled a failure by

the test. I learn a lot by listening to children in the act of reading, and I also observe what they're reading when they're away from me in the classroom.

When I think of evaluation, I know that if I wasn't doing something right, if my children weren't reading and writing, these parents would have a legitimate concern. But my children are enjoying reading and writing. They're learning and growing. They can begin to evaluate their own language learning. . . . For example, I've been in this school now seven years. Sometimes I've had a first grader who is now in the fifth grade. His younger sister is in my present first grade. The older child still has his journal, and the little one brings her first one home. The older one says, "I used to write just like you did. You're really coming along."[39]

Eugene Cain and Vera Milz capture the elements of classroom leadership outlined earlier. They melded these elements into unique relationships with students, producing outcomes that they found desirable. Many of their students enjoyed being led. Orchestration and invention rather than precision marked their efforts; the inexact vocabulary of human relationships rather than tested principles of behavior emerges. Closer to an art form than a science, nonetheless, the techniques of handling materials, people, and content are evident in what these teachers do daily. Their teaching styles differed. Their visions (in which their values were embedded) differed. The school level, subject matter, and student populations differed. Yet they possessed the common elements of classroom leadership.[40]

Note, however, that these snapshots captured what occurred at one moment in one setting. I have no idea whether the leadership portrayed here continued throughout their careers or faded within a few years. If we had career histories of these teachers, supplemented by direct observations of their classrooms over time, we could be more confident about whether such leadership behavior is stable, contingent upon setting and personal circumstances, or other factors.

Based upon my research on teachers and superintendents, my experience as a teacher and administrator, I lean toward the contingency view of leadership. I know teachers who have hit peaks and valleys in their careers when leadership behavior was strong and then weak. When a teacher with a vision alters the existing classroom and works intensely to create that vision (e.g., an open classroom, an individually guided math class, using ten computers in an English room three times a week)—thereby playing out the political and instructional roles with great fervor—then he or she will shift into a managerial mode to keep the vision operating. Over time, as one class follows another, the vision decays, the familiar procedures gain prominence and the teacher slips into routinely managing the classroom. I saw that happen to me at Glenville. But my limited research and experience are insufficient to make anything more than an informed guess, or, at best, an argument.

Familiar images and roles emerged in these vignettes. These teachers cherished notions of being craftsmen/artists; they avoided the language and actions of teachers as bureaucrats/technocrats, although they acted as competent managers in achieving their aims. They seized discretion and acted. In performing the three core roles the dominant patterns appeared to be instructional and political, with the managerial role instrumental in making things happen. The moral vision each had of what their students ought to be permeated classroom activities. It provoked changes in old routines while establishing new ones. That vision, of course, heavily personal in both political beliefs and values, drove (to the degree possible within the constraints in which they worked) the choice and disposition of classroom organization, tasks, pedagogy, and materials.

Are Milz and Cain unique? No. Other teachers perform as classroom leaders at different points in their careers. Books by teachers Sylvia Ashton Warner, Herb Kohl, James Herndon, Eliot Wigginton, Kim Marshall, and other teachers suggest that a larger population exists, generally unobserved but occasionally recognized in newspaper articles or teacher-of-the-year awards. Unrecognized teachers occasionally appear in research studies. Shirley Heath, for example, records the activities of rural and small town teachers in the Southeast who coped with the demands of desegregation by becoming learners and classroom leaders. These teachers drew heavily on the backgrounds of black and white students in their communities to construct a curriculum and pedagogy tailored to these students' strengths and what the school required. They are not in the majority, however. Why that is the case, I will take up in the last chapter.[41]

PRINCIPALS AS LEADERS

There are principals who enact instructional, managerial, and political roles to create independence amidst the organizational constraints surrounding the school. Francis Hedges is one.

The brief description that follows illustrates many of the elements cited earlier. I offer it as another instance of how a principal blends three roles to create a measure of autonomy. This description falls far short of a full portrait of a principal as a leader. It is drawn from published sources that recorded one moment in a particular setting. No one yet knows whether Hedges continued her pattern of leadership or not. This is not a career history. The vignette describes an elementary school principal who displayed these elements of leadership, and infused them into teacher and student relationships in a unique setting as she sought her results.[42]

Francis Hedges, Principal of Orchard Park Elementary, 1982.

The names of the sixty-year-old black principal and the San Francisco bay area school are fictitious. The student body was predominately minority (black 59 percent; Asian 16 percent; Spanish surname 13 percent; white 11 percent, whose socioeconomic status was either low-income or lower middle-income. The school had twenty-five teachers, most of whom were teachers with more than five years experience; five teachers came to Orchard Park just to work with Hedges.

Hedges had been at the school for just over six years. Prior to that she had been a classroom teacher in the district for twenty-one years. She earned a master's degree in educational administration and took a series of positions that ultimately landed her the principalship: reading teacher, program coordinator, and vice-principal. As principal, teachers often found her to be "motherly." She was friendly, smiled often, hugged and embraced both children and adults. Liberal with praise, she often congratulated students and teachers for their achievements.

She was also a strict disciplinarian who spent much time in the cafeteria, corridors, and on the playground during recess, unhesitatingly scolding students when they misbehaved, while also finding time to listen to them. When a serious incident occurred, Hedges would tell a student that she would call his parents. With the student there, Hedges would ring the home or work, put the student on the phone to explain what had happened and why the principal had called. Students viewed the principal as someone who meant what she said.

In the cafeteria, she would ask students to take their trays when they were finished, and on occasion, she would pick up a few that were left and dump them herself. In the corridors, she made sure that students came in the proper entrance, did not run through the halls, or scream. One morning, a boy ran and yelled. Hedges stopped him and warned, "You better start the day on the right foot." Students frequently clustered about her when she toured the playground, asking her questions, telling her of incidents in classrooms. One small girl tugged at her dress and said, "Mrs. Hedges, these are my new clothes." The principal smiled and said, "Oh, you look so nice today."

To Hedges, cultivating social responsibilities in students meant their knowing clearly what the boundaries and expectations were. Within those limits, she would praise them for their good behavior. Often she modeled the behavior she demanded: picking up paper in the corridor; bussing trays in the lunchroom. She wanted order without uniformity; she wanted children and adults to feel responsible and be taken seriously:

> I believe that if we are really going to change behavior of children, we can't just say, "stop that, ah, don't do that," without going a step further and really having some kind of dialogue about what took place, why, and what are the options.

On more than one occasion, she would take students who were in trouble repeatedly and assign them tasks in the building that would, in effect, contribute to the school. For example, Hedges made a few feisty boys become student captains in the auditorium. They had to select other students and together they would set up and take down folding chairs when there were assemblies. On other occasions, student violators of rules would be given a wastebasket and told to pick up playground litter.

She emphasized strongly to teachers the importance of making children "reasonably happy" in school and enhancing their self-confidence. "Some people don't have the same feeling about the humanistic aspects of schools," she said.

> Some teachers are, feel that they are, purely academic and that "my job is to teach the children and I don't have to get into that other area at all." My philosophy is that if we are warm and humane and nurturing, we maximize the learning of children. There is just no way to separate out those basic needs. They [the teachers] don't separate them out in their world . . . so I try to show them that, if as adults we have those needs, then our boys and girls have those human needs also . . . and with warmth and nurturing they'll do better.[43]

Intertwined with these beliefs in the psychological and social development of children is her stress on academic achievement, particularly reading. "I believe that if children don't know how to read they really cannot make it in this world."

> We work hard to try to make sure that in the six or seven years that boys and girls are in elementary school, that they leave this school operating at grade level or above. . . . I'd like to see them at grade level for at least their last two years so that they can go into junior high school as much stronger and more confident children.[44]

Converting beliefs into action, Hedges hired and gave unconditional support to the school's reading specialist, especially when she came under fire from some teachers for placing children in groups at too high a reading level. Hedges endorsed the specialist's decisions.

As with reading, Hedges played a critical role in curriculum. The principal allowed teachers a great deal of independence in choosing materials and instructional tactics. Although she preferred many of the student-centered approaches that would give children discretion to make choices, she also encouraged teacher-centered strategies since she knew that some students needed the structure more than others. Still, she did not miss a beat in drumming up support for her goals and beliefs. She had collected lessons and units on increasing students' self-esteem and had teachers use the materials. When the district mandated a three-year plan of school improvement, Hedges coordinated the writing of the plan and placed her thumbprints all over the document. Her involvement in the curriculum, instructional program, school organization, and physical plant was pervasive.

Hedges directly hired teachers that she wanted and placed them in classrooms at Orchard Park where she felt students would benefit from their presence. She discovered funds and opportunities for teachers to further develop their skills. She assigned students to classes and closely watched their progress by checking with teachers and the reading specialist. She actively participated with the teacher committees in selecting textbooks. Once she arranged with a district office supervisor to pilot social studies books just to secure more texts.

While academic performance, as measured by standardized tests, had been improving steadily, she was concerned about low test scores on the math section of the standardized test. She met with district office staff to figure out ways that teachers and students could improve math achievement. She often visited classes to observe students and teachers. For example, when she visited a substitute who would be taking a regular teacher's class for a month, she saw that the sub had divided the class into two groups. Hedges found a seat next to a boy who was reading to one group. When he finished, she praised him for his reading well. In the other group, the principal helped a girl who labored on a worksheet. Just before the bell rang, she told the entire class how well they were working and how proud the regular teacher would be when she returned.

The principal's relationships with teachers were cordial and firm. They knew where she stood on curricular, instructional, and disciplinary matters. On curricular matters, Hedges actively participated in discussions and encouraged teacher decision making. As one teacher stated:

> Curriculum is developed first of all within circuit meetings [committees of teachers from grade clusters; i.e., K–2, 3–4, and 5–6]. Mrs. Hedges attends about 98 percent of these. She's considered part of the circuit and she adds her ideas and influences. She listens to our ideas first. That's where . . . what is good for the grade levels is reported to the staff and we discuss one another's ideas and then we develop the curriculum from that.[45]

Hedges involved teachers in school-wide decisions through a faculty council that met periodically. She knew that the steadily improving academic achievement of the students was due to the teachers' hard work. So, she protected teacher planning time, prevented, wherever possible, district office paperwork from eroding instructional time, and frequently praised teachers for ideas, lessons taught, and classroom displays. When the district office announced that Hedges was to move to another school, the teachers (and parents) signaled their respect and admiration by organizing a protest to keep Hedges at Orchard Park. She stayed.

Here is a brief description of a principal with a coherent set of beliefs about children's social and intellectual development and teachers' professional growth who maintained order, established stable conditions for instruction to occur, and steered a course that teachers endorsed. She enacted the core roles through daily, small, mundane acts rather than grand gestures, rhetoric, or grandstanding. In persistently exerting competence through a thousand tiny decisions, she made her presence felt. Not to gain personal recognition, Hedges sought to guide and encourage individual growth in children and adults while creating a clear sense of community and providing a direction for the school.

Frances Hedges, Betty Belt, Norris Hogans, and Bob Eicholtz took many of the elements of organizational leadership outlined previously and blended them into a unique set of relationships with students, teachers, and parents. Their styles of principaling differed; each valued particular outcomes more than others; school level and student populations varied. Yet they possessed in common these elements of organizational leadership.

As with the teachers, generalizing beyond these vignettes is risky. What goes on now at Orchard Park, Oakridge, Pioneer, and George Washington Carver Comprehensive High School, I do not know. Nor do I know intimately the history of each of these people. Whether leadership is something constructed out of unique circumstances, ebbs and flows over a particular lifetime, or transcends time and place cannot be determined by these illustrations.

If generalizing about organizational leadership from these brief descriptions is risky, the familiar images and roles common to teachers and administrators still emerge. Principals like Hedges, Belt, Hogans, and Eicholtz pursued images far closer to those of instructional leaders than bureaucrats. However, the image of the principal as instructional leader is more focused at the elementary level, where principals Belt and Hedges worked, than in the high schools, where Eicholtz and Hogans constructed the mission, set the goals, but delegated instructional tasks to trusted subordinates whom they monitored. In short, from the welter of conflicting obligations drawn from students, teachers, the district office, and the community surrounding the principalship, these principals fashioned an area of autonomy to achieve desired ends. Their visions of what their schools should be were translated into scores of routine activities.

The dominant roles they played were instructional and political, although the managerial role was crucial in converting ideas into routine practice. They taught by modeling the behavior they prized. They arranged conditions for improved instruction. Making all of this happen, the infusing of vision into prosaic tasks, of giving meaning to the mundane, became a political process that sought the desirable amidst unrelenting constraints and resistance. Managerial expertise, knowing how to structure tasks and carry them through, became essential in lubricating the political process. The entire configuration is called organizational leadership.

Are these principals unusual. No. There are many such school leaders (often unrecognized), yet they do not represent the majority. Roland Barth, Leonard Covello, and Lucianne Bond Carmichael in such diverse districts as Newton, Massachusetts, New York City, and New Orleans, Louisiana, wrote about their years as principals. Descriptions of Marcus Foster at Philadelphia's Gratz High School, Robert Mastruzzi at New York City's Robert F. Kennedy High School, Robert McCarthy at Brookline High School outside of Boston, and Elliot Shapiro in a Harlem elementary school suggest that many such principals led schools.[46]

The perplexing question of why most principals seldom use the residual autonomy embedded in the post to lead schools is one that I will take up in the final chapter. I now turn to superintendents.

SUPERINTENDENTS AS LEADERS

There are superintendents who use the three core roles, amid the entangling constraints surrounding every school district, to create independence and act like leaders.

Bob Alioto illustrates how a superintendent uses three roles to establish autonomy and lead. This description falls far short of a full picture of a superintendent since it is drawn from published sources written at a certain time in a particular setting. No one knows whether Alioto performed like this before he came to San Francisco or since.

Robert Alioto, 1975–1985

With the forced resignation in 1967 of Harold Spears after a twelve year tenure, the San Francisco Board of Education proceeded to hire and fire four more superintendents. In 1975 they sought a new superintendent.

Representing the city's various ethnic groups, this school board was split over such contentious issues as desegregation, declining enrollments, inadequate funds, school buildings in need of retrofitting under the new state law on earthquake safety, and, of course, ethnic balance among employees at every organizational level. This divided school board presided over a district enrolling over 60,000 students with almost 8,000 employees. The annual budget exceeded 180 million (1978). Into this turmoil and political instability Robert Alioto applied for the superintendency in 1975 along with ninety-three other hopefuls. That summer the board of education selected Alioto (on a 5 to 2 vote). Successive boards renewed his contract on unanimous votes until the early 1980s, when again split votes occurred.[47]

Alioto climbed the customary career ladder: elementary teacher in rural California; principal and later superintendent of a two-school district in Napa, California; an advanced degree at Harvard where he wrote a dissertation on the superintendent's role in collective bargaining; superintendent in Pearl River, New York, a seven-school district, and a move to Yonkers, New York, a district with forty schools. After four years there, he applied for the position in San Francisco. In a career trajectory familiar to many superintendents, Alioto had reached the pinnacle of his career at age forty-four.

"I have the reputation of a son of a bitch and it's deserved. What's more I don't apologize for it," Alioto told a reporter in one of his first interviews after being appointed to the San Francisco post. In Yonkers he had reduced the number of tenured administrators by 25 percent. "When you find someone who is not doing his job then your job as superintendent," Alioto told the reporter, "is to help the person improve. If he is unwilling or unable, then you have the obligation to take him through the due process machinery and terminate him." Told that some associates have described him as arrogant, he said:

> Yes, I can understand that. But they misinterpret my commitment for arrogance. The staff will find that I listen and implement on the basis of staff recommendations. I don't have a magic cook book with quick recipes for solving all of the problems—only commitment.
>
> I'm committed to doing what's right for kids. Sometimes that means I make decisions that are not very popular. Those are only made when I am convinced by my best professional judgment that they are necessary to do a job for youngsters.[48]

Asserting that he leans heavily upon accountability and management, he stated: "I believe in a business approach. School systems for too long haven't had any management and have let resources slip by." When asked about the split board and the history of a swinging-door superintendency, Alioto replied:

> Regardless of the vote, I expect a great deal of unanimity on the board. I wouldn't have accepted this position if I was not absolutely

convinced the board is ready to work cooperatively with me and support the superintendent in the exercise of the prerogatives of his office.[49]

Within two years, Alioto had reorganized the central office, brought in outsiders, demoted others, moved principals, and produced the single major reform of his decade-long tenure, Project Redesign. Project Redesign was an omnibus reform that provided for desegregation, closing of some schools and the opening of new alternative ones, a realignment of grade levels in elementary and secondary schools and curriculum improvement; Redesign became the centerpiece of Alioto's program for bringing stability to a school district jolted by crisis after crisis since 1967.

While Redesign would influence the entire school community insofar as shifts in attendance areas, the mixing of students, more parental choice in selecting schools, the shifting of teachers and principals, it was primarily an organizational change rather than a curricular or instructional reform. By rearranging people and programs into both politically and economically efficient clusters (i.e., creating middle schools and alternative schools to retain middle- and upper-income parents; heading off further desegregation litigation while coping with existing lawsuits), Redesign became the major vehicle for altering the larger organizational arrangements and demonstrating that the school board and superintendent had put the schools on a stable footing. However, few subsequent planned efforts of the magnitude of Redesign were directed at altering what occurred in schools and classrooms while Alioto served as superintendent.

What follows comes form an unusual study of the year that Alioto spent in moving Redesign toward adoption by the board of education. Alioto agreed to have John Feilders, a Stanford University graduate student, shadow him for three months. The dissertation and subsequent book, *Profile: The Role of the Chief Superintendent of Schools*, are unique contributions to the literature on superintendency. I draw from that study for a brief description of what Alioto did.[50]

In the course of a fourteen-hour day, in the midst of getting Redesign approved by the board, Alioto spent over three hours working on the proposed reform's details, talking with board members, district office staff, and parents. As days go with superintendents, this is a very large chunk of time to spend on one project. He did it a little at a time: an hour with a board member, individual conferences with staff, phone calls, and quickie meetings in corridors or in his office. He also visited the two chairmen of the Redesign Task Force where responsibility for working out the myriad details of Redesign (i.e., school closings, openings, shifting students in line with ethnic quotas, and so on) occurred. Finally, he went to the "war room" where an assistant worked to anticipate the expected public opposition to Redesign and develop a strategy to communicate the details of the reform to grease board and community acceptance of the plan.

Alioto knew clearly what he wanted: a comprehensive reform that would introduce sufficient organizational change to bring stability to a troubled district. He also knew that the political climate of San Francisco was such that careful attention had to be paid to daily details, relationships, and group interests. Hence, the unusual amount of time spent in the fourteen-hour day to Redesign.

This eye for detail, relationships, and group interests turned up repeatedly. Alioto spent over one-quarter of his time listening to, speaking with, and attending to board members' concerns. On the particular fourteen-hour day, a few board members, including the black chairman expressed concern over the omission of black teachers from an agenda item paying teachers for summer curriculum work that the superintendent had submitted for that evening's meeting.

Once off the phone with the board members, Alioto met with staff sporadically over the day to find out where the list came from, how were names selected, who made the choices, and why. He found out that his associate superintendent for instruction, John Cleveland, who was also responsible for working with the black community, had produced the list. At a strategy meeting with staff on curriculum matters that afternoon, Alioto entered the room, stopped next to Cleveland and asked:

> "John, what good is it to have a Black Associate Superintendent and have unhappy Blacks in the community? Why aren't you more active in representing them? . . ." John does not reply. Uncomfortable seconds pass. Then suddenly the door swings open and (another staff member enters for the meeting). [Not too long afterwards, Cleveland left his post.][51]

On another occasion, Feilders described a meeting Alioto held with a group of parents angry over the Redesign proposal.

With the help of his key staff members, he prepared to meet the parents by reviewing their complaints, memorizing statistics, and shaping his responses. Then he requested that at the meeting his senior staff join him at the head table to diffuse the effect of the questioners and critics and to show solidarity. He also decided where to set up the table. "I don't want us on a stage. Put the tables and microphones at the same level as the parents." He added, "Have one of our people chair the meeting, not one of theirs." Aides handled the other logistics—the car, driver, the door the superintendent would enter, the seating arrangements, and the police protection.[52]

The busyness of the day was unforgiving. Alioto rushed from one activity to another. Except for an occasional lunch with a trusted associate (where he also absorbs and dispenses information), Alioto seldom relaxed. Quite often he is invited to speak at private business or civic luncheons. These are additional opportunities to deal with details, relationships, and group interests as he sells the schools.

Frequently at luncheons he inventoried the fiscal, administrative, and academic achievements of his tenure. He would mention school mergers to deal with shrinking enrollments, early retirement plans for teachers and administrators, and a plan to create a purchasing unit independent of city hall. Interspersed with these points demonstrating district efficiencies, he would refer to the latest test results that showed improvement, proposals for revised teacher and administrator evaluations, more alternative schools and his idea for a half-hour nightly of compulsory homework.

> Each item [Feilders writes] of his educational program derived from a broad administrative concept that marginally related to actual school and classroom concepts. But to Alioto the items were more than mere rhetoric. "If I thought that I could not affect students," he says, "there would be no reason to be here."[53]

According to Feilders, Alioto questioned the research that suggested a superintendent was only marginally connected ("loosely coupled") to the classroom. Alioto believed that he set a tone in the San Francisco schools. Moreover, in such specific programs as a uniform basal reader for all schools and compulsory homework he felt that he affected daily classroom practice.[54]

Alioto did visit classrooms. He toured schools two or three times a month, dropping in briefly into various classrooms. He met monthly with all school principals and individually for special problems. When

Feilders counted up the time he spent daily on student problems and educational programs (mostly administrative tasks surrounding the testing program and scores), he found it to be 12 percent of his time. Alioto admitted to Feilders that administrative work blocked him from "being more productive out in the schools."[55]

Project Redesign was approved by the board in 1978. In succeeding years, as board members entered and exited the scene, relations with their superintendent remained cordial, marked by great respect for Alioto's achievements in bringing managerial and organizational stability to the district. However, by the early 1980s, more and more board members criticized Alioto for his inattention to curricular and instructional matters, his working a four-member majority while ignoring others, and his increasing independence. After months of open bickering between the board and the superintendent, in the early hours of a July morning in 1985, the board of education voted 4 to 3 to fire Bob Alioto.

Here is a glimpse of a superintendent who believed deeply in his power to shape what happens in classrooms yet spent most of his time with the school board, district office staff, and members of various constituencies inside and outside the district schools. He wanted to make the schools more efficient and effective than he found them. His mission was to bring order and direction to what appeared to be an anarchic, rudderless school district.

Alioto did bring organizational stability to a strife-torn district that had earned a reputation as a graveyard for superintendents throughout the late 1960s and early 1970s. In doing so, he performed the three core roles in a district with a preference for the political. Through mastering the details of San Francisco school politics, he conceived and managed a district reorganization that brought both change and stability. Unmanaged conflicts that had previously torn apart the district and larger community came under a modest degree of control. In a thousand tiny managerial decisions, he made his presence felt at the district office and in the schools (but seldom in classrooms). He had an unerring feel for the symbolic, for what language and what signs touched people's fears and hopes. He knew how to get things done that he prized.

Ella Flagg Young, Frank Cody, Carl Hansen, Paul Sakamoto, and Bob Alioto took many of the elements of organizational leadership and produced their unique synthesis. Their personalities and styles of superintending differed; each valued particular outcomes more than

others; student populations varied. Yet they possessed these elements
of organizational leadership in common.

As with teachers and principals, generalizing about superintendent
leadership beyond these descriptions is risky. No career histories of
superintendents exist. The enigma of whether leadership can be transferred from one setting to another by the same person continues to
puzzle researchers, although it doesn't stop football and baseball team
owners from seeking out coaches and managers who compiled win-
ning records elsewhere. The evidence here is too fragmentary to go
beyond my purpose, which is to illustrate how superintendents
brought the various elements into play.

If generalizing about organizational leadership is impossible from
these vignettes, I still can point to the emergence of historic images in
the three superintendents' performances of core roles. These superintendents varied: if Young, Hansen, and Sakamoto came closer to the
instructional supervisor image, Alioto embodied the administrative
chief conception.

Young, Hansen, and Sakamoto, with such different personal
styles, saw curriculum and instruction as the central tasks of the district. While they necessarily delegated tasks to subordinates given the
size of the operation, they nonetheless saw themselves as administrators who had to give direction and vision to principals and teachers.

Alioto who cared deeply about improving what occurs in classrooms, also believed that an efficiently managed bureaucracy that focused attention on getting things done would, in the long run, benefit
students. Find out who is not doing their job, get the right people, and
let them do what had to be done. He viewed himself as a tough, fair
manager who could identify the problems, construct solutions, find
capable people and shake up a district organization to get it moving in
the right direction. He took initiatives and risks. No instructional
leader, he was nonetheless a political one.

All three superintendents, of course, performed the core roles,
but in different patterns. Alioto and Cody performed the political and
managerial roles most prominently with instruction occupying a small
part. Young, Hansen, and Sakamoto enacted the instructional role
most obviously, yet also performed the managerial and political roles
prominently since the latter ones made it possible to achieve the visions embedded in the instructional one.

By virtue of the organizational niche that superintendents occupy,
all had to be enablers, that is, people who got others to share a moral

vision of what schools can be and then construct the conditions under which that vision can materialize. Through astute use of language, of personal example, of time, of publicizing special moments, and of investing the routine act with meaning, they not only shaped events directly these superintendents helped others get necessary tasks done.

Here again, as with teachers and principals, superintendents found themselves heavily constrained by incompatible expectations and obligations. Yet amid these conflicting crosscurrents, these superintendents had perspectives that nourished a can-do attitude. Rather than seeing a "no" behind every request, they saw sufficient room to manuever, enough space to work and to act as leaders. They transformed their mental images of what their districts could be into prosaic policies and routine procedures. They motivated subordinates and sought desired outcomes.

Are there other such superintendents? Yes. Many have been described in the past: John Philbrick, Ella Flagg Young, William Maxwell, William Torrey Harris, Ben Willis, Harold Spears, and scores of others. From the current generation, Alonzo Crim (Atlanta, Georgia), Floretta McKenzie (Washington, D.C.), and hundreds of other unrecognized school chiefs in urban, suburban, and rural districts, could be identified. They do exist at particular moments in time, but they are not in the majority.

Like teachers and principals, most superintendents hew closer to the image of technocrat/bureaucrat and enact most prominently the managerial role. Not for an entire career, of course; I suspect that over the course of one to three decades, teachers and administrators act as leaders from time to time, but as the years pass eventually slip into a familiar managerial groove that becomes comfortable given the inexorable constraints within which they daily work.

In the final chapter, I consider these constraints on the exercise of leadership—what I call the managerial imperative—in more detail and the implications of the entire argument that I have made thus far for practitioners, policymakers, and researchers.[56]

8

Summary and Implications

Even though teaching and administering today are viewed as separate jobs, since the origin of public schooling both occupations have shared dominant images and core roles that merge the two positions *de facto* into one career, that of educator. Certainly not a novel argument since earlier generations of practitioners and policymakers acknowledged the common purposes of the career, still it is an argument that is less evident, less familiar to a current generation anxious to improve the practice of schooling. The acceptance of separate unions and different agendas is thoroughly fixed in the minds of both lay and professional audiences. Yet common images and roles bind the two occupations together regardless of what reformers, academics, and union leaders say or write.

These dominant images of what teaching, principaling, and superintending ought to be like have reflected larger social forces and the emerging interests of each occupational group. Thus, the pervasiveness of the image of educator as bureaucrat in the classroom or administrative office mirrored frequently the larger social impulses toward greater technical efficiency and increased school productivity. Similarly, the moral view that educators ought to cultivate the best in children reflected the insistence of teachers and administrators that they required much discretion, free of bureaucratic restrictions. These images seldom appeared and disappeared in sequential order. They were present since the origins of public schooling; they were, and are, woven into the fabric of education, stitched together in uneasy patterns just under the surface.

The daily behavior of teachers and administrators emerged from a mix of the images school folk sought, the demands of close and distant partners, the self-generated obligations, the organizational arrangements that shaped the workplace, and, not to be ignored, the choices they made. From a distillation of this blend emerged the three core roles.

The instructional, managerial, and political roles fundamental to teaching and administering produced a common set of tasks performed in very different arenas. These complex core roles tied together teachers, principals, and superintendents, generating in each conflict and autonomy, while creating dilemmas of choice. From choice, arose the potential for leading others. But lead toward what? And how? Here the dominant images of teaching and administering intersect with the core roles. The instructional and political roles played by teachers and administrators contained within them their visions, their hopes for what students and adults should be. Through performing the three roles, educators tried to convert what ought to be into what is.

Yet evidence drawn from numerous studies over the last century have repeatedly shown that a managerial imperative dominated most schools and districts. Most teachers and administrators, over time, mirrored more the technical than the moral image. Leadership occurred (as the ample number of examples cited in the previous chapter suggests) but appeared sporadically and unpredictably. Why?[1]

Answers to this question and the question of (why some teachers and administrators deviate from the dominant managerial pattern and act as leaders) will begin to suggest *possible* implications for policymakers and practitioners interested in altering the press toward the managerial among teachers and administrators. I underscore the word *possible* because this book, while anchored in research and personal experience, is an extended argument in which a number of statements have yet to be tested. What follows is a first attempt to fashion some plausible answers.[2]

WHY DO MOST TEACHERS AND ADMINISTRATORS MANAGE?

Origins of the Positions

In considering teachers, recall that historically they have faced two fundamentally difficult tasks: getting a group of children who must attend school to absorb knowledge, skills, and values deemed acceptable by the community; and ensuring that the class's behavior is mannerly, orderly, and, in general, meets the community's minimum behavioral requirements. Hence, getting children to learn and behave was a high priority for teachers from the first day of class. Managing classrooms, then, was central. Moreover, in organizing a class for instruction (i.e., grouping students, preparing materials, and arranging activities), a teacher always had an eye and ear cocked on the implications for student behavior. Worksheets or group discussions, one group or three groups, quiet time after recess or a boys versus girls game influence classroom order. Never far from the conscious attention of any new or veteran teacher, controlling student behavior while organizing for instruction pressed teachers toward a heavy and sustained emphasis on the managerial role.

The initial rationale for establishing principalships and superintendencies was to have subordinates of the school board perform clerical and administrative tasks. Teachers lacked the time to discharge tasks that affected the entire school, from building maintenance to thrashing unruly children. Such obligations had to be met. As decades passed, such tasks persisted and multiplied as the mission of schooling incorporated broader services to both children and the community (e.g., day care, preschool programs, bilingual education, special services to handicapped children, free lunches, and so on). Hiring clerical and administrative aides reduced somewhat the work load, but the need for managerial oversight persisted.

Also for principals and superintendents, the mission of maintaining order in schools and in the district seldom shifted in importance; it remained central to the community's definition of satisfactory schooling. As organizations established to carry out political ends with the young, classrooms and schools had a central, well-focused function: controlling groups of people to accomplish certain social ends. From the beginnings of each occupation, then, managing assumed a large chunk of time and attention from both teachers and administrators.[3]

Socialization and Training

Except for the priesthood, no other occupation involves almost two decades of informal apprenticeships. From kindergarten through high school, from teacher education to student teaching, from the first classroom job to becoming a principal, from one administrative post to another before appointment to a superintendency, decades pass within different classrooms, different buildings, different offices, but the same institution. Teachers and administrators have spent all but the first few years of their lives in schools watching people practice their trade both expertly and ineptly.

The subtle and obvious absorption of norms and expectations, of habits and beliefs, tend to conserve what is rather than seeking what can be. The tendency to take moderate or high risks, to begin new ventures, or to invest high energy into prized initiatives is low. The dominant bent of those who view the system as filled with steel-lined rules and policies that block new ideas is to comply. Compliance and loyalty produce an orientation toward keeping things as they are. Hence, a leaning toward the managerial.[4]

For administrators in particular, advanced training, especially since the 1920s, incorporated a strong managerial orientation under the influence of the Cubberleys, the Thorndikes, and other administrative progressives. State certification policies tightened further the concentration on efficiently administering schools and districts by requiring courses on finance, facility maintenance, and personnel management. The cumulative effects of socialization, graduate training, and daily experiences encourage teachers and administrators toward the managerial.[5]

Multiple and Incompatible Expectations

The structure of the workplace and the history of each occupation beseiges both teachers and administrators with conflicting demands from individuals and groups to whom they must pay varying degrees of attention. Rather than repeat much of what I have already argued concerning teachers' and administrators' role complexities and how autonomy can emerge from crosscutting demands and obligations, I argue that these contradictory expectations generate an inescapable conflict that requires constant attention.

The need to be on top of things, to have what Jacob Kounin calls "with-it-ness", to prevent a slow-burning brush fire from erupting into a fiery blaze that might disrupt relationships drives teachers, principals, and superintendents to prize routines and activities that maintain organizational stability. The glue that holds the classroom, school, and district together amid the centripetal force of competing demands is administrative tasks. Thus, the managerial role is salient for many teachers and administrators as a conflict-reducing strategy.[6]

Uncertainty in Determining Effectiveness

Faced with multiple and conflicting obligations, teachers and administrators have a tough time deciding not only when they are successful but why. If a teacher feels that students enjoy the class and they are learning, that in no way means that the principal (or superintendent) assesses that same teacher as effective. Parents' delight in a principal who skillfully maintains the school's curriculum and organization may offend teachers who believe the same principal to be ineffective in gaining faculty support for school-wide changes. For a superintendent, does improved SAT scores mean superior performance? Extra lines in the local newspapers? A contract renewal? How many school board agenda items are approved unanimously? Working sixty hours a week?

The criteria, measures, and standards in judging teacher and administrator effectiveness are varied, incomplete, and contested. Moreover, proving that what a teacher or superintendent did caused desired or detested outcomes exceeds the science of measurement, further complicating any judgment of effectiveness.

There is, however, general agreement concerning one task as a measurement of success: management. For a teacher, one looks to see if the students are orderly, working on assigned duties, proceeding through the text, all within a classroom arranged to convey purpose and efficiency. For a principal, one makes sure that the school is clean, the halls are clear, the students and teachers comply with district regulations, schedules are made and kept, and scores of other administrative activities are completed. For a superintendent, one checks for a balanced budget, whether principals and teachers follow procedures, whether personnel are hired and fired without fuss, and whether decisions are made tidily and expeditiously. Thus, focusing on managerial work provides a common yardstick for both teachers and administrators (as well as for all their partners who peek over their shoulders) to use in assessing effectiveness.[7]

Convenience

Within the current structures of schooling, it is simply easier for many teachers and administrators to concentrate on routine managerial tasks and maintain stability than risk increasing the level of conflict and further uncertainty that arises from introducing changes. By "easier" I do not mean that a person works less intensely, puts in less hours, or malingers. By "easier" I mean dealing with less conflict, expending less energy, creating a sense of control over an uncertain, very complex enterprise be it a classroom, school, or district.

A teacher who chooses to alter organizational arrangements (e.g., create novel materials for students; move to a contract plan rather than customary group assignments; use small group instruction most of the time), will invariably have students and parents who will find the changes a joy and those who will find them a disaster. Conflict occurs. A principal determined to increase teacher supervision through frequent classroom visits finds some teachers enthralled with the attention and others thoroughly intimidated. Conflict ensues. A superintendent who works toward reducing class sizes to below twenty students per teacher in the primary grades finds strong support among elementary but not secondary school teachers, among some parents but not others, and a school board split over the value of the policy and its funding. Conflict erupts.

So, it is far easier for teachers and administrators to focus on the managerial, on keeping things as they are rather than altering existing arrangements.[8]

These reasons are plausible. They are rooted in history and the potent influence that workplace structures have upon behavior. In no way, however, do they exhaust the universe of explanations for why most teachers and administrators spend the bulk of their time on managerial activities. I offer these reasons for the managerial imperative to stir the reader to speculate about their persuasiveness and especially to consider possible consequences.

I can suggest a few organizational consequences of the managerial imperative. The press toward maintaining existing structures, norms, and relationships assumes that what is present is better than what can be. In some settings, this assumption is both appealing and preferable (e.g., pressure for fiscal retrenchment during a recession). In other settings (e.g., swift demographic changes in student population), it can hinder action. The drive toward the managerial offers little incentive to look ahead, to respond to environmental changes, and more important, to see emerging problems in their entirety.

Furthermore, workplace structures in which teachers and administrators find themselves not only shape managerial behavior but also produce a fragmented view of problems. Frequently teachers see the "problems" of schooling and their solutions in narrow terms of individuals: if I could only get rid of those three troublemakers from my class;

if I had a more supportive principal; if parents in the community did a better job with their children. The same is true for principals and superintendents who frequently define problems in individual terms or more of the same resources. In short, hierarchial, fragmented, and complex work settings cultivate splintered, narrow, and incomplete framing of problems and their solutions.

The result is ad hoc, constricted problem-defining. Problems are broken into tiny parts that can be easily managed by individuals isolated from one another (i.e., teacher problems, principal problems, and so on). Thus, the managerial imperative is enhanced further by viewing solutions in narrow, individual terms rather than broader, organizational ones. These consequences, I believe, are both subtle and real.

But in trying to understand why most teaching and administrative behavior is managerial and its potential consequences, I don't want to be diverted from pursuing a more important question: What explains the existence of teachers and administrators who, in doing all the managerial work, somehow go beyond it and act as leaders? This question is crucial because answers may suggest that far more potential for school improvement exists in what teachers and administrators do daily, provided (and here is the catch) that policymakers focus on altering the basic designs of schooling to tap hidden sources of leadership.[9]

INVESTING MEANING INTO THE MUNDANE: WHY SOME TEACHERS AND ADMINISTRATORS LEAD

Although managerial behavior is the norm (and one that is essential for maintaining stability in formal schooling), leadership occurs more frequently than believed, is often hidden from public view, is largely unexamined by researchers, and, on occasion, is stunted by policymakers who enforce their views of what administrators and teachers should do.

Teachers, principals, and superintendents develop, over time, visions of what classrooms and schools should be. Rooted in their beliefs, experiences, and values, these visions (their political perspectives), harnessed to a core of managerial skills and a willingness to use some discretionary time, infuse the routine acts of teaching and administering with instructional meaning. By "routine acts" I mean the daily duties that teachers and administrators ordinarily perform, such as goal setting, planning, organizing work schedules, deciding who gets what and when, monitoring activities, assessing the quality of work, verbal and nonverbal exchanges, and scores of other low-profile, prosaic tasks.[10]

Within the organizational constraints and crosscutting obligations in which teachers and administrators find themselves entangled, those who lead construct patterns of leadership anchored in the mundane.

Moreover, I argue that there is no one best way of leading in a classroom, school, or district. No simple formula conveys the diversity in context, style, and goals that mark teachers and administrators as leaders. Leadership, to those who seek a formula, may be even more confounding in that it is seldom transportable. A first-rate suburban sixth grade teacher may last a few months in an inner-city elementary school, for example. Or a big city high school principal working in a small, affluent suburban high school may find that what worked previously is no longer applicable.

Finally, such leadership exists in many classrooms, schools, and superintendents' offices. By no means a majority, nonetheless, there are many mainstream teachers and administrators who act as leaders quietly and unobtrusively at different points in their careers. Partial evidence for these claims, I have offered in the vignettes of teachers, principals, and superintendents. These illustrations were incomplete but suggestive of my view of leadership. Thelma Katz, Betty Belt, Bob Eicholtz, Frances Hedges, and Paul Sakamoto have yet to appear as leaders in journal articles, newspaper interviews, or on television talk shows. They are uncertified by noneducators as leaders. I see them as mainstream educators who demonstrate how a political perspective (often unarticulated, but insistently moral) wedded to managerial competencies invests instructional and administrative routines with institutional meaning.

So what? What possible significance is there in viewing teacher and administrative leadership in the manner I do? Of major significance, I believe, is whether cultivating the ordinary practice of leadership by teachers and administrators can contribute to persistent attempts by reformers to improve schooling. Reformers have frequently ignored the enabling conditions necessary for educators to lead, thereby smothering rather than nourishing classroom, school, and district leadership. Furthermore, encouraging teacher and administrative initiative and risk-taking will inexorably raise the issue of common purpose. What ends should educational leaders in classrooms and schools seek? What role should schools play in this society?

Let me now consider the possible implications of the argument that I have made thus far in the book concerning images, roles, and leadership and its connection to school improvement. While I believe that these arguments have consequences for a variety of issues current in the last decade of the twentieth century, I will concentrate on school improvement because of its connection to leadership and because it has historically fixed the attention of practitioners, researchers, and policymakers on the question of what societal role schools should play. Should schools reinforce existing advantages that children bring to school, or should they enhance student talents regardless of background so each can contribute to society? The periodic surges of school reform over the last few centuries that seized public attention were merely visible punctuation marks for a persistent grammar of school improvement and a redefinition of the social role of schooling.

In focusing this discussion of implications on school improvement, I will touch briefly on the extensive efforts of the federal government since 1965 and the explosion of state efforts in the 1980s to alter what occurs in schools and classrooms. In summarizing the lessons learned from both research and practice on trying to implement school improvement efforts that were either mandated or voluntarily embraced, I will connect what has been learned to the arguments advanced in this book about images, roles, and leadership.

SCHOOL IMPROVEMENT

Historically, major efforts to improve teaching and administering have come from outside the schools. Amateur and professional reformers affiliated with universities, school districts, or lay coalitions have sought changes in schools, from the elimination of one-room rural schools to the use of desktop microcomputers, from the use of federal subsidies for vocational education to the banning of science texts that treat evolution as a fact. On occasion these reformers called for state intervention. For example, at the turn of the century states mandated that public schools teach the physical harm done to the body and morals of youth due to smoking, alcohol, and drugs. Or, in a later decade, reforms lobbied successfully for the Smith-Hughes Act (1917), which subsidized the training of high school boys and girls in specific occupations. For the most part, however, school improvement efforts concentrated on districts. Coalitions of reformers organized into state, regional, and national networks pressed local boards of education to institute particular improvements.[11]

Nonetheless, organizational changes from the top and pressures for reforms from the outside characterize most of the efforts to improve schools. Of course, teachers and administrators have initiated changes from the bottom, but as schooling has become larger, more complex, and bureaucratic, such internal moves (unaided by external forces) become increasingly difficult.[12]

First and Second Order Changes

To distinguish among planned changes introduced into schools, consider the experiences of the National Air and Space Administration (NASA).

In the mid–1980s, NASA endured a number of grave setbacks with the tragic destruction of the Challenger shuttle and two unmanned rockets within three months. By all accounts, an agency that had numerous successes with the lunar landings, shuttle flights, which included space walks and satellite repairs, screeched to a halt with the deaths of seven astronauts.

With such public scrutiny, NASA's new leadership had to define the problem clearly: Was the Challenger accident a design problem, a lapse in quality control, or some mix of the two? Defining the problem became crucial since the definition would chart the direction for changes in NASA's formal structure, relationships with government contractors, and a score of other rippling effects. Similarly, for school reforms over the last century, there is a need to determine whether school problems were defined as design or quality control issues or some mix of the two.

First-order changes are reforms that assume that the existing organizational goals and structures are basically adequate and what needs to be done is to correct deficiencies in policies and practices. Engineers would label such changes as solutions to quality control problems.

For schools such planned changes would include recruiting better teachers and administrators, raising salaries, distributing resources equitably, selecting better texts, materials and supplies, and adding new or deleting old content and courses to and from the curriculum. When such improvements occur, the results frequently appear to be fundamental changes or even appear to be changes in core activities, but actually these changes do little to alter basic school structures of how time and space are used or how students and teachers are organized and assigned. First-order changes, then, try to make what exists more efficient and effective without disrupting basic organizational arrangements or how people perform their roles. The compensatory education programs of the 1960s and since (including Title I of the Elementary and Secondary Education Act and Chapter 1) are instances of first-order reforms. The school effectiveness movement with its emphasis on high expectations, strong instructional leadership, academic performance in basic skills, aligning goals with curriculum, texts, and tests is a recent instance of a cluster of first-order, planned changes.[13]

Second-order changes, on the other hand, aim at altering the fundamental ways of achieving organizational goals because of major dissatisfaction with current arrangements. Second-order changes introduce new goals and interventions that transform the familiar ways of doing things into novel solutions to persistent problems. The point is to reframe the original problems and restructure organizational conditions to conform with the redefined problems. Engineers would call these solutions to design problems.

Going from the one-room school house with one unsupervised teacher and a group of children ranging in ages from six to sixteen to an eight-room building divided into grades and a formal curriculum where a teacher is supervised by a principal is a second-order change that happened throughout the late nineteenth century in urban schools and the first half of the twentieth century in rural areas. Other second-order changes have been efforts to create open classrooms (sometimes called "informal education"), a core curriculum in secondary schools for an entire morning or afternoon, proposals to give vouchers to parents to use in choosing a school, open space architecture in new buildings, a non-graded school and the abolition of local school boards and lay governance of education. These examples suggest basic changes in one or more areas of school operations.

Second-order changes, then, involve visions of what ought to be that are different from those embedded in the existing organization. Putting those visions into practice alters fundamental roles, routines, and relationships within an organization.

The history of school reform has been largely first-order improvements on the basic structures of schooling established in the late nineteenth century. Incremental improvements to schooling that maintained existing arrangements (e.g., graded school, self-contained classrooms with one teacher and thirty students, varied curricula, fifty-minute periods in secondary schools) have been the dominant pattern, punctuated occasionally by second-order changes (e.g., progressive pedagogy, open-space architecture, team-teaching) that have been adapted to the contours of the existing arrangements. Hence, over time, first-order changes paradoxically strengthen organizational stability.

Researchers examining past efforts to improve schooling have found common characteristics to those first- and second-order reforms that were institutionalized, in contrast to those that left a few or no traces. School improvements that endured were a mix of both kinds of changes, with first-order ones dominant. They were structural in nature (e.g., graded schools in mid-nineteenth century America), created new constituencies (e.g., vocational education curricula; guidance counselors; Title I teachers), and were easily monitored (e.g., Carnegie units; certification requirements for teachers). Researchers concluded that such instructional second-order reforms as team teaching, inquiry learning, open classrooms, and individualized instruction were installed and dismantled, barely denting existing practice.[14]

The last two decades have provided more illustrations of important first-order improvements that have the full force of state and federal law, ample dollars, and regulatory muscle. Since 1958 when Congress passed the National Defense Education (NDEA), thereby launching a response to the Soviet challenge of American scientific supremacy, the federal government has been directly involved in school improvement. Spurred by NDEA, curriculum projects blossomed in the academic disciplines; new textbooks and technologies, new modes of teaching were introduced in a deluge of experimental projects subsidized by federal funds.

With the spread of the civil rights movement and a growing national sensitivity to minority aspirations for equal opportunities, President Lyndon Johnson and the Congress produced the Elementary and Secondary Education Act of 1965. Expanded federal regulations over the next fifteen years aimed to improve the academic performance of minority, low-income children (Title I, ESEA), provide access and improved schooling for handicapped children (P.L. 94–142) and unleash broad innovations in all aspects of the school program (Title III, ESEA). The next decade and a half saw federally funded programs move to the states that took over the improvement effort, penetrated local districts that operated the programs, or, in some cases, entered individual schools.[15]

With the election of Ronald Reagan, the federal presence receded to be replaced by a philosophy of deregulation, commitment to state and local leadership in school improvement, and reduced federal funding. From equity concerns that translated into myriad categorical programs heavily regulated by the federal bureaucracy, the encouragement of innovation and intervention to open up locked doors to excluded children, the Reagan administration brought a different agenda that emphasized academic excellence, productivity, performance standards, individual competition, state and local initiatives, and parental choice.[16]

From the laws, mandates, and billions of dollars spent since the early 1960s, what kinds of changes sponsored by federal intervention have lasted in states and districts? What order of changes endured?

- organizational changes that required a new layer of specialists, such as programs that pull children out of their regular classes to receive additional help, for example, remedial experts, vocational education personnel, bilingual and Chapter 1 (formerly Title I, ESEA) staff.

- procedural changes that guarantee student rights (e.g., due process). P.L. 94–142 mandated new procedures for working with handicapped children and their parents.

- pupil classification systems for differentiating categories of children, for example, English-speaking, gifted, and handicapped children.

- increased teacher specialization produced new certification categories, such as remedial reading, bilingual education, English as a second language, and classifications within special education for both teachers and aides.

All of these changes were either rule changes or further staff specialization. The reforms created new constituencies and were easily monitored, but hardly transformed existing organizational structures. Little or no sustained impact on curriculum or classroom instruction appears to have occurred.[17]

Most consequences of federal efforts to improve schooling suggest first-order changes. Schools were seen as failing to provide necessary resources, let alone quality services for certain populations, and worse, had excluded groups of children entirely. To promote quality, that is, to provide an equal education, federal policymakers tried to improve schools as they were rather than altering substantially the structures, roles, and relationships in states and districts.

This is no trivial pursuit. Expanding equal opportunity in the delivery of services and the treatment of children different from the mainstream is a massive, if not intimidating, undertaking. The changes that have occurred and will continue to accrue to these federal interventions have been superseded in the 1980s by activist state governments filling the vacuum created by the Reagan administration in reducing the federal role in school improvement.[18]

STATE EFFORTS AT SCHOOL IMPROVEMENT

Others have analyzed well the origins and spread of the excellence in schooling movement that state governors and legislatures initiated in the 1980s. They have examined the legal mandates, regulations, and particular indicators of excellence that emerged in these reports: spending more time in school on an academic curriculum, higher graduation requirements, more homework, fact-filled textbooks, tests, tougher requirements for screening new and veteran teachers while recognizing the best and the brightest among them. Rather than cover the same issues, I will concentrate on the major premises of these reforms as they touched curriculum and instruction, and determine whether they concentrated on design or quality control issues.[19]

Two central assumptions (largely unspoken and unexamined) guided the actions of governors, legislators, and state superintendents determined to improve schools. First, these policymakers assumed that what caused academic excellence to erode (as measured by declining test scores and fewer students taking math and science) were district school boards and superintendents who let standards slip. With spines made out of rubber bands, locals could not be fully trusted was the assumption.

Second, policymakers assumed that state laws and regulations could reach into schools and classrooms and reshape teacher performance sufficiently to improve what students learn. They assumed that state mandates could take hundreds of districts (with even larger numbers of principals and teachers) historically loosely tied to state policymakers' intentions and realign them tightly to what state officials desired and produce gains in student academic performance. Not only will states set goals and standards, they'll direct how districts should go about schooling all children. There are, in effect, right and wrong ways to get students to learn.

Both assumptions further regulated local schooling and concentrated policymaking into the hands of state officials, who, as a consequence of taxpayer revolts and judicial decisions on school funding, allocate increasing amounts of state dollars to districts. Both assumptions are wired to a conception of student learning, teaching, principaling, and superintending that is closer to the bureaucrat/technocrat than the craftsman/artist image. This is most clearly seen in California, New York, and a number of southern states anxious to use public schools as an anchor for economic growth, such as Texas, Florida, Arkansas, Mississippi, Tennessee, and South Carolina. My analysis will focus on these pacesetting states that specialized in what I call technocratic reforms.

Based on these two unexamined premises and a technical conception of how teachers and administrators should carry out their tasks, these reforms used research findings drawn from studies of low-income, largely minority elementary schools and the presumed benefits of corporate management strategies in promoting employee productivity. Armed with these research findings, a series of laws, regulations, dollar-backed incentives, sanctions, and mandates showered local school boards.[20]

- Laws that mandated the longer school day and more days in school each year come directly from research that demonstrated strong connections between how much time students spent in classrooms on instructional tasks and gains in standardized test scores in elementary schools at particular grades in reading and math (e.g., California, Texas, South Carolina, Florida).[21]

- Laws that raised graduation standards and established that student placement, promotion, and retention be based on their mastery of specific skills and knowledge rely heavily on research findings on effective schools. The phrase *high expectations,* for example, refers to adults' positive attitudes toward students and is viewed as a necessary condition for producing higher achievement. (By 1985, over half of the states had legislated such requirements with forty-three having raised graduation requirements.[21]

- Laws that mandated state tests to be given at various grades in a student's career can be traced to the research on effective schools and teacher effectiveness that frequently used standardized achievement test results as the primary measure to determine program success. Also, impetus for more frequent and broader display of test scores comes from policymakers' concern for easily understood and displayed evidence of school performance— the notion of an educational boxscore or, to shift metaphors, a profit-loss statement that conveys a sense of public accountability to the public. Shaping the perceptions of the general public is important business since their vote will determine whether or not schools should receive more funds. (By 1985, over forty states had increased or begun state assessment programs.)[22]

- Laws that increased state testing and tied curricular content to test items, while wiring both to curriculum goals and a teacher's daily lesson plans, produced, measurement-driven instruction. Such legislative aims were derived from research findings on classroom and school effectiveness (e.g., California, South Carolina, and Texas).[23]

- Laws that stipulated higher entry-level teacher salaries and merit pay schemes, competency tests for new and veteran teachers, stiffer evaluation procedures, and career development programs draw heavily from private sector wisdom on what will motivate the best and the brightest in the teacher corps and will screen out low performers. These laws incorporate the familiar incentives in the private sector that those at the bottom of the organization, motivated by recognition and dollars, will seek positions and perform well.[24]

Governors, legislators, and state superintendents speak easily and often of the importance of local control, that without the principal and teacher no improvement will occur, and that the state is merely reasserting its constitutional responsibilities to establish goals and standards, however, those words cannot obscure how state policymakers have reduced the discretion of local boards, superintendents, principals, and teachers to determine how to run their schools.

States have moved swiftly into the role of regulator. If deregulation is *de rigeur* at the federal level, few could say the same for the state's role in schooling. The Texas State Board of Education, for example, has ordered local school board members to complete twenty hours of training on their duties under the new reform legislation, and each board is to record in its minutes which members have completed the training. The success of these reforms rests on the bold assertion that schools and classrooms can, indeed, be tightly coupled to state mandates to produce desired outcomes.[25]

Are these first-order or second-order changes? Apart from the attempted realignment of local/state relations in those pacesetter states mentioned earlier, which I would label as an effort to alter a fundamental relationship in governance equal to changes that occurred at the local level in the early decades of this century, the bulk of improvement efforts aim to make the existing system more efficient and effective, not alter fundamental roles and arrangements in districts, schools, and classrooms. The historic design of public schooling instituted in the late-nineteenth century, with all of its additions, remains intact. Thus, first-order changes seem to prevail in state interventions heavily loaded with regulations targeted at governing teacher and administrator decisions. If correct, the cumulative effects of these changes will be to strengthen the managerial imperative and instructional regularities while preserving the fundamental design of schooling.

This point of first-order reforms strengthening existing structural arrangements of schooling (e.g., how time and space are used; isolation of teachers; Carnegie unit, etc.) is crucial in understanding why the bureaucrat/technocrat conception of both students and professionals will persist alongside the managerial role. Both are embedded in the original designs of schooling.

The familiar tendency of public officials to announce that reforms are successful will divert attention from this basic point. They must sustain public attention, political momentum, and funding. In the mid–1980s, for example, California State Superintendent Bill Honig declared that the California reforms were a success, based on a Stanford researcher's 1985 study of increased high school enrollments in math and science. U.S. Secretary of Education William Bennett announced in 1986 that state reforms were working since Scholastic Aptitude Test scores have risen over previous years. Such remote productivity indicators of efficiency (and not effectiveness) fall short of persuading the uninformed much less the skeptical observer. No one yet, for example, fully knows what principals do in their schools or what teachers do in their classrooms as a consequence of these measures.[26]

Nonetheless, from these vigorous state efforts in the 1980s a few obvious results linked to the arguments advanced in this book have surfaced.

- The image of teachers and administrators as somewhere between a bureaucrat carrying out state directives and a technocrat applying scientifically derived rules to schooling again reemerge. Buried within laws, mandates, productivity measures, and programs aimed at improving student performance and holding educators accountable is the picture of a principal and teacher efficiently executing orders from above. For those teachers and administrators more comfortable with the craft or artist image, this surge of reform proves annoying, if not enervating.

- The centralizing and bureaucratizing impulses at the heart of these reforms strengthen the managerial role in teachers and administrators. Authority and information flow downward in these state reforms, and the task for local educators is to put into practice what others judge as effective. Such a direction encourages a managerial perspective rather than one in which independent judgments are made, initiatives taken, and leadership displayed.

- If teacher and administrative discretion is a necessary (but not sufficient) condition for leadership, one would expect that the enabling conditions for exercising initiative, creativity, and the like aimed at helping children would sink under the weight of these state efforts targeted at producing schools and classrooms driven by rules, test items, and easily displayed numbers. In other words, were state policymakers' assumptions about aligning local districts into a de facto state-operated system of schooling to work, then one would expect discretion (which is a natural by-product of loosely coupled organizations) to shrink; one would expect that educators' attention and ingenuity would be drawn to making the numbers look better rather than increasing the overall quality of the services.[27]

I say "expect" because few state policymakers, responsible for such laws, or researchers know what has occurred in schools or classrooms as a consequence of these recent reforms. Until that knowledge surfaces, I suspect that at least two outcomes (and their myriad mutations) are possible. First, the measurement- and rule-driven reforms will fail to achieve fully their intentions. Wiring curriculum and instruction to high-stakes tests will occur, but the business of schooling is for educators to make daily decisions about other people; such human judgments cannot be programmed by others or made routine by a set of rules.

In such organizations, there is a long history of visible and token adherence to external mandates, while stable core processes within schools and classrooms persist. Anyone familiar with teachers' use of technology knows that machines can be bought and delivered to schools and placed in teachers' rooms. None of that guarantees serious use of the advanced technology. Anyone familiar with large bureaucracies knows the ways that principals can comply minimally with district office directives if they find them too intrusive or disruptive for their schools.[28]

A second outcome may well be the partial success of these mandates, driving some teachers and administrators to do pretty much what the policymakers want. Curriculum would be rewritten and scripts of units and lessons for teachers produced. Superintendents would inspect principals (recall New Brunswick, New Jersey's implementation of effective schools research). Principals would closely inspect whether teachers were teaching what was supposed to be taught. Teachers would inspect students through frequent testing. Evaluations of superintendents, principals, and teachers would be linked to how well the implementation of directives is being carried out. The dream of a direct link from the state capital into each classroom would then materialize.

In such a bureaucratic scenario, anchored in top management's passion for control, discretion would be further reduced but not eliminated. Teachers and administrators would become civil servants carrying out routine procedures. Such instructional management systems exist today in Washington, D.C., Atlanta, Georgia, and many other districts, but evidence of this occurring on the scale of a state has yet to emerge.

Some hints of teacher reactions to this direction have appeared. Frances Fowler, a sixth grade Tennessee teacher, pondered the consequences of the state's Basic Skills First Program.

> If all five components of the new state-mandated K–8 curriculum are implemented, and if each segment involves the amount of record-keeping for me that the math segment did last year, the time will come when I have to thumb through 3,360 pages of teachers' guides to plan my lessons, administer 280 tests each year, and maintain 450

individual student charts and 75 pages of class record sheets. Moreover, if I ever learn how to operate the computer down the hall, I will
have to enter the test results on five floppy disks.

Fowler described a meeting between teachers and a representative
from the state department of education to launch the program in the
local schools. Concerns about the amount of time and the lack of help
in tracking student progress on all of the skills had been raised previously with this state department staffer. This time, the teachers,
Fowler reports, were no longer "stony-faced; they were openly muti-
nous." Teachers asked who was going to record all the results.

Staffer: "Your aides."

Teachers: "What aides?!"

Staffer: "Well, your better students can fill out charts during their
P.E. [physical education] time."

Teachers: "They're *required* to go to P.E."

Staffer: "You could fill out charts during your lunch period."

Teacher: "Somehow, I'd planned to eat lunch then."

Staffer: "There just isn't enough time in education. *You will have to
make time.*"

Fowler understood. "We could make time by giving our students
busywork to do while we filled out charts. We could make time by
doing the recordkeeping before and after school. The problem was
ours to solve."[29]
Her anger, of course, will go away in time. She will work out
compromises between these externally imposed obligations and her
sense of what students need. She was fortunate in one respect: she
expressed herself publicly, dispelling some of that corrosive anger.
Many of her colleagues will seek other alternatives.
Another potential consequence of this movement toward curricular uniformity and instructional standardization is the silent, pervasive
spread of fatigue and cynicism among teachers and administrators.
Hundreds of objectives, detailed lesson plans, numerous tests, and
much recordkeeping persuades some teachers that they are more
clerks than schoolmasters. If anything, state curricular mandates such
as in Texas threaten to deskill teaching.

Equally frustrating to teachers is the use of test scores, drop-out rates, course enrollments, and other productivity measures to sell schools. Because most insiders know that the numbers quickly change from year to year, that data are haphazardly collected, and that students who are the source of much data often unintentionally provide inaccurate information, teachers and administrators come to mistrust what is presented to the public as crisp, hard facts. Worse, they smirk.

What attracts and keeps teachers and administrators working hard at their jobs for years is not the chance to keep records, grade tests, or produce better numbers but inner rewards, that is, relationships with children and adults, the satisfaction in seeing growth that is seldom found in paper-and-pencil tests. Many teachers and administrators will find less pleasure and more strain in their jobs and choose to leave.[30]

Therefore, actual and potential leadership in schools and classrooms will either atrophy or get diverted into novel forms of resisting directives aimed at standardizing behavior and holding school people accountable. Initiative, inventiveness, and imagination among those who take the moral view of teaching will be channeled into guerilla skirmishing, covert resistance, or apathy. Educators will resist, using methods they have used for years, in order to accomplish what they believe is necessary in their classrooms and schools. Often quietly and alone, such resistance (even sabotage) has been an alternative for those at the bottom of hierarchial organizations who are the target of policies adopted by those at the top.[31]

The negative implications that I see for current state reform efforts to improve schooling can be offset by constructive approaches. The line of argument I have set forth suggests other directions for policymakers interested in school improvement and the cultivation of local leadership. State policymakers, I believe, are genuinely interested in making schooling better. They do want teachers and administrators to act as professionals and help children learn. I do not question their intentions. I question their assumptions about whether a state can get students to learn more and better by altering curriculum and instruction in thousands of schools and tens of thousands of classrooms, using policies, regulations, incentives, sanctions, and dollars as their primary tools (I was about to write weapons). I question policies infected with conceptions of teaching and administration that constrict independence and strengthen managerial leanings. In short, I question strategies of control infused with massive distrust of teachers and administrators.

After all, once the laws are passed, the regulations put in the mail, the state department of education tries to enforce, monitor, and, in general, persuade schools to comply. State bureaucracies are rough-edged, blunt instruments largely unequipped to achieve fine-grained legal outcomes for classrooms and schools. What a governor, legislature, or state board of education have at their disposal are not teachers, principals, superintendents, parents, or school board members. They have policies. They have regulations. They have threats. They have reports due at the end of the month. They have review teams that inspect schools every three to five years. They have dollars.

So the state department of education tries to insure that the hundreds of thousands of teachers, the tens of thousands of principals, and the hundreds of superintendents and school boards comply. Rivers of paper, occasional inspections, newspaper exposés, complaints, and the publishing of district and school indicators signal the governor, the legislature, the commissioner of education, and the state board of education the degree of compliance.

Not unlike the bold attempt by federal policymakers to realign their relationship with state and local school agencies, an effort that lasted no more than a decade and a half, few can predict with confidence how long such reform momentum by the states can be sustained. Now, it is appropriate to consider these largely first-order changes undertaken by the states and federal government over almost three decades and ask a frank question: What has been learned from the federal and state experience about improving schools? The follow-up question would be to take what has been learned from research and practice and assess the implications of those lessons for the arguments laid out in this book.

WHAT HAS BEEN LEARNED FROM STATE AND FEDERAL SCHOOL IMPROVEMENT EFFORTS?

From the enormous body of research findings and practical experience accumulated by teachers and administrators, I have extracted lessons and converted them into guiding principles for policymakers interested in school improvement. Readers are familiar with my experience as a practitioner and academic and the arguments laid out in earlier chapters. My experience and research-based arguments acted as filters for selecting the following guiding principles that bear on school improvement.[32]

TEACHING AND ADMINISTERING WITHIN AND AMONG SCHOOLS VARY. DO NOT PRESCRIBE WHAT SHOULD OCCUR IN THOSE CLASSROOMS AND SCHOOLS. What teachers in classrooms and administrators in schools do is make decisions about other people. They deal in human judgment. While their actions are shaped to a great extent by the general structural arrangements within which they work, these same actions are also influenced by the particular conditions they face, the time that events unfold, and their conceptions, beliefs, and experiences. Variation in performance is inexorable. Although at some general level clear similarities exist across context, time, and beliefs, still classrooms, schools, and districts differ enough in these factors to give pause to anyone who is bent on generalizing about what should be done.

Because of these inevitable variations within and between schools, it is impossible to prescribe policies from afar, that is, from federal, state, and district offices that tell teachers and administrators what they must do about curriculum and instruction or in operating a school. In short, there is no one best system of teaching, principaling, or superintending for policymakers to adopt.[33]

IMPROVEMENT IS TIED TO EACH SCHOOL SITE. Anyone familiar with schooling knows the palpable differences between schools in the same neighborhood. Informed parents shop for schools, not classrooms.

With all of the criticism of the effective schools movement and its research from both academics and practitioners, one fact has stubbornly emerged: Substantial changes that touch the inner core of classroom activities occur at the school site where principal and teachers work together with students to achieve common aims. The literature on effective schools, reinforcing the folk wisdom of practitioners, has underscored the importance of building commitment to the goals among those who do the daily work and holding them responsible for outcomes. The intangibles of a school culture that prizes achievement (however defined) for both adults and children repeatedly turns up in practitioner anecdotes and researchers' findings. In effect, the organization that can alter teacher and student behavior most directly and in sustained fashion is the school. This is not to argue that the district is irrelevant or less important. Indeed, there is sufficient evidence that district efforts can enhance or hinder school performance. It is only to make especially clear the inherent potency of the single workplace where combined efforts of adults and children have the most telling effects.

IN ORDER TO PRODUCE DURABLE IMPROVEMENTS AT THE SCHOOL SITE, TEACHERS AND PRINCIPALS REQUIRE A LARGER DEGREE OF INDEPENDENCE

THAN NOW IS GRANTED BY MOST LOCAL AND STATE AGENCIES. The impulse to control continues to permeate the thinking about planned change among policymakers. Policies aimed at teachers and principals, especially in inner city schools, offer little legitimate discretion in making decisions about organizational conditions within which they work. Yet school-site decisions spell the difference between how faithfully district, state, and federal policies are implemented.

Reform by remote control, which is transforming classrooms and schools through regulations—a familiar strategy practiced by governing bodies—will yield compliance at some level with easily monitored procedures and paperwork, but will do little to alter the core activities that occur in the workplace.

In arguing that more formal discretion be extended to teachers and administrators (as contrasted to the negative freedom common in organizations where little supervision occurs and people pretty much do what they like), I assume that no pool of imagination and creativity is simply waiting to be tapped at the local level. Nor do I assume that teachers and administrators have a special monopoly on goodwill and the knowledge of what is best for children; any romantic ideas I may have held eroded in watching my colleagues in McKeesport, Cleveland, Washington, D.C., and Arlington, Virginia. I have seen altruism and racism; I have seen fiery engagement with ideas and anti-intellectualism; I have seen colleagues sacrifice money and time for their students and seen others identify vested interests, such as salaries and fringe benefits, with the best interests of children.

Yet—and this is a crucial "yet"—these teachers and administrators are all we have. They do the work. They need to be helped. They need to be seen as potential heroes who perform essential social tasks that cannot be regulated from afar. A better balance than exists now needs to be struck between expanded autonomy for teachers and administrators and ways of demonstrating accountability to the larger community.

EFFECTING CHANGE DEPENDS ON WHAT THE ON-SITE IMPLEMENTERS THINK AND DO AND THE QUALITY OF HELP THEY RECEIVE. The process of adopting, implementing, and institutionalizing school improvements aimed at changing teacher and administrator behavior is heavily dependent upon their:

- Understanding clearly what it is to be done.
- Commitment to doing what is intended.

- Having the discretion to make alterations in the changes.

- Tailoring the desired improvements to the contextual conditions of the settings.

- Having tangible and sustained help to effect the improvements.[34]

The sum of these guiding principles adds up to a larger reliance upon the infantry of reform: the men and women who staff schools. These principles rely far less upon the goodwill or designs of policymakers, who legislate and preach but seldom enter a classroom or school to see the results of their laws or sermons. If proposed changes that are intended to alter substantially what occurs in classrooms are to have a durable effect, they must come to grips with the existing organizational structures in elementary and secondary schools and the need for broader teacher and administrator discretion.

All of these principles say little about the goals of school improvement. Implicit in this analysis is that policymakers and practitioners who wish to improve schooling share similar goals. Because such an assumption is flawed, I now discuss how these principles fit some goals better than others.

GOALS FOR SCHOOL IMPROVEMENT AND EXISTING STRUCTURES

Policymakers determined to improve schooling have differed among themselves for decades as to what is desirable. Some sought increased efficiency in spending public funds; some sought enhanced effectiveness in student performance; some wanted more scientists and engineers; others wanted schools where intellectual engagement flourished; others wanted schools where students reasoned critically; others wanted schools to take on parental obligations, such as teaching children proper sexual behavior, the evils of drug abuse, and how to get a job; others wanted schools where even the slowest and least able student achieved. A grab-bag of goals both noble and complex, inspired and surprising paraded by the public. So what?

Inspired by reformers, over the last century filled with pocketfuls of worthy intentions and driven by varied conceptions of what schools should do, a jerry-built architecture of schooling and a jumble of old and new blueprints for the efficient mass production of schooling arose. Conflicting goals produced graded schools and self-contained classrooms, promotion policies, Carnegie units, fifty-minute periods, vocational and sex education, and mandated achievement tests. All were once novel solutions to momentary problems defined by reformers and put into practice to improve schooling.

Yet these and other reforms created over the decades a Rube Goldberg machine ill-designed to achieve a growing list of goals. Each generation of policymakers and reformers added goals and organizational mechanisms designed to achieve specific aims. The total effect of these innocent, helter-skelter designs stacked one atop another was a disorderly array of intentions and structures mismatched to broad educational goals for children and professionals in schools. The consequences for non-mainstream children (the immigrants, disadvantaged, and others) had been largely negative. Noble intentions misaligned with traditional structures produced unsatisfying results which persuade taxpayers that schools are doing poorly. Another effect has also been to deeply divide educators into adversarial factions without a sense of common purpose.

The mismatch can be seen in how some aims are consistent (and how some are not) with existing organizational arrangements that have been present in schools for the last century. Certain goals considered important by reformers, researchers, policymakers, and parents, call for structural changes. Goals for students to be treated as individuals, to learn to think for themselves, to seek an engaged practice of citizenship, and to develop a sense of caring for others, have little chance of succeeding within the current structures of schooling, except in those instances where extraordinary people overcome the compelling imperatives embedded in these structures. Those policymakers and practitioners seeking such goals would advocate second-order reforms to create different school structures better aligned with desired aims.

The goal of increased reasoning skills within schools, organized as they are, is one instance of this fundamental conflict. Corporate officials, governors, legislators, superintendents, and district officials share in common the goal of cultivating critical thinking and problem solving within the nation's youth. National reports repeatedly emphasize the need for public school graduates to be flexible, independent thinkers.

But state mandates in the mid–1980s, wedded to the existing structural conditions within schools and the practical pedagogy that teachers invented to cope with these conditions, are in severe conflict. Regulations that detail curricular content, specify textbooks, and assess student performance through multiple-choice test items pour wet concrete over that practical pedagogy. The core repertoire of instructional practices finds students listening to lectures, doing worksheets at their desks, reciting from textbooks, and seldom asking questions. Such work demands little application of concepts, little imagination, and very little intellectual engagement.

Eager reformers, unaware of how the practical pedagogy that arose came in response to difficult working conditions and of the dulling effects of such practices on students' reasoning skills, have repeatedly exhorted teachers to teach students to think. Teachers are caught between using a repertoire that works (given the structures within which they labor) and responding to reformers' pleas. When they do the former, they are labeled as unimaginative; when they try to incorporate new materials and learn new approaches, researchers swiftly point out the lack of results or the persistence of old patterns, leading reformers to blame teachers anew.

This dilemma has no simple solution. Glitzy materials aimed at producing thinkers, special courses for teachers on how to teach reasoning, new multiple-choice items that supposedly assess students' "higher order thinking skills" will not end the dilemma. To teach students to reflect, to question, and to solve problems, teachers must, at the least, work in settings that allow them ample time and resources to engage in these kinds of tasks.

If policymakers desire to have children increase their reasoning and problem-solving skills, they will need to see clearly the fundamental conflict between current school structures and this important goal and then move to realign those commonplace, unquestioned structures to fit a pedagogy that strives for intellectual engagement. To align the classroom setting to a teaching that centers on such engagement and student involvement, reformers and policymakers will need to begin with the organizational imperatives that largely govern teacher routines, that determine the use of time and space in schools and classrooms, and that shape how and by whom instructional decisions are made. If policymakers become aware of the mismatch between goals and structural arrangements, the DNA of schooling, and if they strive to achieve such a goal as improved reasoning skills, they begin a very different journey toward school improvement.

I doubt, however, that the reformers of the 1980s have such a journey on their agenda. There is a fundamental acceptance of schools as they are. Reformers today have little appetite for basic changes in schools even when a desired goal is unachievable within the present structures.

This is how I see the lessons that have been learned and the actions that need to be taken. At first glance, this appears as a pessimistic rendering of the potential that now exists for substantial school improvement, yet I see it as an optimistic assessment of what can be. After all, a clearer view of what the fundamental problems are offers a more hopeful beginning than errant chasing after seductive solutions for ill-framed problems or a quick skip over the misfit of goals and structures.

But what about the central and fundamental dilemma for school improvement as designed by state and federal policymakers? How to strike a balance acceptable to both implementers and external audiences between practitioner autonomy and bureaucratic accountability, between helping teachers and administrators do what has to be done and holding them responsible for their performance? These dilemmas will persist in schools, redesigned or not. I now turn to the implications drawn from lessons learned in previous interventions and the arguments set forth in this book for policymakers, practitioners, and researchers.

THE DILEMMA OF AUTONOMY AND RESPONSIBILITY

The conventional means of holding teachers and administrators accountable at all levels of government is through rule-making. Fiscal regulations, for example, call for production of paper trails that can be monitored in periodic audits. Program regulations and procedures that require keeping records, documenting what occurs, and submitting reports are monitored by occasional on-site inspections, but are more often monitored by systematic examining of the paper sent into the appropriate office. It comes as no surprise, then, that reports in triplicate, files covering everything from purchasing to attendance, and enormous collections of data that often go uninspected, much less used, fill office after office in school districts. Bureaucratic procedures is the common way of holding educators accountable.

There are other means. By concentrating upon outcomes such as test scores, dropout rates, numbers of students continuing their schooling, and similar markers, both educators and noneducators can supposedly determine whether teachers and administrators have met their responsibilities. Focusing upon outcomes, has decided benefits for administrators and policymakers and fewer benefits for those who work in schools and classrooms. Some policymakers have married this stress upon results to sharing these outcomes with the public through publishing school-by-school test scores and other comparisons of performance on varied measures. The premise is that teachers and administrators will become more responsible if results are available to the community. The undesirable outcomes would trigger community pressure for improvement. This is accountability by bullying. The substantial negatives linked to concentrating upon outcome measures and having them become public signs of success have begun to emerge.[35]

Another approach to accountability is to simply render an account, as Milbrey McLaughlin puts it. Describing what occurs in classrooms and schools, calling exemplars and misfits to both lay and public attention contributes to what teachers and administrators see as their responsibility. Exemplars are recognized; misfits and incompetents are handled as they appear in these accounts. Informally, this occurs in schools and districts where there is sufficient pride in what is currently occurring and self-confidence in dealing forthrightly and fairly with the unfortunate exceptions who perform inadequately. It is uncommon, however.[36]

Also uncommon in public schooling is professional responsibility. For example, teachers working with teachers, principals with teachers, and superintendents with principals, holding joint responsibility for what occurs, remains rare in districts. Professionals holding one another accountable is sought in law and medicine but continues to have many flaws in actual operation. Except for occasional schools where such solidarity arises informally and the infant efforts to introduce teacher-shaped licensing procedures and peer review among teachers, little of this collegial responsibility yet exists in public education.

The dominant manner of accountability remains regulatory with occasional mixes of other approaches. Embedded within it, of course, are images of teachers and administrators as bureaucrats. The managerial imperative becomes even more compelling with this strategy of coercing responsible behavior from teachers, principals, and superintendents. Alternative means of assuring accountability such as teacher-run schools or schools freed from the constraints of lay control contain images of both teachers and administrators as moral actors capable of exercising choice and holding themselves accountable for their judgments.

In ending this discussion of accountability, I want to make clear
that regulations accompanied by familiar forms of accountability are
often necessary as a governmental response to social problems of in-
justice, health, and safety. Local agencies may neglect such issues, and
in a federal system another governing body may need to intervene.
The point is that a balance is necessary between local, state and federal agencies in existing structures of governance that permits sufficient discretion to those delivering a service while monitoring
performance in a flexible manner. Striking that balance is no easy task.
Maintaining a flexible tension requires sensitivity from both policymakers and practitioners.[37]

The primary implication of these guiding principles is a federal,
state, or district strategy of school improvement that focuses less on
control through regulation and more on vesting individual schools and
educators with the independence to alter basic organizational arrangements (if necessary) to reach explicit goals and standards.

Years of research and the practical experience of teachers, principals, and superintendents, including the more recent school effectiveness literature, has underscored the importance of concentrating upon
the unit that gets the work done, building commitment toward a common goal and providing aid to those who do the work and holding
them responsible for the outcomes. Corporate wisdom on unleashing
innovativeness and energy to achieve higher profits points to trusting
those at the bottom of the organization to do the right thing, while
holding them responsible. For public education, the school is the unit
of improvement and accountability, and the teachers and principals are
the key participants who need independence, assistance, and oversight
to reach goals and standards in their unique way. How that occurs
depends upon how closely reformers attend to such basic governance
issues as who should control the schools.

Assuming that the reform movement will continue for the immediate future at the state or federal levels, what could such agencies do?
The temptation to offer a new blueprint is strong. I resist it because
previous blueprints of school reform seldom stood up once they left
the drafting table. Moreover, I believe that fundamental changes in the
formal structures of schooling are necessary to reach certain aims of
educating children and bringing together teachers and administrators
into one profession. The goals for schooling that I would rank highest:
intellectual engagement, learning to reason and problem solve, cultivate caring for others, and the practice of citizenship, may be ones
that all readers would not accept. Hence, given this history of other

blueprints and my belief that for certain goals new redesigned schools are necessary, why offer a detailed plan?

Far more important is that policymakers (informed fully by teacher and administrator judgments) could use these guiding principles to generate specific policies aimed at building teacher and administrator leadership capacities and tailored to fit varying contexts and different times. If policymakers see the wisdom of redesigning schools to enhance incentives for teachers and administrators to reach goals of improved schooling, there are many ideas that can strike a fruitful balance between professional autonomy and accountability. A blueprint, then, would be both unwise and inconsistent with my basic trust in teachers and administrators to use their imagination and ingenuity to determine the best approaches to use.

Readers may find this a pale way to end a book on images, roles, and leadership in the practice of schooling. The impulse to end with a tightly argued solution to the complexities I have documented both in my career and other educators is strong. I resist it because what counts most, in my judgment, are not solutions but the framing of problems. There are far too many true believers who carry around neatly packaged solutions in search of problems to solve; there are far too few practitioners and scholars around who reframe situations that have been defined as problems.

By concentrating on how teaching and administering have become divorced from one another over the last century, yet in images and roles they have much in common, I have tried to reframe the problems of schooling in a slightly different manner. In blending the historical with the personal, I have tried to show how the career of one educator is inexorably entangled in the ways schools have been put together, how dominant images and roles have been enacted by teachers and administrators, and how a narrow but significant margin for leadership exists in schools and districts dominated by a managerial imperative and perverse incentives. To view the issues of improved schooling through the bifocal lens of a practitioner and scholar offers a perspective that concentrates on the designs of schools, on the DNA of schooling that drives teacher, administrative, and student behavior in ways that often escape the attention of well-motivated reformers.

To make schools places where teachers and administrators share common purposes, have the wherewithal and desire to help children grow in mind and character, one begins with a question: What is the problem? This book has been an answer to that question.

Notes

INTRODUCTION

1. The divisions that I see between teachers and administrators deeply concern both educators and policymakers. Among the many national reports published in the mid-1980s, for example, a few (e.g. National Governors, Association's *Time for Results*) called for cooperation across occupational boundaries. Also, the National Education Association and the National Association of Secondary School Principals joined to produce *Ventures in Good Schooling*, a series of portraits of teachers and principals working together in their schools. *Education Week*, September 24, 1986, p. 8. In David Hogan, *Class and Reform* (Philadelphia: University of Pennsylvania Press, 1985), he describes the 1915 controversy over the Chicago Teachers Federation when school board member Jacob Loeb convinced his colleagues to deny teachers the right to belong to any organization linked to trade unions. Aimed at Margaret Haley, leader of the Teachers Federation, Loeb said: "Teaching is not a trade, it is a profession and one of the noblest professions." pp. 209–209.

2. Lee Shulman, "Paradigms and Research Programs in the Study of Teaching," in Merlin C. Wittrock (ed.) *Third Handbook of Research in Teaching* (New York: Macmillan, 1985), p. 27. He calls the type of knowledge i present in this book "conceptual inventions, clarifications, and critiques."

3. This definition draws from many sources and will be elaborated in chapter 7. See James McGregor Burns, *Leadership* (New York: Harper and Row, 1978), pp. 1–48; Philip Selznick, *Leadership in Administration*

(Evanston, Ill.: Row, Peterson, 1957); Chester Barnard, *The Functions of The Executive* (Cambridge. MA: Harvard University Press, 1938).

1. TEACHING: IMAGES AND ROLES

1. "Classroom Propaganda," *San Jose Mercury,* March 19, 1985, March 20, 1985.

2. *Washington Post,* October 13, 1980, and May 24, 1981; also two direct observations of Mrs. Porter in May, 1981.

3. Alice Rinehart, *Mortals in the Immortal Profession,* (New York: Irvington Publishing Inc., 1983) pp. 352–53.

4. I use the word *image* interchangeably with *conception, metaphor,* and *picture.*

5. See Larry Cuban, *How Teachers Taught* (New York: Longman Inc., 1984); Barbara Finkelstein, "Governing the Young: Teacher Behavior in American Primary Schools, 1820–1880," (Unpublished Ed.D dissertation, Teaching College, Columbia University, 1970); Nancy Hoffman, *Womens 'True' Profession* (New York: McGraw-Hill, 1981); David Tyack, Robert Lowe, Elisabeth Hansot, *Public Schools in Hard Times* (Cambridge, Mass.: Harvard University Press, 1984).

6. The image of a staircase comes from Elliot Eisner, *Educational Imagination,* (New York: Macmillan Co., 1979) p. 69. The term *bureaucrat/technocrat* has an entangled geneology. Charles Kerchner and Douglas Mitchell in "Labor Relations and Teacher Policy," *Handbook of Teaching and Policy,* ed. Lee Shulman and Gary Sykes (New York: Longman, Inc., 1983), pp. 214–238, developed a framework for viewing teaching as labor, craft, professional, and artistic. While I found this way of viewing teaching as work useful, the category of "labor" was too constricting to convey the unique position of teacher as *both* a boss (of students) and subordinate (of principal). The bureaucrat is expected to be impartial, objective, consistent, and exercise limited discretion in executing a standard array of routines. Hence, the idea of a bureaucrat with its connotation of civil servant carrying out orders from above captures the subordinate status. In *Street Level Bureaucracy* (New York: Sage Foundation, 1980), Martin Lipsky specifically includes teachers as street-level bureaucrats who serve clients, as do nurses, police officers, and social workers.

The technocrat exercising managerial authority nicely embraces the other dimension of administering a classroom, of being in charge. Harry Wolcott used the label in *Teachers and Technocrats* (Eugene, Oregon: Center for Educational Policy and Management, 1977) in his study of the South Lane school district (Oregon). As Wolcott and others use technocrat, it means a rationality embedded in science and technology and geared to achieving efficiency. See also Arthur Wise, *Legislated Learning: The Bureaucratization of the American Classroom* (Berkeley: University of California Press, 1979), pp. 94–101. He describes "rationalistic teaching" and cites competency-based teacher education as an exemplar of this approach to teaching. See also Robert V. Bullough, Jr., Andrew Gitlin, and Stanley Goldstein, "Ideology, Teacher Role, and Resistance," *Teachers College Record*, 86 (Winter 1984), pp. 342–43.

The use of dichotomies to separate how teachers and others view their work is common. See, for example, Harry Gracey, *Curriculum or Craftmanship* (Chicago: University of Chicago Press, 1972), p. 3, where he uses such terms as *production teaching* (similar to bureaucrat/technocrat) and *craftsman* (similar to craftsman/artist) to describe the faculty in an elementary school. In Philip Jackson's, *The Practice of Teaching* (New York: Teachers College Press, 1986), two traditions in teaching are described: the "mimetic" and the "transformative," similar to the two images that I use. See Chapter 6, pp. 115–45.

While I use a dichotomy, it is shorthand for a continuum, not mutually exclusive categories. Other researchers have analyzed these competing terms less in polar terms and more as tensions within, for example, teachers who attend to bureaucratic goals (e.g., classroom order, sorting out students by grades) and care for students' individual needs; R. Dreeben, *The Nature of Teaching* (Glenview, Ill.: Scott, Foresman, 1970). See also A. and H. Berlak, *Dilemmas of Schooling: Teaching and Social Change* (New York: Methuen, 1981). Until more is known about the cognitive maps in teachers' minds, I suspect that the notion of images arrayed along a continuum would be a more generous notion. I can imagine teachers who hold both images, variations of each, etc. See C. Clark and P. Petersen chapter in *Third Handbook of Research in Teaching*, ed. E. Wittrock (Washington, D.C.: American Educational Research Assoc., 1986) Also, I assume that these images change over time. An eager neophyte entering the classroom at age twenty-one may have visions of teaching that will be quite different than after two decades of sustained contact with the organizational imperatives embedded in schooling. Theodore Sizer's composite portrait of Horace in *Horace's Compromise* picks up such changes in teachers (Boston: Houghton Mifflin, 1984).

7. See Barak Rosenshine and Robert Stevens chapter in the *Third Handbook;* Kerchner and Mitchell in Sykes and Shulman's *Handbook of Teaching and Policy*.

8. See Alan Tom, p. 126, for revised version of his example *The Moral Craft of Teaching* (New York: Longman Inc. 1984). A question arises whether these images of the technical and moral are gender-linked. Is the image of the bureaucrat/technocrat based on male traits the artist/craftsman and moral meaning of the conception on female traits? Although such gender-based

dichotomies have been explored frequently, the accounts of both male and female teachers and administrators and formal studies of gender issues among administrators, I could find no substantial body of evidence that clearly links sex to images. Among female superintendents, for example, there is Ella Flagg Young (Chicago, 1909–1915), Susan Dorsey (Los Angeles, 1922–1929), Ira Jarrell (Atlanta, 1944–1960), and Floretta McKenzie (Washington, D.C., 1980–), the images they have projected in their writing and what has been written about them are mixes of both the technical and moral, of the negotiator-statesman, administrative chief, and instructional supervisor. To assert this, however, is not to close the door on the point of gender-linked roles. It remains open in my mind.

For a summary of the literature on women as principals, see Joan Meskin, "Women as Principals: Their Performance as Educational Administrators," in D. Erickson and T. Reller, *The Principal in Metropolitan Schools:* McCutchin, 1979) pp. 323–47; Neal Gross and Anne Trask, *The Sex Factor and the Management of Schools* (New York: John Wiley (New York/& Sons, 1976); for a brief historical analysis of women in administration, see Tyack and Hansot, *Managers of Virtue* (New York: Basic Books, 1982), pp. 180–201.

9. The view of teacher as a clinician, for example, who diagnoses specific forms of learning difficulties and prescribes educational remedies is anchored in the view of a professional who has access to a body of knowledge and combines that knowledge with beliefs and theories to render independent judgments. See Clark and Petersen in the *Third Handbook*. Yet a number of writers question whether teachers are professionals since such a reliable body of knowledge with a solid theoretical base is missing, as is the conceptual framework, vocabulary, and usual paraphernalia of professional control over entry and monitoring of performance. See Dan Lortie, *Schoolteacher* (Chicago: University of Chicago Press, 1975), p. 136.

10. The linkages between images and behavior have been noted repeatedly in human affairs. From cognitive psychology to advertising, from the hiring of image-makers by ambitious candidates for public office to the deep concern for the effect of television and films on the young, the awareness of the power of pictures in people's heads (as Walter Lippman first put it in *Public Opinion* in 1922 [New York: Free Press, 1965, pp. 3–20]) continues to intrigue observers. See, for example, Kenneth Boulding, *The Image* (Ann Arbor: University of Michigan Press, 1961); Daniel Boorstin, *The Image: A Guide to Pseudo-Events in America* (New York: Atheneum, 1971); Richard Schickel, *Intimate Strangers: The Culture of Celebrity* (New York: Doubleday and Co., 1985). What remains difficult to link are the images that teachers have and daily practice. What are the connective tissues that join ideas to action in a classroom? A few researchers have explored the nature of the intersection. See D. Jean Clandinin, "Personal Practical Knowledge: A Study of Teachers' Classroom Images," *Curriculum Inquiry*, 15, No. 4, (1985) pp. 361–385.

Images of teaching, of course, are wedded to images of students as learners. Teacher as bureaucrat/technocrat implicitly sees students as passive objects to whom things must happen (i.e., teachers dispense information and students absorb it). No relationship need exist. Emotions either get in the way or are irrelevant. Teacher as craftsman/artist implies an interactive view of students as an audience or as clients. In either case, students are seen as beings capable of expressing feelings and of judging for themselves whether they wish to participate in a relationship with the teacher. For a general description of the conceptions of students that teachers and other adults have had over the last few centuries, see John Cleverly and D. C. Phillips. *Visions of Childhood* (New York: Teacher College Press, 1986).

11. Carl Kaestle, *Joseph Lancaster & the Monitorial Movement* (New York: Teacher College Press, 1973). Also see Carl Kaestle, *The Evolution of an Urban School System* (Cambridge, Mass., Harvard University Press, 1973).

12. Kaestle, *Lancaster,* pp. 80–81.

13. Manual of the System of Primary Instruction Pursued in the Model Schools of the *British and Foreign Schools Society,* London, 1831, pp. 48–54.

14. Kaestle, *Lancaster,* pp. 80–81.

15. Ibid., p. 95.

16. See Cuban, *How Teachers Taught,* pp. 17–38; David Tyack, *One Best System* (Cambridge, Mass.: Harvard University Press, 1974), pp. 80–88.

17. Joseph Rice, *The Public School System of the United States* (New York: Arno Press, 1969), pp. 97–98.

18. Alfred D. Chandler, Jr., *The Visible Hand* (Cambridge, Mass.: Harvard University Press, 1977).

19. For a general description of these critics, see Tyack, *One Best System,* pp. 126–147, 182–198; Raymond Callahan, *Education and The Cult of Efficiency* (Chicago: University of Chicago Press, 1962).

20. Ellwood P. Cubberley, *The Portland Survey* (Yonkers, NY: World Book Co., 1916), pp. 118–119.

21. Wolcott, *Teachers and Technocrats,* p. 17.

22. Ibid., p. 19.

23. Ibid., pp. 148–149.

24. Ibid., p. 75.

25. Ibid.

26. President's Commission on Excellence in Education, *A Nation at*

Risk (Washington, D.C.: U.S. Government Printing Office, 1983).

27. See Barak Rosenshine, "Teaching Functions in Instructional Programs," Paper delivered at National Institute of Education Conference at Airlie House, Virginia, February, 1982.

28. Gilbert Highet, *The Art of Teaching* (New York: Vintage Books, Inc., 1950); E. B. Castle, *The Teacher* (London: Oxford University Press, 1970).

29. Lortie, pp. 68–70, 266; Philip Jackson, *Life in Classrooms* (New York: Holt, Rinehart, and Winston, 1968), pp. 143–150; Tom, pp. 98–119.

30. Tom, 129–135; Elliot Eisner, *The Educational Imagination*, p. 153; N. L. Gage, *The Scientific Basis for the Art of Teaching* (New York: Teachers College Press, 1978), pp. 15–16.

31. Donald Schon, *The Reflective Practitioner* (New York: Basic Books, 1983), pp. 21–75.

32. Horace Mann, *Annual Report of The Secretary of the Board of Education of Massachusetts, Years 1845–1848* (Boston: Lee and Shepherd, 1981), pp. 24–26.

33. Henry Barnard, ed., *Memoirs of Teachers and Educators* (New York: Arno Press, 1969), pp. 436–437.

34. National Education Association, *Journal of Proceedings and Addresses, 1884* (Washington, D.C.: National Education Association, 1884), p. 46.

35. See Wayne Fuller, *The Old Country School* (Chicago: University of Chicago Press, 1982), pp. 101–109.

36. David Cohen, "Innocent Inventions" (Paper presented at American Educational Research Association, San Francisco, April, 1986).

37. Reginald D. Archambault, ed. *John Dewey on Education* (New York: Random House, 1964), pp. 430–433.

38. See Tyack, *One Best System*, pp. 23–27.

39. City College of New York, Workshop for Open Education, "Recollections of A One-Room Schoolhouse," Interview with Marian Brooks, April, 1985; also see Margaret Nelson, "From the One Room Schoolhouse to The Graded School: Teaching in Vermont, 1910–1950." *Frontiers*, 7 (1983), pp. 14–20.

40. Brooks, pp. 8–9.

41. See Agnes DeLima, *Our Enemy The Child* (New York: New Republic, 1925); Patricia Graham, *Progressive Education: From Arcady to Academe* (New York: Teachers College Press, 1967).

42. Jesse Newlon, "The Need of a Scientific Curriculum Policy for Junior and Senior High Schools," *Educational Administration and Supervision*, 3 (May, 1917), p. 267.

43. Jesse Newlon and A. L. Threlkeld, "Denver Program of Curriculum Revision" in National Society for the Study of Education, 26th Yearbook, *Curriculum Making*, Part 1 (Bloomington, Ill.: 1926), pp. 231–233.

44. In 1927–1928, there were 1,400 Denver teachers, of whom 27 percent (376 teachers) served on curriculum committees. While only 10 percent of the elementary staff worked that year on committees, almost half of all secondary teachers served. The process had begun five years earlier and by 1927 between 30 to 40 percent of all Denver teachers had participated in curriculum revision. Also see section on Denver in chapter 2 of Cuban, *How Teachers Taught*.

45. Highet, p. vii.

46. Jackson, *Life in Classrooms*, p. 175.

47. Louis Rubin, *Artistry in Teaching* (New York: Random House, 1985); Ken Macrorie, *20 Teachers* (New York: Oxford University Press, 1984), p. xi.

48. See Lortie, pp. 73–79; for a more recent statement on professionalization of teaching, see Linda Darling-Hammond, "Valuing Teachers: The Making of a Profession," *Teachers College Record*, 87 (Winter, 1985), pp. 205–218.

49. See Barbara Finkelstein, "Governing the Young: Teacher Behavior in American primary Schools, 1820–1880," (Unpublished Ed.D dissertation, Teachers College, Columbia University, 1970), pp. 22, 86; also see Barbara Finkelstein, "The Moral Dimensions of Pedagogy," *American Studies* (Fall, 1974), pp. 81–2, 84. Also, Nancy Hoffman, *Womens (True) Profession: Voices from the History of Teaching* (Old Westbury, New York: Feminist Press, 1981).

50. Teacher-centered instruction means that a teacher controls what is taught, when, and under what conditions within the classroom. Usually, the teacher does most of the talking, teaches to the whole group, and focuses upon subject matter and skills. Student-centered instruction means that the students exercise a substantial degree of direction and responsibility for what is taught, how it is learned, and for any physical movement within the classroom. Usually in such classrooms, instruction occurs in small groups and individually, ample materials are available to students, and seating arrangements encourage exchanges between students. See Cuban, *How Teachers Taught*, pp. 3–4.

51. John Goodlad, *A Place Called School* (New York: McGraw-Hill, 1983); Theodore Sizer, *Horace's Compromise: The Dilemma of the American High*

School (Boston: Houghton-Mifflin, 1984).

52. See Louis Smith and William Geoffrey, *The Complexities of the Urban Classroom* (New York: Holt, Rinehart and Winston, 1968).

53. Walter Doyle, "Classroom Organization and Management," in Wittrock (ed.) *Handbook of Research in Teaching*, p. 394.

54. Ibid.

55. Ibid., 394–395.

56. Willard Waller, *The Sociology of Teaching* (New York: John Wiley, 1965), preface; Seymour Sarason, *The Culture of the School and the Problem of Change* (Boston: Allyn and Bacon, 1971); Hugh Mehan, *Learning Lessons* (Cambridge, Mass.: Harvard University Press, 1979).

57. I have drawn these roles from the following sources: Richard Scott, "Professionals in Bureaucracies: Areas in Conflict," in Howard Vollmer and Donald Mills, *Professionalization* (Englewood Cliffs, N.J.: Prentice-Hall, 1966), pp. 265–175; Lee Shulman, "Autonomy and Obligation: The Remote Control of Teaching," in Shulman and Sykes, pp. 484–504; Walter Doyle, "Classroom Organization and Management;" Dan Lortie, *Schoolteacher;* Thomas Green, The Activities of Teaching (New York: McGraw-Hill, 1971). In describing the three primary roles, I exclude such often cited roles as "caring," "counseling," or "nurturing." Such expected and actual behaviors are included in personal traits that many (but not all) teachers bring to bear in enacting their primary roles. For analytic purposes, I distinguish between roles and personal attributes that each teacher stamps uniquely into the performance of these roles.

58. Green, p. 4; see Bruce Joyce and Marsha Weil, *Models of Teaching* (Englewood Cliffs, N.J.: Prentice-Hall, 1972).

59. Few researchers or practitioners have openly acknowledged the political role within either the classroom or school. Robert Hess and Judith Torney, *The Development of Political Attitudes in Children* (Chicago: Aldine, 1967); Harmon Zeigler, *The Political Life of American Teachers* (Englewood Cliffs, N.J.: Prentice-Hall, 1967) either focused upon children's political attitudes and the school's impact upon them or the teacher's political role outside the classroom. Herbert Kohl, *On Teaching* (New York: Schocken Books, 1976) devotes a section to the conventional view of politics. He urges readers to find out about the school and district organizational hierarchies, who the formal and informal power brokers are (e.g., school secretary), the importance of knowing the community and getting its support, and teachers' unions. Closer to the sense of my use of the word *political* is Sara Lighfoot, "Politics and Reasoning: Through the Eyes of Teachers and Children," *Harvard Educational Review*, 43 (May 1973), pp. 197–244 and John Schwille, Andrew Por-

ter, and Michael Gant, "Content Decision Making and the Politics of Education," *Educational Administration Quarterly*, 16, no. 2 (Spring 1980), 21–40. How the political climate outside schools affects what teachers teach and how they teach has been explored by Howard K. Beale, *Are American Teachers Free?* (New York: Charles Scribner's Sons, 1936).

In Freeman Elbaz's study of Sarah, an English teacher, Sarah is aware of her political role as a teacher, "but does not appear to act on this knowledge." She is less aware of her work in the classroom as political action. Elbaz points out that Sarah "shrinks from the obligation to determine by her evaluation which students will go on to the university." She views this process as "phony rather than as an act with very significant consequences both personal and political." Freeman Elbaz, *The Teacher's "Practical Knowledge,"* (New York: Nichols Publishing Co., 1980), p. 52.

60. Tyack and Hansot, *Manager of Virtue*, pp. 105–114; Wallace Sayre, "Additional Observations on the Study of Administration," *Teachers College Record*, 60, (Oct. 1958).

61. The generic definition of "political" leans upon David Easton's *A Framework for Political Analysis* (Englewood Cliffs, N.J.: Prentice-Hall, 1965). The example comes from Alan Tom, pp. 78–88. However, he does not extend the point on teaching as moral behavior into political action as I do, although he does discuss Paolo Friere's work on the relationship between teacher and student; Nel Noddings in *Caring* argues that the teacher's relationship with a student is inescapably moral: "A teacher cannot 'talk' this ethic. She must live it, and that implies establishing a relation with a student. Besides talking to him and showing him how one cares, she engages in cooperative practice with him. He is learning not just mathematics or social studies; he is also learning how to be one-caring. By conducting education morally, the teacher hopes to induce and enhance moral sense in the student" (Berkeley: University of California Press, 1984), p. 179. John Dewey's *Ethical Principles Underlying Education* (1897) argues that moral growth of the child is the central task of the school: "The school is fundamentally an institution erected by society to do a certain specific work—to exercise a certain specific function in maintaining the life and advancing the welfare of society. . . . Hence the necessity of discussing the entire structure and the specific workings of the school system from the standpoint of its moral position and moral function to society." Also see Maxine Greene, "Philosophy and Teaching," in *Third Handbook of Research on Teaching*, p. 481: "most [philosophers] do, indeed, recognize that moral and political values are inescapable in the teaching enterprise." Also see Margaret Buchmann, "Role Over Person: Morality and Authenticity in Teaching," *Teachers College Record*, 87, no. 4 (Summer 1986), pp. 529–543. The historic role of American teachers as moral exemplars is summarized in Finkelstein, "The Moral Dimensions of Pedagogy." Philip Jackson's category of "transformative teaching" as a

tradition among teachers, according to Jackson, "seeks moral ends" with children, *Practice of Teaching*, pp. 127–128.

For many writers who see schools as instruments of the larger society that recreate the social relationships existing in the culture, schools are both intensely political and moral. See Michael Apple, *Ideology and Curriculum* (London: Routledge and Kegan, 1979); Henry Giroux, *Ideology, Culture, and the Process of Schooling* (Philadelphia: Temple University Press, 1981); Jean Anyon, "Social Class and School Knowledge," *Curriculum Inquiry*, 11, no. 1 (1981); Paul Willis, *Learning to Labor* (Lexington, Mass.: Heath, 1977); Michael Katz, *The Irony of Early School Reform* (Boston: Beacon Press, 1968).

62. These decisions are often called managerial or instructional rather than political. The point is that from the teacher's view such acts are labeled managerial or instructional, yet to an outsider such decisions contain political content (i.e., connected to the institution's goals), use political tools (e.g., bargaining, exerting control), and have political consequences. Much depends upon the teacher's degree of political awareness in making managerial and instructional decisions to determine whether the political content, actions, or consequences are intentional or not. If the teacher is unaware of the political content, actions, or consequences, does that make their actions any less political?

The point of how conscious the person is about the political content or process is crucial. Is a decision made by a teacher or the manner of putting that decision into practice political if the person is unaware of the larger political issues, personal, or organizational goals? It is the difference between the self-perception of the actor and the perception of the observer. Many would argue that explicit intentions (i.e., conscious awareness) is essential for political behavior since the awareness is central to building coalitions, undertaking negotiations, and striking compromises.

To researchers who write within the broad perspective of cultural reproduction, that is, the school shapes students who fit into the larger society socialized to its values, such as Michael Apple, Henry Giroux, and others (although sharp differences exist between these and like-minded writers), teachers are agents of the larger culture who help transform children into compliant adults embracing norms, values, and dominant views of society, including work roles. They would prefer to make teachers conscious of the role they play in order to make teachers agents of social change (i.e., consciously political to seek different ends). See Levin and Carnoy for their summary of these "critical functionalist writers" in *Schooling and Work in the Democratic State* (Stanford: Stanford University Press, 1985).

Most teachers, then, unaware of the larger social meaning of their daily activities, are, therefore, tacitly political in embracing without question the dominant beliefs of the culture and perform their assigned roles of socializing students to accept existing norms. Other teachers, however, more conscious of what goes on in schools may resist their assigned roles. Teachers, for example, who seldom use the desktop computer allocated to the classroom or teachers who use a planning period to run personal errands have been used as examples of teachers resisting the intrusion of bureaucratic demands. Although such acts are ambiguous and difficult to interpret since they depend greatly upon determining the teacher's consciousness and intention, writers have explored such actions and have labeled them teacher resistance. See Stanley Aronowitz & Henry Giroux, *Education Under Siege* (South Hadley, Mass.: Bergin & Garvey Publishers, 1985), pp. 96–109.

63. Sizer, *Horace's Compromise;* Cohen, Farrar, and Powell, *The Shopping Mall High School;* Cusick, *Egalitarian Ideal* (NT: Longman, Inc., 1984); Ernest Boyer, *High School* (New York: Harper & Row, 1985) note the concept of a contract or deal between teachers and students.

64. See Walt Haney, "Testing Reasoning and Reasoning About Testing," *Review of Educational Research*, 54 (Winter, 1984), pp. 597–654.

65. I examined two forty-minute videotaped lessons of Thelma Katz's kindergarten class; interviewed her twice over the telephone for a total of two hours; and had her read a draft of what I wrote for correction of errors in fact or interpretation. The quotes come from the transcription of the interviews.

2. DRIFTING INTO TEACHING AND STAYING AWHILE

1. A description of the entire project is included in Larry Cuban, *To Make a Difference: Teaching in the Inner City* (New York: Free Press, 1970).

3. PRINCIPALING: IMAGES AND ROLES

1. Paul R. Pierce, *The Origin and Development of the Public School Principalship* (Chicago: University of Chicago Press, 1935) p. 8.

2. Ibid., pp. 8, 14.

3. Tyack, *One Best System*, pp. 44–45.

4. National Education Association, Bulletin of Department of Elementary School Principals, "Elementary School Principalship," vol. 7, no. 3 (April, 1928), pp. 206–207.

5. Frank McMurry, *Elementary School Standards* (Yonkers, New York: World Book Co., 1913); Ellwood P. Cubberley, *The Principal and His School* (Boston: Houghton Mifflin Co., 1923).

6. From the very origins of the post, principals spent a portion of their time working with parents (e.g., handling complaints, establishing mothers' clubs, planning what used to be called vacation, or summer, schools, and so

on) interpreting the school to the community, and in general playing what educators, in an age dominated by corporate vocabulary and the glitter of advertising, were fond of calling public relations. The phrase is a euphemism for political behavior (i.e., maintaining and expanding public support of one's school). However, such activities, noted as early as the 1880s by Paul Pierce in his history of the position, seldom coalesced into a dominant image of the principalship in either graduate schools or in professional associations. Such actions were often seen as important by practitioners, but probably were transformed into the prosaic language of "community relations" because of the earlier taint of partisan politics that previous generations of school administrators knew full well. The growing professionalization of the principalship made anything smelling of partisan political behavior noxious. See chapters in Pierce, pp. 123–51 and Wallace S. Sayre, "Additional Observations on the Study of Administration," *Teachers College Record*, 60 (October, 1958). Sayre points out the political tabus and what he calls "serviceable myths."

7. See Pierce, pp. 25–56.

8. Cited in "Elementary School Principalship," Bulletin of Department of Elementary School Principals, 7 No. 2 (April, 1928), pp. 162–63; also see report of F. Lee Forman, principal of Arapahoe School in *Eleventh Annual Report*, Board of Education, District No. 1, Arapahoe County, Colorado (Denver), September 1, 1885, pp. 86–87.

9. McMurry, *Elementary School Standards*, p. 186.

10. See Callahan, chapters 1–3.

11. See Tyack and Hansot, *Managers of Virtue*, pp. 105–140.

12. Ellwood P. Cubberley, *The Principal and the School* (Boston: Houghton and Mifflin, 1923), p. 19.

13. Pierce, p. 58; *Twelfth Annual Report of Board of Education of Cincinnati, Ohio*, 1841, p. 51.

14. *Seventeenth Annual Report of Board of Education of St. Louis, Missouri*, 1871, p. 188; for a practitioner's view of the principalship, see Superintendent J. M. Greenwood's report to the school board in *Annual Report of the Public Schools, Kansas City, Missouri*, 1895–1896, p. 61.

15. *Annual Report, Kansas City*, 1895–1896, pp. 84–94, 104–194.

16. Ellwood P. Cubberley, *School Organization and Administration* (New York: World Book Co., 1923), pp. 43–44.

17. Pierce collects many of their duties from annual reports of school boards. Independently, I have examined annual reports from Boston, Denver, Kansas City (Missouri), and Syracuse.

18. See, for example, Kent Petersen, "The Principal's Task," *Administrator's Notebook*, 26 no. 8 (1977–1978); W. J. Martin and D. J. Willower, "The Managerial Behavior of High School Principals," *Educational Administration Quarterly*, 17 (Winter, 1981); Van C. Morris, Robert Crowson, and Cynthia Porter-Gehrie, *The Urban Principal* (Chicago: University of Illinois at Chicago Circle, 1981); also see Roland Barth and Terence Deal for a summary and analysis of principals' writings that focus on busyness, emotional and non-rational elements to the post, and frequent conflicts, "The Principalship: Views from Without and Within," (Washington, D.C.: National Institute of Education, 1982, pp. 21–23.

19. Frank McMurry, "Educational Aspects of the Public School System of The City of New York," Report to Committee on School Inquiry of the Board of Estimate, 1911–1912, p. 335.

20. Cubberley, *The Principal and the School*, p. 191.

21. Cayce Morrison, "The Principalship Develops Supervisory Status," *Tenth Yearbook*, Department of Elementary School Principals, 10, No. 3 (1931), p. 160.

22. "Elementary School Principalship," p. 208; that pattern persisted in a massive survey of elementary principals in 1968 (Elementary School Principals, *The Elementary School Principalship* (Washington, D.C.: National Education Association, 1968), p. 51 and for high school principals, National Association of Secondary School Principals, *The Senior High School Principalship*, vol. 1 (Washington, D.C.: National Education Association, 1978), p. 20.

23. See Terence Deal and L. Celotti, "How Much Influence Do (And Can) Educational Administrators Have on Classrooms?" Phi Delta *Kappan*, 61, No. 7 (1980), pp. 471–473. See description of principal's role in "Who Will Teach Our Children," *Report of the California Commission on the Teaching Profession* (November, 1985), pp. 32–36. It focuses on the principal as facilitator for teachers who act as instructional cadre of leaders in school. Also Nancy Pitner, "Substitutes for Principal Leader Behavior," Educational Administration Quarterly (Spring 1986). Also see Adam Urbanski, "Lessons Learned from Evaluating Administrators," *Education Week* (2/26/86), p. 24. Approximately 1800 Rochester, New York, teachers evaluated 172 principals and other supervisors. They gave administrators high marks for treating staff as professionals and low marks for instructional leadership. Urbanksi argues that principals are like hospital administrators who manage and set a tone but never tell "surgeons to cut a little to the left or a little to the right."

24. Barth and Deal analyze major works written by academics between 1970–1981. They underscore a dominant theme of leadership, pp. 18–20.

25. Labels for such leaders run from Ed Bridges' "White Knight" in "The Principalship as a Career," in Erickson & Reller, *The Principal in Metropolitan Schools* to "Water Walkers" in Sheila Huff, Dale Lake, and Mary Lou Schaalman, *Principal Differences* (Boston: McBer and Co., 1982).

26. See, for example, James Lipham and J. A. Hoeh, *The Principalship: Foundations and Functions* (New York: Harper & Row, 1974); Chester Finn, Jr., "Better Principals, Not Just Teachers," *Wall Street Journal*, 2/18/86. Also, California School Leadership Academy (sponsored by State Department of Education): "The CLSA's purpose is to train aspiring/practicing administrators . . . in instructional leadership competencies which support opportunities for student success, particularly in academic learnings." (CSLA brochure n.d.)

27. See David Armor, "Analysis of the School Preferred Reading Program in Selected Los Angeles Minority Schools," Santa Monica, Calif.: RAND, 1976; Elizabeth Cohen, Russell Miller, Anneke Bredo, Kenneth Duckworth, "Principal Role and Teachers Morale Under Varying Organizational Conditions." Mimeographed, Stanford, California, Center for Research and Development in Teaching, Stanford University, 1977.

28. Ronald Larkin, superintendent of the New Brunswick (N.J.) Schools sent me the material described here. New Brunswick, New Jersey, "Manual for Principals To Implement Improvement Program," (1984) I–1.

29. Ibid., I–1, I–3.

30. Ibid., Introduction, (8/16/84–TP16).

31. Washington, D.C., Atlanta, Georgia, and other districts enrolling large numbers of low-income minority children have implemented competency-based curricula and produced manuals for teachers and principals to follow.

32. There is much written on the principal's roles. Charles Bidwell, "Some Effects of Administrative Behavior: A Study in Role Theory," *Administrative Science Quarterly*, vol. 2, no. 2, (1957), pp. 163–81; E. Bridges, "Bureaucratic Role and Socialization," *Educational Administrative Quarterly*, vol. 1, no. 2 (1965), pp. 19–28. See A. Blumberg and W. Greenfield, *The Effective Principal* (Boston: Allyn and Bacon, 1980) in which the political dimension of principaling is specifically described. Leithwood, K. A. and Montgomery, D. "The role of the elementary school principal in program improvement," *Review of Educational Research;* M. A. Thomas, "A Study of Alternatives in American Education," *The Role of the Principal*, vol. 2 (Santa Monica, Calif.: RAND, 1978). For a thorough review of the research literature on principals (and superintendents) that notes the popularity of role theory among academics, see E. Bridges, "Research on the School Administrator: The State of the

Art, 1967–1980," *Educational Administrative Quarterly,* vol. 19, no. 3 (Summer 1982), pp. 12–33; and Norman Boyan, "The Description and Explanation of Administrative Behavior," *Handbook of Research on Educational Administration,* ed. Norman Boyan (New York: Longman, 1987).

33. Bruce McPherson & John Lorenz, "The Pedagogical & Andragogical Principal—The Consummate Teacher," *NASSP Bulletin,* 69, (May, 1985), pp. 55–60.

34. As superintendent of the Arlington County public schools (1974–1981), I visited Belt over thirty times at Oakridge Elementary. In addition, we conferred over her school's annual plan and I was also her evaluator for three of the seven years. Since leaving the superintendency, we have exchanged letters and I conducted three phone interviews with her in 1985.

35. I have read two articles that Eicholtz wrote; I attended the school assembly where he received a standing ovation which occurred during my site visit for the National Secondary School Recognition Program, an effort sponsored by the U.S. Department of Education (May, 1983). In addition, he wrote one letter and I interviewed him twice by phone during the fall of 1985.

36. See Harry Wolcott, *Man in the Principal's Office* (New York: Holt, Rinehart and Winston, 1973), chapters 5 and 6.

37. The moral dimension of political choices is often submerged in daily routines. On occasion, events erupt suddenly to reveal the moral ground on which principals stand. A recent U.S. Supreme Court decision upheld the principal's right to suspend a high school student in Spanaway, Washington, for making a "lewd and indecent" nominating speech to an assembly. The Court ruled that "schools must teach by example the shared values of a civilized social order" and have broad freedom to punish what principals determine "inappropriate" speech in classrooms or assemblies (*New York Times,* 7/8/86). For a broader treatment of moral dimensions in administrative work see Thomas B. Greenfield, "The Decline and Fall of Science in Educational Administration," *Interchange,* vol. 17, no 2 (Summer 1986), pp. 57–80; Mary Ann Raywid, "Some Moral Dimensions of Administrative Theory and Practice," American Educational Research Association, San Fran., (April 1986); D. A. Erickson, "Moral Dilemmas of Administrative Powerlessness," *Administrator's Notebook,* vol. 20, no. 8 (1972). Also see Barth and Deal on literature written by principals that acknowledge competing interests, natural conflict, and so forth, pp. 36–37.

38. Dale Mann, *The Politics of Administrative Representation* (Lexington, Mass.: D. C. Heath, 1976); Arthur Blumberg and William Greenfield, *The Effective Principal: Perspectives on School* (Boston: Allyn and Bacon, 1980); sometimes researchers call political activity, "street-level" policymaking. See

Robert Crowson and C. Porter-Gehrie, "The Discretionary Behavior of Principals in Large City Schools," *Educational Administration Quarterly*, 16 (1980), pp. 45–69, on how principals bend rules. Some researchers call political work "boundary-spanning" (e.g., reaching out to parents and the immediate community or district office), see M. P. Koza and W. Levy "School Organization and Community Participation," *Administrator's Notebook*, 26 (9) (1978), pp. 1–4. Also see portraits of principals who openly assert their political activity such as Atlanta's Norris Hogans in Sara Lightfoot, *Good High Schools* (New York: Basic Books, 1983) or the brief description of Marcus Foster in Tyack and Hansot *Managers of Virtue*, pp. 234–237 and New York City's Elliot Shapiro in Nat Hentoff, *Our Children Are Dying* (New York: Four Winds Press, 1966).

39. Philip Jackson, "George Washington Carver Comprehensive High School School: Schools for the Poor" *Daedalus*, 110 (no. 4) (Fall 1981), pp. 39–57.

40. Letter from Betty Belt to author, September 23, 1985.

41. I recognize that "leadership style" or "managerial style" has a long history in various research traditions studying the practice of administration. I am familiar with the various literatures that stress autocratic/democratic styles, task- oriented/relationship/oriented approaches and Theory X/Theory Y. Researchers have produced over a score of different dimensions that have been used to describe style as a way of capturing executive or managerial behavior. The work on principals and school improvement done at the University of Texas's Research and Development Center for Teacher Education in the mid–1970s and early 1980s, for example, embraced the concept of style (their phrase was "change facilitator style") as the conceptual framework to use in analyzing principal behavior. Gene Hall, Shirley Hord, Leslie Huling, William Rutherford, Suzanne Stiegelbauer, "Leadership Variables Associated with Successful School Improvement," Report No. 3164, American Educational Research Association (April, 1983), Montreal, Canada.

Researchers have also expressed deep reservations about the concept of style as a tool for understanding organizational leadership. Criticisms point to the array of conflicting definitions of *style*, or of the difficulty that researchers have in categorizing observed behaviors (e.g., delegation of a task to a subordinate) without knowing the person's intentions (e.g., did the delegation occur because of the manager's belief in giving responsibility to people to gain productivity or as a tactic to create less conflict in a particular situation). Also criticisms have been made that emphasis on style minimize organizational context, and situational differences. See McCall, Jr. and Michael Lombardo *Leadership: Where Else Can We Go* (Durham, N.C., Duke University Press, 1978). F. E. Fiedler, *A Theory of Leadership Effectiveness* (NT: McGraw-Hall, 1967). I am persuaded both by the criticisms and my experience with so many different superintendents, principals, and teachers that style as a conceptual tool is sufficiently flawed as to be useless with practitioners since it exaggerates personal traits while minimizing organizational setting.

42. For an example of a seemingly apolitical principal whose actions have political consequences, see the case of Jonathan Rolf in David Dwyer, G. Lee, N. Filby, B. Rowan, and C, Kojimoto, *Understanding the Principal's Contribution to Instruction: Seven Principals, Seven Stories* (San Francisco: Far West Laboratory, 1985). Jonathan Rolf heads an affluent suburban elementary school and appears to be apolitical; another one of the studies describes Ray Murdoch, the principal of a rural elementary school, who is as consciously political as a principal could be.

4. PERVERSE INCENTIVES: MOVING BACK AND FORTH BETWEEN CLASSROOM AND ADMINISTRATION

1. See Carl Hansen, *Amidon Elementary School* (Englewood Cliffs, New Jersey: Prentice-Hall, 1962) and *Danger in Washington* (West Nyack, N.Y.: Parker Publishing Co., 1968). Also see Larry Cuban, *Urban School Chiefs Under Fire* (Chicago: University of Chicago Press, 1976), chapter 2 on Washington, D.C.

5. SUPERINTENDING: IMAGES AND ROLES

1. Theodore Reller, *The Development of the City Superintendency in the United States* (Philadelphia: Theodore Reller, 1935), p. 31.

2. C. T. Onions, ed., *The Shorter Oxford English Dictionary*, third ed., Vol. 2 (Oxford: Clarendon Press, 1973), p. 2192.

3. *Annual Report of the School Committee of The City of Boston, 1857* (Boston: J. E. Farnell and Co., 1858), p. 18.

4. For histories of the origins of the city superintendency, see Reller and Thomas Gilland, *The Origin and Development of the Power and Duties of The City School Superintendent* (Chicago: University of Chicago Press, 1935), and Joseph Cronin, *The Control of Urban Schools* (New York: Free Press, 1973).

5. Larry Cuban, *Urban School Chiefs Under Fire* (Chicago: University of Chicago Press, 1976), pp. 114–126; Arthur Blumberg, *The School Superintendent* (New York: Teachers College Press, 1986) interviewed twenty-five New York state superintendents and devoted a chapter to the images of superintending that emerged from these discussions. Blumberg clustered the images into superintendent as leader and inducer of change; his interviewees used

such metaphors as theatrical director or producer, symphony orchestra conductor, coach, trout fisherman, and football quarterback, pp. 32–44.

6. Reller, pp. 52, 295. In Cuban, *Urban School Chiefs*, I had used the phrase "teacher-scholar" in place of "instructional supervisor."

7. Cuban, *Urban School Chiefs*, p. 115.

8. National Educational Association, *Journal of Proceedings and Addresses, 1880* (Washington, D.C.: National Educational Association, 1880), p. 313.

9. Many of Young's ideas first appear in her doctoral dissertation, *Isolation in the Schools* (Contributions to Education, No. 1) (Chicago: University of Chicago Press, 1901).

10. Tyack and Hansot, *Managers of Virtue*, p. 207.

11. See Ronald Johnson, "Captain of Education: An Intellectual Biography of Andrew Draper" (Unpublished doctoral dissertation, University of Illinois, 1970).

12. National Educational Association, *Journal of Proceedings and Addresses, 1884* (Washington, D.C.: National Educational Association, 1884), p. 284.

13. Ibid., (1890), pp. 463–464.

14. For some historians to argue that an efficiency movement took administrators by storm after the corporate community had become entranced by Frederick Taylor's version of scientific management is to ignore the strong, unrelieved pressures within which earlier generations of superintendents had to work to keep the costs for schooling children within bounds. Barbara Berman, "Business Efficiency, American Schooling, and Public School Superintendency: A reconsideration of the Callahan Thesis" *History of Education Quarterly* (Fall 1983), pp. 297–319, challenges Callahan's use of evidence. Her research on teacher education reveals a deep concern for economical use of public funds. My reading of numerous annual reports in the middle and late decades of the nineteenth century in Boston, Denver, New York City, Kansas City (Missouri), and Syracuse confirm a persistent search by superintendents and boards for ways of stretching limited funds to accomplish grand aims in both the business and instructional sides of school operations. See, for example, Boston's John Philbrick's annual reports for 1857 and 1862 for repeated references to "efficiency," the tables that list expenditures per "scholar," the amount of real estate taxes spent on the schools, the rate of increase and explanations for those increases. *Annual Reports*, 1856, pp. 136–38; 1862, pp. 11–12; 231–38.

15. National Educational Association, *Journal of Proceedings and Addresses, 1873*, p. 253; (1904), pp. 264, 272.

16. William Chancellor, *Our Schools: Their Administration and Supervision* (Boston: D.C. Heath, 1904), pp. 89–90.

17. Reller, p. 101.

18. National Educational Association, *Journal of Proceedings and Addresses 1904*, p. 264.

19. Few women served as superintendent between 1870 and 1970. In twenty-five cities in that period, six women (3 percent) were school chiefs. See Appendix in Cuban, *Urban School Chiefs*.

20. A common way of determining what superintendents did was to inventory what the school board regulations and duties assigned to the post were. See Arthur Chamberlain, "The Growth and Enlargement of the Power of the City School Superintendent," University of California, *Publications*, 3, no. 4 (May 15, 1913); W. S. Diffenbaugh, *School Administration in the Smaller Cities* Bureau of Education Bulletin, (1915), no. 44 (Washington, D.C.: Department of Interior, 1915).

21. *Twenty-Eighth Annual Report of the Board of Education of Syracuse, 1876* (Syracuse: Masteurs and Stone, 1876), pp. 121–129 and 13.

22. Ibid., p. 135.

23. Ibid.

24. Ibid., pp. 135–136.

25. Ibid., p. 134.

26. Chancellor, p. 134.

27. See Gilland, pp. 252–261.

28. See Tyack and Hansot, *Managers of Virtue*, pp. 114–207.

29. Fred Ayer, "The Duties of Public School Administrators," *American School Board Journal* (1929), March, pp. 39–41; April, pp. 39–41; June, pp. 58–60.

30. Cuban, *Urban School Chiefs*, p. xii.

31. See Peter Gronn, "On Studying Administrators at Work," *Educational Administration Quarterly*, 20 (1), (1984), pp. 115–129; for a broader critique of a scientific approach to examining administration, see Thomas Greenfield, "The Decline and Fall of Science in Educational Administration," *Interchange*, 17 no. 2 (Summer 1986), pp. 57–80.

32. Lars Larson and his colleagues did time-and-motion studies in *The Nature of a School Superintendent's Work* (Carbondale, Illinois: College of Business and Administration, Southern Illinois University, 1981). For a study of superintendents that argues for examining what school chiefs think, see

Nancy Pitner and Rodney Ogawa, "Organizational Leadership: The Case of the School Superintendent," *Educational Administration Quarterly*, 17, (Spring 1981), pp. 45–66. John Feilders combined interviews, time and motion studies and a dash of ethnographic methods in his study of superintendent Robert Alioto in San Francisco, "Action and Reaction: The Job of an Urban School Superintendent," (Unpublished doctoral dissertation, Stanford University, 1979).

33. See the American Association of School Administrators, "The Superintendent as Instructional Leader," (Washington, D.C.: American Association of School Administrators, 1957) for the dominant ideology with the constant awareness that most superintendents spend their time on noninstructional tasks. Also see Roald Campbell, "Guilt Feelings for the Superintendent," *American School Board Journal* (August 1958), pp. 11–12. A 1939 report of interviews with 135 school board members and 175 school employees stated that the highest percentage (62%) of the 310 people said they expected their superintendent to have the "ability to stimulate and encourage growth among members of the teaching staff." The second highest percentage (60%) was for the statement: "ability to organize members of the teaching staff so there is freedom for and encouragement to make creative contributions to instructional improvement," American Association of School Administrators, "The Superintendent of Schools And His Work," (Washington, D.C.: American Association of School Administrators, 1940), p. 19.

34. Henry Mintzberg, *The Nature of Managerial Work* (New York: Harper and Row, 1973). In this study, Mintzberg lays out ten roles for managers (one of his subjects was a school superintendent); The ten roles I consolidate into the three I use.

35. *Annual Report of the School Committee of the City of Boston, 1857*, pp. 27–28. The picture of Philbrick that emerges from the annual reports and that which Michael Katz draws of the same superintendent at the end of his tenure in 1876, that is, a portrait of an administrator only interested in uniformity and adherence to bureaucratic rules, differs. Yet both pictures may be accurate. They touch different parts of a long career and the impulse toward efficiency is evident in Philbrick's annual reports as is his determination to be a teacher of teachers. In short, competing images of what a superintendent should be and may occur within the same official over a period of years. See Michael Katz, *Class, Bureaucracy and Schools* (New York: Praeger Publishers, 1971), pp. 56–104.

36. N. L. Engelhardt, "The Status of the Superintendent of Schools," *American Educational Digest*, 44 (July 1925), pp. 494–496.

37. For one illustration of this role as viewed by a superintendent, see Richard Doremus, "The Superintendent as Teacher," *Educational Leadership*,

42 (February 1985), pp. 82–84.

38. See Rosemary Donatelli, "The Contributions of Ella Flagg Young to the Educational Enterprise," (Unpublished dissertation, University of Chicago, 1971), pp. 279–429.

39. Ibid., pp. 359–369; Joan Smith, *Ella Flagg Young, Portrait of a Leader* (Ames, Iowa: Educational Studies Press, 1976), pp. 183–184.

40. Cuban, *Urban School Chiefs*, pp. 30–56.

41. Hansen, pp. 66, 151.

42. Carl Hansen, *Four Track Curriculum for Today's High School* (Englewood Cliffs, N.J.: Prentice-Hall, 1964).

43. Philip Hallinger and Joseph Murphy, "The Superintendent's Role in Promoting Instructional Leadership," *Administrator's Notebook*, 30, no. 6 (1982); Larry Cuban, "Transforming the Frog into a Prince: Effective Schools Research, Policy and Practice at the District Level," *Harvard Educational Review*, 54, (1984), pp. 129–151.

44. Tyack and Hansot, *Managers of Virtue*, pp. 114–144.

45. Aaron Gove, "Duties of the City Superintendent," National Educational Association, *Journal of Proceedings and Addresses, 1884*, pp. 26–33.

46. Chicago Board of Education, *Fifty-Sixth Annual Report, 1909–1910* (Chicago: Board of Education, 1910), pp. 75–87.

47. Ibid., pp. 75–77; Donatelli, pp. 342–346.

48. The same point I raised earlier with teachers and principals about values and beliefs and their degree of self consciousness about both applies to superintendents. Others who have argued the importance of the political dimension to superintending are: Joseph Viteritti, *Across the River: The Politics of Education in the City* (New York: Holmes and Meier, 1983); Blumberg, *School Superintendent;* Lesley Browder, "A Suburban School Superintendent Plays Politics," in Michael Kirst, ed. *The Politics of Education at the Local, State, and Federal Level* (Berkeley, CA: McCutchar, 1970); William Boyd, "The School Superintendent: Educational Statesman or Political Strategist," *Administrator's Notebook*, 22 (9) (1974).

49. See Tyack and Hansot for a delightful vignette of Cody, pp. 144–152.

50. Frank Cody, "The Superintendent: His Administrative and Supervisory Staff," *School Executive Magazine*, 49, (February 1930), pp. 259–262. Cody and other superintendents (as well as academics) often divided the job into three parts. See, for example, Ellwood P. Cubberley's chapter on the

superintendent in *Public School Administration* (Cambridge, MA: The Riverside Press, 1916).

51. Smith, pp. 195–196.

52. Ibid., pp. 193–194, 257.

53. See Cuban, *Urban School Chiefs*, pp. 33–56.

54. Beverly Carter, "Paul Sakamoto: A Case Study in Leadership" (Unpublished report for Education 221C, Stanford University, 1985).

55. Ibid., p. 11.

56. Ibid., 15–18.

57. Scott Pfeifer, "The Mountain View-Los Altos Union High School District's Teacher Evaluation System" (Unpublished report, Stanford University, 1985).

58. Carter, p. 21.

59. Ibid.

60. Pfeifer, p. 4.

61. See Luvern Cunningham, *The American School Superintendency: A Summary Report, 1982* (Washington, D.C.: American Association of School Administrators, 1982; also see Charles Fowler's parody of these exaggerated expectations in "How Does Your Superintendent Measure Up?, *American School Board Journal*, February, 1977. Fowler was superintendent at that time in Fairfield, Connecticut.

6. FROM HIGH SCHOOL TEACHER TO SUPERINTENDENT TO PROFESSOR

1. This description comes from Larry Cuban, "Shrinking Enrollments and Consolidation: Political and Organizational Impacts in Arlington, Virginia, 1973–1978." *Education and Urban Society*, 11, (May, 1979), pp. 367–395.

2. Ibid.

3. Twice a year Bettye Dudley, my secretary, would set up forms for both of us to record what I did, who I met with, where I went. I draw from those records to construct what I did.

4. F. Fuller, "Concerns of Teachers: A Developmental Characterization" *American Educational Research Journal*, 6, (1969), pp. 207–226.

7. FROM IMAGES AND ROLES TO LEADERSHIP

1. The negotiator-statesman image for superintendents (one that I constructed in my research on school chiefs) is missing from the other two occupations. The awareness that political behavior disguised as statesmanship was apparent among superintendents—it was an imperative that could not be ignored— may account for its presence among superintendents. Its absence for teachers and principals may be in response to the potent tabus surrounding political activity that arose in the early decades of this century.

2. Not unusual in public bureaucracies where professionals serve others, being a boss and a subordinate simultaneously applies to doctors, lawyers, accountants, and others.

3. C. B. Silver is cited in Sharon Feiman-Nemser and Robert Floden, "The Culture of Teaching" in Wittrock, ed. *Handbook of Research in Teaching*, p. 509; this isolation has been observed and studied numerous times. I have already cited Ella Flagg Young's dissertation on *Isolation in the School* (1901). Also see Sarason, Lortie, and Gertrude McPherson, *Small Town Teacher* (Cambridge, Mass: Harvard University Press, 1972).

4. See, for example, Schon, pp. 326–338.

5. For examples of the cross-cutting expectations that teachers face, see McPherson and Lortie; for principals, see Morris, *Urban Principal;* for superintendents, see Feilders, *Profile: The Role of the Chief Superintendent of Schools* (Belmont, CA: Pitman Learning, Inc., 1982).

6. The busyness of teachers and administrators has been documented by numerous researchers. For teachers, see Doyle, "Classroom Organization and Management;" for principals, I have already cited a number of time-and-motion studies of a principal's day. For superintendents, the Larson and Pitner and Ogawa studies document a superintendent's day.

7. Paul Lawrence and Jay Lorsch, *Organizations and Environment* (Boston: Graduate School of Business, Harvard University, 1967); James March and Johan Olsen, *Ambiguity and Choice in Organizations* (Bergen, Norway: Universitetsforlaget, 1976); Karl Weick, "Educational Organizations as Loosely Coupled Systems," *Administrative Science Quarterly*, 21 (1976), pp. 1–19; Charles Bidwell, "The School as a Formal Organization," in James March, ed. *Handbook of Organizations* (Chicago: Rand McNally, 1965); James March, "Footnotes to Organizational Change," *Administrative Sciences Quarterly*, 26, (December 1981), pp. 563–577.

8. Rose Coser, "The Complexity of Roles: Seedbed of Individual Autonomy,: in L. Coser, ed. *The Idea of Social Structure* (New York: Harcourt, Brace, and Jovanovich, 1975), pp. 237–264; Neal Gross, Ward Mason, A.

McEachern, *Explorations in Role Analysis* (New York: John Wiley, 1958), p. 319–320; the concept of complexity in roles is frequently used by sociologists in studying schools. See McPherson, Lortie, and Neal Gross, *Who Runs Our Schools* (New York: John Wiley, 1958).

9. Lee Shulman, "Autonomy and Obligation," in Shulman and Sykes, pp. 484–504. Also see Michael Lipsky, *Street-Level Bureaucracy: Dilemmas of the Individual in Public Services* (New York: Russell Sage, 1980).

10. Coser, pp. 237–264; Clark and Petersen describe teacher choice and use the phrase "interactive decisionmaker." David Dwyer and associates who studied the principal point out repeatedly the choices that confront the school head. Similarly, Gross and his associates do the same in *Explorations in Role Analysis.*

11. Robert Crowson and Van Morris, "Administrative Control in Large-City School Systems: An Investigation in Chicago," *Educational Administration Quarterly,* 21, no. 4 (Fall 1985), pp. 51–70; also see Joseph Murphy and Philip Hallinger, "The Superintendent's Role in Promoting Instructional Leadership."

12. State school reforms in the mid-1980s tried to align closely curricular goals with tests and instruction. These efforts are examined in the next chapter.

13. Gertrude McPherson captures crisply the complexity and ambivalence teachers have for principals: "What the teacher is saying to the principal, then, is: 'Leave me alone. Don't interfere in my classroom. Don't tell me how to teach. Protect me form all who challenge me. Support my decisions. And show you care about and appreciate me' "; "What Principals Should Know About Teachers" in D. A. Erickson and Reller, *The Principal in Metropolitan Schools* (Berkeley, CA: McCutchan, 1979), p. 241.

14. I have profited from Rebecca Hawthorne's dissertation in conceptualizing these categories of expectations and analyzing the operational curriculum of the classroom.

15. Michael Lipsky's work on professionals in public bureaucracies has helped me considerably in framing these ideas. For an application of Lipsky's concepts of street-level bureaucrat, see Crowson and Porter-Gehrie article on the principal.

16. Ruth Coser uses the phrase in her article.

17. See Lipsky and Coser for further elaboration of these points.

18. See Gross, Mason, and McEachern, pp. 281–318 for my abridgment of their arguments and concepts.

19. Ibid., p. 284 for a variation of the example.

20. Seymour Sarason's *The Culture of the School* first called my attention to the principal's orientations to the organization as an important variable. Also see Morris, *Urban Principals* for a further elaboration of the point that a principal's perspective on what can or cannot be done within the system shapes what the person does.

21. Warren Bennis and Burt Nanus, *Leaders* (New York: Harper and Row, 1985), p. 4; Louis Pondy, "Leadership is a Language Game" in Morgan McCall, Jr. and Michael Lombardo (eds.) *Leadership: Where Else Can We Go?* (Durham, N.C.: Duke University Press, 1978), p. 88.

22. Clifton Fadiman, ed. *Little, Brown Book of Anecdotes* (Boston: Little, Brown, 1985), p. 252.

23. See Ralph Stogdill, *Handbook of Leadership* (New York: Free Press, 1974), chapter 1, for different approaches to defining and viewing leadership.

24. The science of management is anchored in Frederick Taylor's time-and-motion studies in the early decades of the twentieth century. "Scientific management" and numerous offspring have stressed the rationality of top managers in organizing the behavior of subordinates. Writers within that diverse tradition are: L. Sayles, *Managerial Behavior* (New York: McGraw-Hill, 1964; Peter Drucker, *The Practice of Management* (New York: Harper and Brothers, 1954); G. Odiorne, *Management by Objectives* (New York: Pittman, 1956).

25. Writers who have viewed leadership in this manner are: Philip Selznick, *Leadership in Administration* (Berkeley, CA: University of California Press, 1957); Chester Barnard, *The Functions of the Executive* (Cambridge, Mass.: Harvard University Press, 1938 and 1968); Burns, *Leadership;* Bennis and Nanus; and T. Peters and R. Waterman, *Search for Excellence* (New York: Harper and Row, 1982).

26. Michael Cohen and James March, *Ambiguity and Leadership* (New York: McGraw-Hill, 1974). In organizational folklore such notions are found in the gag-line of the leader seeing people going one way and catching up with the supposed followers, or the Knights of Columbus ritual in Boston of having someone "lead" a billy goat in a parade to teach humility and that the leader is often the led. Anthony Lukas, *Common Ground* (New York: Alfred Knopf, 1985), p. 24.

27. Robert Reich and John Donald, *New Deals* (New York: Random House, 1985) pp. 5–7. Also see Jeffrey Pfeffer, "The Ambiguity of Leadership" *Academy of Management Review*, 2 (197), pp. 104–112. Also Bobby Calder, "An Attribution Theory of Leadership,: in Barry Straw and Gerald

Salancik (eds.) *New Directions in Organizational Behavior* (Chicago: St. Clair, 1977), pp. 179–204. Among educational researchers, who question the attribution of success to leaders, see Edwin Bridges, "The Nature of Leadership,:" in L. Cunningham, W. Hack, and R. Nystrand (eds.) *Educational Administration: The Developing Decades* (Berkeley, CA: McCutchan, 1977).

28. For one analysis of such views within social science research, see James Meindl, Sanford Ehrlich, and Janet Dukerich, "The Romance of Leadership," *Administrative Science Quarterly*, 30, (1985), pp. 78–102.

29. Ibid.; also see Dan Duke, "The Aesthetics of Leadership," *Educational Administration Quarterly* 22 no. 1 (Winter 1986), pp. 7–27.

30. Let me be clear on this point of vision that enjoys so much enthusiasm among policymakers, researchers, and practitioners in the late 1980s as the irreducible element in any notion of leadership. See, for example, Linda Shuve and Marion Schwenhut, "Leadership: Examining the Elusive," 1987 Yearbook (Washington, D.C.: Association for Supervision and Curriculum Development, 1987). All visions, however, are not equal; some are better than others. What makes some better or worse depends upon a number of criteria that can be applied to pictures of the future. I offer a few of my criteria by which I judge visions of those who view themselves as leaders:

- clarity: is the vision understood by followers?
- fit: does the vision fit followers' aspirations?
- history: is the vision consistent with or depart from the history of the organization?
- flexibility: can the vision expand, shrink or be modified by followers?
- moral principles: is the vision anchored in a set of ethical values?

Consider one example of the last criterion. Progressive reformers in the early decades of this century had a vision of schooling that embodied the values of technical efficiency for what students, teachers, and administrators ought to do and be. Ellwood P. Cubberley, just to cite one of the spokesmen for this vision, was clear on the mission of the school, the roles of teachers and administrators, and the importance of modeling the organization after the industrial or business corporation. The technocratic values embedded in that vision appealed to many and annoyed others. Hence, some visions are viewed as embraceable or not depending on an observer's or participant's accepting the values implicit in the vision. Visions, then, are declarations of moral intentions.

31. Because this view of leadership embraces the concept of a relationship, both Barnard and Selznick stress the importance of motivating and communicating clearly with followers in drawing their attention towards organizational goals.

32. Transforming the abstract into the concrete requires the leader to use words and ceremonies to get followers to sense the deeper meanings of

organizational routines and prosaic daily tasks.

33. Both Barnard and Selznick emphasize the importance of the unique in organizations and the leader's responsibility to call followers' attention to what is unique and how to nurture it.

34. Pondy, pp. 94–97. In Burns, *Leadership*, he makes clear that being a leader is of little import without achieving desired ends. See pp. 422–423.

35. These arguments form my view of leadership for teachers and administrators. I have drawn these concepts from earlier research that I have done on superintendents and teachers. I have also drawn from my experiences as a teacher and administrator, many of which I refer to in this book. While professional leadership in a public bureaucracy is considered by some as an oxymoron, I believe that it is possible and have constructed this framework upon that belief.

36. David Berliner, "Executive Functions of Teaching," (paper presented at the annual meeting of the American Educational Research Association, New York City, 1982).

37. Philip Sterling, *The Real Teachers* (New York City: Vintage Books, 1972), pp. 221–27.

38. Ibid., pp. 228–46.

39. Ken Macrorie, *Twenty Teachers,* (New York: Oxford University Press, 1984), pp. 79–91.

40. These vignettes are of teachers who lead students. As mentioned earlier, I narrowed the concept of teacher as leader to the classroom. There are many instances of teachers who lead adults *outside* the classroom: in teaming with colleagues; as a member of a school's faculty; as a director of a project; as an officer in a professional association. Such leadership outside the classroom contains the same elements described previously but extends beyond the classroom where the teacher is *expected* to lead. Not all teachers are expected to provide professional leadership to their colleagues. Some do, most do not. Leadership in both domains is essential, but I concentrate only on the classroom.

41. Shirley B. Heath, *Ways with Words* (London: Cambridge U. Press, 1983), chapters 8–9.

42. David Dwyer, G. Lee, Bruce Barnett, B. Filby, and Brian Corvan, *Frances Hedges and Orchard Park Elementary School: Instructional Leadership in a Stable Urban Setting* (San Francisco: Far West Laboratory, 1984).

43. Ibid., p. 11.

44. Ibid., p. 22.

45. Ibid, p. 42.

46. Lucianne Carmichael, *McDonough 15;* (New York: Avon Books, 1982); Leonard Covello *The Heart is the Teacher* (New York: McGraw-Hill, 1958); Nat Hentoff, *Our Children Are Dying* (New York: Four Winds Press, 1966).

47. *San Francisco Chronicle,* June 18, 1975; Feilders, *Profile,* pp. 15–18.

48. *Chronicle,* June 18, 1975.

49. *San Francisco Examiner,* June 18, 1975; *Chronicle,* June 18, 1975.

50. Feilders, *Profile,* pp. 5–13.

51. Ibid., p. 74.

52. Ibid., p. 68.

53. Ibid., pp. 53–54.

54. Ibid., 109.

55. Ibid., pp. 54, 95.

56. There is a less obvious and untidy question that arises from this chapter on teachers and administrators as leaders. To envision the teacher and administrator as a leader is one thing. To transform that vision into practice within an organization where both occupations are bosses and subordinates requires rethinking whether leadership at one level in a public bureaucracy shrinks or expands autonomy at another level. See Figure 10 on p. 195. In short, can a school district have teachers, principals, and superintendents as leaders.

I believe that the answer is yes on two grounds: first, the degree of looseness in district organizations is such that, left untouched by bureaucratic hands anxious to wire organizational layers together, there is room for each person to exert leadership in their domain in a variety of ways without the next level knowing too much about what is happening, except in those instances where conflict arises; second, I believe that there are large numbers of teachers and administrators who desire to lead but the managerial imperative (a concept I develop in the next chapter) depresses that desire, leaving little incentive to take initiative.

Of course, I also believe that not all teachers and administrators desire to be leaders, that is, wave-makers and risk-takers. Personalities, preferences, and circumstances filter out many educators who have little desire to pursue leadership opportunities.

Having argued that, I also believe (and I label these as beliefs, not facts) that organizations can be structured to identify and cultivate those who wish to lead at various levels. Can an organization prize leadership openly, encouraging initiative and responsibility, moderate risk-taking and retain accountability? Can incentives be invented that reward responsible initiatives aimed at meeting and transforming organizational goals rather than the conventional perverse ones that shrink initiative?

From the examples of football and baseball teams, corporations, and some public organizations, I believe the answer is yes. The issue is whether an organization explicitly accepts untidiness in structure and variation in leader performance. Creating structures and incentives that nourish multi-level leadership, of course, can come from those who have the authority and power to make such changes and from those who have struck out on their own and built exemplars of such places to work. It is far from an easy task.

8. SUMMARY AND IMPLICATIONS

1. Numerous descriptions of teaching over the century have character-ized teaching as class-tending, keeping order and making sure that children were kept busy. Concern over the lack of intellectual engagement in the midst of academic busyness appeared repeatedly. See, for example, Joseph Rice (1896), Robert and Helen Lynd, *Middletown* (New York: Harcourt and Brace, 1929); Willard Waller (1930s); and, more recently, John Goodlad, *A Place Called School*, Cusick (1984), and Sizer (1984).

2. There are connotations associated with managing and leading that need elaborating. We are now within a period when managing is increasingly viewed as insufficient; it is technical work that is marginally important but not equivalent to "leading." Not always the case in this culture. Recall educators' embrace of scientific management in the early twentieth century and its dom-inance in certain occupations (e.g., engineering and in graduate schools of business). In the 1980s, *leadership* is the buzz word. The two concepts are not polar opposites; they are related but separable. Organizational leadership requires technical skills of managing resources (including people) and activi-ties; when these technical skills are harnessed to goals beyond maintaining things as they are (which in some instances may be all that can be expected), then we enter the area of leadership that takes initiatives and risks, transform-ing existing goals and even adding new ones. Given my career, one punctu-ated by intentional and unanticipated changes, I value both managerial and leadership concepts; I do not believe that to *merely* manage is to engage in some low-level activity unrelated to important outcomes. In effect, we need educators to be both leaders and managers. For teachers and administrators to solely manage without harnessing their skills to goals, beyond maintaining the status quo for long periods of time, is harmful to children's as well as adults' intellectual and moral growth. I have argued that the structural arrange-ments in schools create an acute press toward the managerial, not toward leading, as I have defined it. Abraham Zelznick goes further and argues that managers and leaders are, indeed, different people psychologically. A

manager and a leader have different views of themselves and approach goals, careers, and relationships differently. See "Managers and Leaders: Are They Different?" in Eliza Collins, ed., *Harvard Business* Review's *Executive Success: Making It in Management* (New York: John Wiley & Sons, 1983), pp. 123–39. While such a case can be made, I hold that both managing and leading are activities that frequently occur during an educator's career in tandem, separately and, in some instance, simultaneously.

3. See, for example, D. J. Willower, V. Eidell, and W. F. Hoy. "The School and Pupil Control Ideology" (University Park, Penn.: Penn State, 1967).

4. Dan Lortie's work on teachers underscores this point. See *Schoolteacher*, pp. 230–235; also Joseph Blase, "The Socialization of Teachers," *Urban Education*, 20 (October 1985), pp. 235–256; for administrators, see Tyack and Hansot, *Managers of Virtue*, pp. 217–223.

5. Tyack and Hansot, *Managers of Virtue*, pp. 168–194.

6. See J. S. Kounin, *Discipline and Group Management in Classrooms* (New York: Holt, Rinehart and Winston, 1970).

7. Earlier chapters dealing with the daily work patterns of teachers, principals, and superintendents have repeatedly stressed the managerial tasks that dominate the work.

8. Deep reluctance to alter existing arrangements has been a theme in the observation of Dan Lortie, Willard Waller, and John Goodlad on teachers. For principals, see Seymour Sarason and Harry Wolcott. For superintendents, see Tyack and Hansot.

9. Before answering the question, I need to review briefly a paradox produced by researchers on teachers and administrators. The early dominance of psychologists on the application of scientific principles to education, the low status often associated with working directly with teachers, and the high cost attached to sending individual researchers into classrooms and schools produced traditions in applied research that relied heavily upon a handful of methods. Experimental designs that control particular variables, followed up by responses on questionnaires, for example, are useful in isolating particular behaviors and linking them to particular outcomes. In specifying the relationships between particular variables and outcomes, researchers further splinter knowledge into researchable bits but leave practitioners scratching their heads over its utility or meaning for classrooms and schools.

Such research, however, fails to describe totally what teachers and administrators actually do, link perceptions with behavior, or point to causal connections. When researchers do observe teachers and administrators directly, a preferred tool has been variations on time-and-motion studies that leaned heavily on frequency counts of tasks. Although that has helped fill in important gaps in what we know, such approaches fail to extract meaning from what these educators do. More recently, occasional ethnographies and case studies from other disciplines have wed time-and-motion studies with the intentions, thoughts, and values of a teacher or administrator over an extended period of time.

The results of decades of varied research designs and methods applied to teaching and administering are a potpourri of skills, attitudes, values, and behaviors that have little coherence (much less application) for practitioners and policymakers. From this research has arisen at least two views of teaching, principaling, and superintending. On the one hand, descriptive and experimental studies argue that what teachers and administrators do is varied, fragmented, disjointed, complex, and frequently unconnected to the central mission of each occupation. On the other hand, the normative literature on what each should do and research findings on teacher and school effectiveness assume (and in many cases, argue) the importance of the teacher, principal, and superintendent to school improvement and productivity. This paradox results from narrowly conceived research designs that often concentrate on what can be examined, measured, and reduced to numbers, the equally narrow view of schools as relatively simple organizations with technical processes called instruction or management, and, finally, a narrow version of desired student outcomes. Given this paradox, it is no surprise that information and concepts about leadership as a phenomenon in classrooms and offices has been incomplete and frequently unstudied.

Thus, the use of varied research methods (such as ethnographical, direct observations of participants, sociological case studies, historical analyses of schools and their staff) construct fuller, more complete portraits of teachers and administrators in action (or inaction) that come closer to resembling and understanding the nature of both occupations. Combining all of these research approaches to my studies of teachers and administrators, my supervising of hundreds of teachers and scores of principals over the last three decades, and my collaborating over the years with numerous practitioners, I argue that leadership is more evident than researchers have either sought or found.

In making this argument, I found the work of David Dwyer and his associates on principals most helpful. Their direct observations and probing interviews of the subjects produced the idea that certain principals invested meaning into the routines they and the staff faced daily. Dwyer's work outlined how principals go about the elusive business of giving meaning to the mundane. While I have criticized some elements of this line of research, in the main, I have found his work consistent with my studies of superintendents, my observations of teachers (and also Ken Macrorie's studies of teachers). Moreover, Dwyer's insights intersect with my observations of both teachers and administrators who I would label leaders.

For critiques of research methods on teaching and administering, see Lee

Shulman, "Paradigms and Research Programs in the Study of Teaching;" Edwin Bridges, "Research on the School Administrator: The State of the Art, 1967–1980" *Educational Administration Quarterly*, 18, (3) (1982), pp. 12–33.

10. David Dwyer, "Understanding the Principal's Contribution to Instruction," *Peabody Journal of Education*, 63, no. 1 (Fall 1986), pp. 13–18. In Michael Cohen and James March's study of college presidents, they link routine competency as an essential to making a bureaucracy work. Also see Tom Peters, "Symbols, Patterns, and Settings," *Organizational Dynamics* (Summer 1977).

11. See David Tyack and Thomas James, *Law and the Shaping of Public Education* (in press).

12. Very different views of school reform over the last century can be obtained from: David Tyack, *The One Best System;* Michael Katz, *Class Bureaucracy, and Schools;* Diance Ravitch, *The Troubled Crusade* (New York: Basic Books, 1983), and Lawrence Cremin, *The Transformation of the School* (New York: Random House, 1961).

13. Paul Watzlawick, John Weakland, and Richard Fisch, *Change: Principles of Problem Formation and Problem Resolution* (New York: Norton, 1974). I need to make two further points about the distinction between orders of change.

First, the terms "first-order" and "second-order" may confuse some researchers who recall Type I and Type II errors from statistics. For practitioners, occasionally, the phrases may be awkward because "first-order" seems more important than "second-order" which is the opposite for those who see structural changes as being more significant. I am less concerned over labels. Whatever the names are, I want to distinguish between two levels of change. Simply calling attention to the difference in magnitude of changes is my purpose in distinguishing between the two kinds of reform.

Next, "first" or "second-order" changes are results of first and second-order problem-framing. When problems are defined in individual terms, of the securing of more resources, or gaining more authority for those already in power, this is first-order framing of problems. Second-order definition of problems seek broader, integrated perspectives that take into account how the environment, organization, and individual intersect to create issues. In short, first and second-order changes imply ways of framing problems as much as generating solutions.

14. Michael Kirst, David Tyack, and Elisabeth Hansot, "Educational Reform: Retrospect and Prospect" *Teachers College Record*, 81 no. 3 (Spring 1980) pp. 253–270; Michael Kirst and Gail Meister, "Turbulence in American Secondary Schools: What Reforms Last," *Curriculum Inquiry*, 15 no. 2 (1985), pp. 169–186.

15. Michael Kirst, "Teaching Policy and Federal Categorical Programs," in Shulman and Sykes, pp. 426–448; Michael Fullan, *The Meaning of Educational Change* (New York: Teachers College Press, 1982), pp. 216–231.

16. David Clark and Terry Astuto, "The Significance and Permanence of Change in Federal Educational Policy, 1980–1988" (Bloomington, Indiana: University Council for Educational Administration, January, 1986), pp. 4–8.

17. Kirst, "Teaching Policy and Federal Categorical Programs," p. 41.

18. Much of the periodic shifting in targets of reform, i.e. expanding access for excluded students to emphasizing higher standards in academic performance, depends upon which meanings are attached to the concept of excellence. To some, excellence means broader access of quality schooling to the excluded; to others, excellence is defined in terms of meritorous performance. For an analysis of this point, see Madhu Suri Prakash and Leonard Waks, "Four Conceptions of Excellence," *Teachers College Record*, 87 (1) (1985), pp. 79–101.

19. See *Harvard Educational Review*, "Symposium on the Year of the Reports,: 54 (1) (February 1984), pp. 1–31; Joseph Murphy, Pete Mesa, Philip Hallinger, "School Effectiveness: Checking Progress and Assumptions and Developing a Role for State and Federal Government," *Teachers College Record*, 86 (1) (1985), pp. 615–641.

20. For an advocate's view of state reform, see Michael Kirst, "State Policy in an Era of Transition," *Education and Urban Society*, 16 no. 2 (February 1984), pp. 225–237; for a critical view, see Linda Darling-Hammond and Arthur Wise, "Beyond Standardization: State Standards and School Improvement," *Elementary School Journal*, 85 no. 3 (1985), pp. 315–336.

21. California, Texas, South Carolina, and Florida, for example, passed laws extending the time children spend in schools. For a critical review of the research upon which these laws were based, see Henry Levin, "About Time for Educational Reform," (Stanford, CA: Institute for Research on Educational Finance and Governance, 1983), no. 83–A19.

22. See a summary of state legislation on curriculum, tests, and other items in *Education Week*, February 6, 1985, pp. 11–29.

23. James Popham, "The Merits of Measurement-Driven Instruction," Phi Delta *Kappan*, 68 (9) (1987), pp. 679–682; for a sharply critical view, see George Madaus, "Testing and the Curriculum" (Boston College: Center for the Study of Testing and Evaluation, 1986). Walt Haney provides a useful history and explication of the testing movement and its strengths and limits in "Testing Reasoning and Reasoning about Testing," *Review of Educational Research*, 54 (4) (1984), pp. 597–654.

24. Samuel Bacharach, "Career Development, Not Career Ladders," *Education Week*, March 12, 1986, p. 28.

25. Michael Killian, "Local Control: The Vanishing Myth in Texas," Phi Delta *Kappan*, 65 (11) (1984), pp. 192–195; *Education Week*, March 5, 1986.

26. Pam Grossman, Michael Kirst, Worku Negash, and Jackie Schmidt-Posner, "Curricular Change in California Comprehensive High Schools: 1982–83 to 1984–85," Policy Paper no. PP85-7-4 (Stanford, CA: Policy analysis for California Education, 1985). For U.S. Secretary William Bennett's comments on state reforms turning the nation's schools around, see James Hertling, "Bennett Says 'Wall Chart' Shows Gains," *Education Week*, February 26, 1986. One of the few studies where researchers listened to teachers and their reactions to state-driven reforms is the Linda Darling-Hammond and Arthur Wise's study cited earlier.

27. Peter Blau studied employment counselors who were judged on the basis of how many job-seekers they placed; they skimmed their case loads for easy-to-place clients; District of Columbia police reduced the incidence of serious crime by reporting that most burglaries involved less than fifty dollars, thereby dropping many crimes that were serious (as measured by dollars) into a less serious reporting category. Peter Blau and Richard Scott, *Formal Organizations* (Scranton, Pa: Chandler Publishing Co. 1962) pp. 178–180. Or the New York City sanitation workers who failed to complete their routes and then hosed down their garbage so their trucks would weigh the proper quota assigned by superiors when they appeared at the dump. The tendency toward underreporting and bending numbers to deceive is accelerated by introducing bureaucratic accountability devices: some schools, respond by not testing certain groups of students; teaching actual test items to students; actual fiddling with the results, and so on. See Lipsky, pp. 166–167 and S. Stringfield & A. Hartman, "Irregularities in Testing: Ethical, Psychometric, and Political Issues," (Chicago, Ill: Paper presented at the annual meeting of the American Educational Research Association 1985).

28. Cuban, *Teachers and Machines*, pp. 51–71.

29. "Why Reforms Go Awry," Frances Fowler, *Education Week*, November 6, 1985, p. 24.

30. Geoffrey Isherwood and Wayne Hoy, "Bureaucracy, Powerlessness, and Teacher Work Values," *Journal of Educational Administration* 11 (May 1973); Cecil Miskel and Ed Gerhardt, "Perceived Bureaucracy, Teacher Conflict, Central Life Interest, Voluntarism, and Job Satisfaction,: *Journal of Educational Administration*, 12, (May 1974); Harold Cox and James Wood, "Organizational Structure and Professional Alienation: The Case of Public School Teachers," *Peabody Journal of Education*, 58, (October 1980).

31. For an examination of teacher resistance, see Robert Bullough, Jr., Andrew Gitlin, and Stanley Goldstein, "Ideology, Teacher Role, and Resistance," *Teachers College Record*, 86 (no. 2) Winter, 1984), pp. 339–358.

32. The literature on planned change is massive, especially for state and federal initiatives. I cite a few works that I have found useful: Fullan, *The Meaning of Educational Change;* Paul Berman and Milbrey McLaughlin, "Federal Programs Supporting Educational Changes," vol. 8 (Santa Monica, CA: Rand, 1978); Michael Huberman and Matthew Miles, *Innovation Up Close* (New York: Plenum Press, 1984); Paul Berman, "Educational Change: An Implementation Paradigm," in Rolf Lehming and Michael Kane (eds.) *Improving Schools: Using What We Know* (Beverly Hills, CA: Sage Publications, 1984); Kirst, "Teaching Policy and Federal Categorical Programs:" Richard Elmore and Milbrey McLaughlin, "Steady Work: The Task of Educational Reform," (Washington, D.C.: National Institute of Education, 1984).

33. Jane David and Susan Peterson, "Can Schools Reform Themselves? A Study of School-Based Improvement Programs," (New York: Carnegie Corporation, 1984); Milbrey McLaughlin, "Implementation as Mutual Adaptation" in Dale Mann (ed.) *Making Change Happen* (New York: Teachers College Press, 1978).

34. Fullan, pp. 107–214; Cuban, *Teachers and Machines;* D. Crandall, "Training and Supporting Linking Agents," in N. Nash and J. Culbertson (eds.) *Linking Processes in Educational Improvement* (Columbus, Ohio: University Council for Educational Administration, 1977).

35. See George Madaus, "Testing and the Curriculum;" Lee Sproull and D. Zubrow, "Performance Indicators in School Systems: Perspectives from Organizational Theory," *Educational Administration Quarterly*, 17 (3) (1981) pp. 61–79; Jane David, "Improving Education with Locally Developed Indicators" (Center for Policy Research in Education, University of Wisconsin, 1987).

36. These points come from a series of conversations with Milbrey McLaughlin.

37. See Lipsky, pp. 166–167.

Index

Abortion, class discussion of, 1, 33
Achievement Directed Leadership,
    66–68
Active instruction, 4
Adaptations, organizational, 184–90
Administrative chief, superintendent as,
    115–16
Administrators
    American Association of School
        Administrators, 113
    autonomy, 182, 187–90, 246–49
    career paths, 172
    contradictory expectations, 183, 222
    effectiveness, determining, 223
    loyalties, conflicting, 182, 187
    origin of position, 221
    socialization and training, 221–22
    as solo practitioners, 181–82
    teachers, common ground with,
        179–83
    teaching, desire to resume, 102–103
    see also Principals; Superintendents
Alioto, Robert (superintendent), 210–17
Amidon Plan (Washington), 135–36,
    138–39, 141–42
Art of Teaching, The (Highet), 23
Artist, teacher as. See Craftsman/artist,
    teacher as

Atlantic, The, 45
Author's experiences
    as assistant principal, 84–93
    career choices, 48–49
    as college student, 41–42
    as elementary instruction aide,
        101–102
    as graduate student, 150–51
    as high school student, 41
    as master teacher
        Cardozo High School, 49–51
        Roosevelt High School, 104–110
    as professor, 171–72, 173
    as staff development director, 96–102
    as student teacher, 42–43
    as superintendent, 149–75
    as teacher
        Coolidge High School, 102
        Glenville High School, 45–48
        McKeesport Tech, 43–45
        Roosevelt High School, 93–96,
            104–110

Bargaining. See Unions
Barnard, Chester, 193
Barnard, Henry, 196
Barth, Roland (principal), 210
Bell, Andrew, 7

Bell, Ed (principal), 75–76, 81–83
Belt, Betty (principal), 70–83, 209, 226
Bennett, William, 235
Bennis, Warren, 190
Berliner, David, 196
Black Boy (Wright), 89
Black Panthers, 94
Blackboard Jungle (film), 45
Blacks. *See* Minorities
Boston School Committee, 55, 112, 132
British and Foreign School Society, 7
Brooks, Marian, 20–21
Buddha, 15
Budgets, 153, 184, 189
Bureaucrats
  administrators as, 181
  principals as, 54–57, 65
  teachers as, 3–15, 181
Burns, James McGregor, 193
Business, school as, 56–57

Cain, Eugene (teacher), 197–200, 203, 204
Carmichael, Lucianne Bond (principal), 210
Carmichael, Stokely, 95
Carstensten, Carol (teacher), 105
Case Western Reserve University, 45
Catholic University, 93, 169
Chancellor, William (superintendent), 118–19, 125–26
Chicago, University of, 114, 134
Choices, 186–90
City schools. *See* Urban schools
Civil Rights, U.S. Commission on, 95–96
Civil servant, teacher as, 5
Cleveland Plan of 1892, 115
Cody, Frank (superintendent), 140, 146, 215, 216
Collective bargaining. *See* Unions
Competency-based curricula, 14–15
Conant, James B., 196
Conflicting expectations, 183, 188–90, 222
Consolidation, 154–55

Convenience, 223–25
Covello, Leonard (principal), 210
Craftsman/artist, teacher as, 3–6, 15–20, 23–25
Creery, William (superintendent), 117
Crim, Alonzo (superintendent), 77, 217
Cubberley, Elwood P., 11, 56–59, 61, 65, 68, 151, 196, 222
Curriculum design, 22–23
Curriculum reforms
  competency-based, 14–15
  mastery learning, 14–15
  for uniformity, 156–57
  Washington, D.C. (1970s), 1–2
  see also Reforms

D.C. Gazette, 110
Darwin, Charles, 32
Davis, Myrtle (teacher), 105–109
Declaration of Independence, teaching of, 32
Deex, Oliver (principal), 45–46
Department of Elementary Principals (NEA), 64
Department of Superintendence (NEA), 113
Dewey, John, 9, 18–20, 114, 134
Direct instruction, 4, 14–15
Discipline
  in monitorial schools, 8
  moral vs. technical approach, 5
Doyle, Walter, 27–28
Draper, Andrew (superintendent), 115
Drillmaster, teacher as, 26

Economic Opportunity, Office of (OEO), 51, 88, 90
Education, National Institute of (NIE), 171
Effective schools movement, 4, 14–15
Eicholtz, Bob (principal), 72–83, 179, 209, 226
Elementary Principals, Department of (NEA), 64
Elementary and Secondary Education Act of 1965, 12, 229, 230–31
Enabler, teacher as, 24

Excellence in Education, National
Commission on, 14
Expectations, conflicting, 183, 188–90,
192

Factory school as, 4, 9
Family life, superintendent's, 166–70
Finkelstein, Barbara, 25–26
Feilders, John, 212–14
Ford, Glenn, 45
Foster, Marcus (principal), 210
Fowler, Frances (teacher), 237–38

George Washington University, 160
Goals, instructional, 155–56
Gove, Aaron (superintendent), 115–16,
119, 123, 137–38, 146
Grange, Red, 190
Great Depression, teaching of, 32
Greenwood, James W. (superintendent),
113, 119

Hansen, Carl (superintendent), 86–88,
91, 97–98, 128, 134–39, 141–42,
146, 215–16
Harpers magazine, 45
Harris, William Torrey, 58, 113, 119,
217
Heath, Shirley, 204
Hedges, Francis (principal), 204–209,
226
Henley, Ben (superintendent), 96,
98–100
Herndon, James, 204
Highet, Gilbert, 23
Hispanics. *See* Minorities
History, classroom's, 28
Hobson v. Hansen, 98, 142
Hogans, Norris (principal), 77–78, 81,
83, 209
Honig, Bill (state superintendent, Calif.),
235
Howard University, 88, 89, 93

Iacocca, Lee 191–92
Images of teaching

moral, 3–6, 32–33
technical, 3–6
Immediacy in classroom, 27
Improvements. *See* Reforms
Instructional leader, principal as, 57–59,
69–74
Instructional supervisor, superintendent
as, 113–15, 131–36
Intellectual overseer, teacher as, 26
Interpreter of culture, teacher as, 26

Jackson, Philip, 23–24
Jesus, 15
Jim Crow, 46, 47
Johnson, Lyndon, 12, 95, 230
Jones, Lewis (superintendent), 113
Juvenile Delinquency, President's
Committee on, 50

Katz, Thelma (teacher), 34–39, 179,
226
Kennedy, John F., 49–50, 141, 191
Kennedy, Robert F., 141
King, Martin Luther, 46, 95, 191
Kohl, Herb, 204

Lancaster, Joseph, 7, 8, 9, 16, 54, 116
Leadership
defined, 190–96
expectations, multiple and
incompatible, 222
origins of, in schools, 220–21
potential for, in schools, 183–90
principals, 204–210
reasons for, in schools, 225–27
socialization and training for, 221–22
superintendents, 210–17
teachers, 196–204
Life in Classrooms (Jackson), 23–24
Lombardi, Vince, 191
Lutheran Church, 111

Machine, school as, 4, 9
Macrorie, Ken, 24, 200–202
Managers
principals as, 74–76

superintendents as, 136–39
teachers as, 30
Mann, Horace, 16–18, 196
Manning, William (superintendent), 98
Marshall, Kim, 204
Mastery learning, 14–15
Mastruzzi, Robert (principal), 210
Maxwell, William (superintendent), 119, 217
McCarthy, Robert (principal), 210
McKenzie, Floretta (superintendent), 217
McLaughlin, Milbrey, 247
McMurry, Frank, 56
Michigan State University, 142
Military organization, school as, 56–57
Milz, Vera (teacher), 200–203, 204
Minorities
    in Arlington, Va., schools, 152
    author's experiences, predominantly black schools, 45–51, 84–110
    Black Panthers, 94
    Carmichael, Stokely, 95
    Carver High School (Atlanta), 77–78
    civil rights movement, 12
    Cooley High School (Detroit), 197–200
    King, Martin Luther Jr., 46, 95, 191
    monitorial schools for, 7
    in Mountainview/Los Altos, Calif., schools, 143–44
    Pioneer High School (Whittier, Calif.), 72–74, 80–81
    Roosevelt High School (Washington), 93–96, 104–110
    in San Francisco schools, 213
    Students Non-Violent Coordinating Committee (SNCC), 95
    U.S. Commission on Civil Rights, 95–96
    see also Urban schools
Mintzberg, Henry, 128–30
Mitchell, Bertha (teacher), 41, 42
Model School Division (Washington), 85–86, 141–42
Monitorial schools
    decline of, 9

development of, 7
discipline in, 8
modern principalship, origins in, 54
structure of, 7
Moral approach to teaching, 3–6, 32–33
Multidimensionality in classroom, 27
Muzzey, David Saville, 46
My Pedagogic Creed (Dewey), 19–20

Nation, The, 45
"Nation at Risk, A," 14
National Aeronautics and Space Administration (NASA), 228
National Commission on Excellence in Education, 14
National Council of Education, 18
National Defense Education Act (NDEA), 230
National Education Association (NEA), 64, 113, 114, 140
National Teacher Corps, 51
National Institute of Education (NIE), 171
National Teachers' Association, 113
Negotiator, superintendent as, 116–19, 139–45
New York Free School Society, 7
Newlon, Jesse, 22
Nineteenth-century schools, 7–10, 16–20, 25–26

Office of Economic Opportunity (OEO), 51, 88, 90
Oregon, University of, 12

Parity Plan (Mountainview/Los Altos schools), 143–44
Parker, Francis, 9
Parks, Rosa, 46
Peace Corps, 49–51, 90, 91
Personal life, superintendent's, 166–70, 175
Philbrick, John (superintendent), 123, 132–33, 217
Pierce, Cyrus, 17–18
Pittsburgh, University of, 41–43

Planning, Program and Budgeting
Systems (PPBS), 12
Poitier, Sidney, 45
Politicians,
principals as, 76–81
superintendents as, 116–19, 139–45
teachers as
decline of partisan politics, 31
in moral education, 32–33
negotiation with students, 33
patronage, 31
practice, 30–34
testing, 33–34
Porter, Dorothy (teacher), 2, 15
President's Committee on Juvenile
Delinquency, 50
Principals
accountability, 65
autonomy, 65, 182, 187–90, 246–49
career paths, 172
Department of Elementary Principals
(NEA), 64
duties, 59–69
effectiveness, determining, 223
expectations, contradictory, 183, 222
history, 53–54, 221
individual experiences, 70–81,
205–209
as leaders, 204–210
loyalties, conflicting, 182, 187
roles of
administrator, 60
bureaucrat, 54–57
complexity, 185–87
images and descriptions of,
discrepancy, 64–66
instructional leader, 57–59, 69–74
manager, 74–76
merging of images, 67–69, 219–20
patterns in discharging, 81–84
politician, 76–81
public relations, 76
supervisor, 60
in scientific management movement,
56
socialization and training, 221–22
as solo practitioners, 181–82

time, distribution of, 60–63
see also Administrators
Professionals
principals as, 54, 59–60
teachers as, 3, 5, 10–11, 19–23
*Profile: The Role of the Chief Superintendent
of Schools* (Fielders), 212
Progressive education movement, 22–23
Project Redesign (San Francisco),
212–15
Proposition 13 (California), 13, 80, 143
Publicness of classroom, 28

Quincy School, 54, 132

Reagan, Ronald, 231
Reforms
Amidon Plan (Washington), 135–36,
138–39, 141–42
competency-based curricula, 14–15
direct instruction, 14–15
effective schools movement, 4, 14–15
Elementary and Secondary Education
Act of 1965, 12, 229, 230–31
federal, generally, 12
first-order changes, 228–30
goals, 243–46
lessons of, 240–43
mastery learning, 14–15
nineteenth century, 16–20
Planning, Programming and Budgeting
Systems (PPBS), 12
progressive education movement,
22–23
Project Redesign (San Francisco),
212–15
School Planning, Evaluation and
Communications System (SPECS),
12–14
second-order changes, 228–30
state intervention, 227–28, 232–40
Title I, 12, 229, 230–31
see also Curriculum reforms
Research for Better Schools (RBS),
66–68
Rice, Joseph, 10

Role complexity, generally, 185–87
Rubin, Louis, 24

Sabbaticals, 174–75
Sakamoto, Paul (superintendent),
    142–46, 215, 216, 226
Salaries
    discrepancies, teachers vs.
        administrators, 103–104
    see also Unions
Saturday Review of Literature, 45
Schmidt, Richard (teacher), 1, 33
Scholastic Aptitude Test, 158–59, 235
School Administrators, American
    Association of, 113
School boards
    Boston School Committee, 555, 112,
        132
    superintendents, relations with,
        126–27, 139, 153–56, 160–66,
        170–71
School Planning, Evaluation and
    Communication Systems (SPECS)
    design of, 12–13
    development of, 12
    teacher's reactions to, 13–14
    testing, role of, 13
Science, teaching as, 17–18
Scientific management movement, 56
Scott, Hugh (superintendent), 100
Selznick, Philip, 193
Semiprofessional, teacher as, 5
Shapiro, Elliot (principal), 210
Silver, C. B., 181–82
Simultaneity in classroom, 27
Sizer, Theodore, 33
Smith, Edward (superintendent), 123–25
Smith-Hughes Act, 227–28
Sociology of Teaching, The (Waller), 196
Socrates, 15
Spears, Harold (superintendent), 128,
    210, 217
Staff development
    author's experiences, as director of,
        96–102
    Teachers Innovation Fund (Arlington,
        Va.), 157

Stanford University, 150–51, 171–72
State education departments, 160,
    227–28, 232–40
Statesman, superintendent as, 116–19,
    139–45
Sterling, Philip, 198–99
Stevenson, R. W., 115
Student-centered practices, 26–27
Students Non-Violent Coordinating
    Committee (SNCC), 95
Superintendence, Department of (NEA),
    113
Superintendents
    American Association of School
        Administrators, 113
    autonomy, 246–49
    career paths, 172
    duties, 123–31
    effectiveness, determining, 223
    family of, effects of job on, 166–70
    individual experiences, 114–15,
        123–26, 132–33, 140–45, 210–15
    as leaders, 210–17
    origin of position, 111–12, 221
    roles of
        administrative chief, 115–16
        complexity, 185–87
        instructional supervisor, 113–15,
            131–36
        manager, 136–39
        merging of roles, 219–20
        negotiator/statesman, 116–19,
            139–45
        patterns in discharging, 145–47
        public relations, 118, 139
        shifting of roles, 120–23
    school boards, relations with, 126–27,
        139, 153–56, 160–66, 170–71
    socialization and training, 221–22
    time, distribution of, 125–31, 163–66
    see also Administrators

Talladega College, 198
Tarbell, Horace (superintendent), 113
Taylor, Frederick, 56
Teacher-centered practices, 26

Teachers
  administrators, common ground with,
    179–83
  autonomy, 182, 187–90, 246–49
  career paths, 172
  effectiveness, determining, 223
  expectations, contradictory, 183, 222
  individual experiences, 1–2, 34–39,
    41–51, 105–109, 197–203
  as leaders, 196–204
  loyalties, conflicting, 182, 187
  origin of position, 220–21
  roles of
    bureaucrat/technocrat, 3–15, 181
    civil servant, 5
    complexity, 185–87
    conflicting, 28–29
    craftsman/artist, 3–6, 15–29
    drillmaster, 26
    enabler, 24
    instructional, 29
    intellectual overseer, 26
    interpreter of culture, 26
    manager, 30
    merging of roles, 219–20
    politician, 30–34
  socialization and training, 221–22
  as solo practitioners, 181–82
  thought processes of, 6
Teachers Innovation Fund (Arlington,
  Va.), 157
Technical approach to teaching, 3–6
Test scores, 158–59, 235
Title I, 12, 229, 230–31
To Make a Difference (author's work), 96

U.S. Commission on Civil Rights,
  95–96
Unions
  and administrators, conflicting
    expectations, 189–90
  author's experiences with (Arlington,
    Va.), 160–61

National Education Association, 64,
  113, 114, 140
  and technical approach to teaching, 4
  see also Salaries
United Planning Organization (UPO),
  88–90
Unpredictability in classroom, 28
Urban schools
  Carver High School (Atlanta), 77–78
  development of, 9–11
  early critics of, 9–11
  modern principalship, origins in,
    53–54
  Urban School Chiefs Under Fire (author's
    work), 128
  Urban Teaching Project/Urban Teacher
    Corps, 84–93, 104–110
  see also Minorities

Venereal disease, class discussion of,
  106–109
Vietnam, 95
Volunteers in Service to America
  (VISTA), 90

Waller, Willard, 196
Warner, Sylvia Ashton, 204
Washington Post, 158–59, 165
Watson, Tom, 191
Wayne, John, 192
Wesley, John, 111
Wigginton, Eliot, 204
Willis, Benjamin (superintendent), 128,
  217
Wolcott, Harry, 75–76
Wright, Judge Skelly, 98, 142
Wright, Richard, 89

Young, Ella Flagg (superintendent),
  114–15, 134, 138, 140–41, 146,
  179, 215–17
Youth as a Minority (author's work), 110